To Ree
"Dig Deep"
Love Strokes

Digging deep for *Change*

Susan R. Anderson

Digging Deep For Change

Susan R. Anderson

For my big sister Brenda:

I miss you more than I can say…

Acknowledgements

I'd like to express my deep appreciation to my family, and close comrades (you know who you are) for their constant support and never-ending encouragement. I could not have done this without you all. Thank you for putting up with my constant yammering about this book, and talking me off the edge when I felt like jumping.

To my editor extraordinaire, Holly Kothe of The Espresso Editor: Thank you Holly for your sound advice, expertise and patience as I stumbled through my rookie season as a published author. Your guidance goes above and beyond the call of duty. You totally rock!

Special thanks to Graphic Designer Charlotte Harding of The Libros Book Cover Shop, for her artistic flair, in bringing my book cover to life.

To my three awesomely beautiful daughters: Your love is what fuels my heartbeat, my pride and joy is in you. You three characters are my reason for giving it all I've got, and then some each day. Your constant support as I wrote this book means the world to me…thank you for your patience while I was in the process. Mommy loves you more than I could ever express.

To my best friend and absolutely, remarkable husband Craig Anderson:

Your faith in me has been unshakable, my gratitude is endless.

Thank you for boosting me atop of your shoulders, so I can reach higher for my dreams, and thank you for catching my fall, when I stumble along the way.

You make it easier to dance in the rain, because we always dance together… I love you.

Contents

Introduction.............. 2

The Onset — 3
Early Activation of an Addiction…….............. 4
Daddy…………..……. 5
Mama…………..……. 9
The Divorce……………. 12
Mr. Samuel…………….. 15
Silent Suffering…………. 17

The Progression — 22
Teen Years…………….. 23
Stuffing Emotions………. 24
Lies My Mirror Told Me... 26
Finding My Way……….. 28

The Dependence — 31
Now Pronounce You…Broken……………. 32
Searching for a Savior – Darryl………….. 37
Home Again…………….. 48
Mama's House…………... 51
Hope Deferred…..……... 57
Blinded by Love or Something Like It………. 59
Addiction and Disorder…... 75

The Mission — 79
The Paradigm Shift………. 80
The Launch of a Journey…. 93
Shelly's Great Shape……… 100
The Dawning of a New Day………………….. 117
Step 1…Step 2..(349.2)…... 120

The Pursuit — 130
Learning to Fly Solo……................... 131
Caution: Incentive Engaged (332.0)…………... 136

Earning my Wings………... 143
Butt-Kicking Mode (312.7)…………………. 146
Whose Body is this Anyway? (276.8)…………. 152
The Woe of the Plateau (277.1)…………. 155

The Setback — 162
Hey Friend, Where Ya Been?……………… 163
Make Way for Mama…………………. 171
This is Only a Test (271)……………............ 174
Love Don't Leave Here Anymore………….. 181
A Crisis of Christian Conscious (256)……….. 186

The Comeback — 191
Happy NEW Year! (231).. 192
Permission to Shine (211).. 201
Overcast on Sunshine……. 208
Strut! (185.5)……………. 216
Coming Full Circle (174.0)…………………. 229

The Collapse — 234
Decisions…………………. 235
Reluctant Departure……… 239
Brenda's Call……………. 243
When it Rains…it Pours…. 263

The Heartache — 271
Social Media Medicine (200)……………. 272
Juggling Act………………. 280
The Horrors at Hudson General………….. 281
Code Red…………………. 286
August 17…………………. 288
A Brother's Love…………. 293

Contents

The Plummet	*301*
Dodging the Bullet……..	302
Donuts and Setbacks…...	304
An Affair of the Heart….	311
Caught Up………..……	316
Broken Vows Revealed…	325

The Affliction	*332*
Peace, Be Still……….....	333
Mama's Season……..….	336
Suspension of a Sound Mind………..…..	341
Home is Where the Fear Is……………...	342
The Spirit of Fear…….....	345

The Awakening	*349*
When Did I Give Up on Me?.......................	350
"Getting It"…………….	352
Facing the Truth……..….	357
Cleaning House…….…..	360
Strongholds Released….…	364

The Rise	*367*
FILED, STAMPED……….	368
The Lightbulb Moment……	374
Get it Together……………	377
Delays and Deception……..	381

The Revival	*386*
The Strength of a Woman…………………	387
Finding a Good Thing…..	388
"Yes…Yes…Yes."……...	397
Mama's Gift……………..	403

The Journey	*411*
Ties that Bind……………	412
D Day Arrives…………..	416
Pieces that Fit……………	419
The Countdown…………	424
Transitioned in Love……..	426
Choices, Chances, Changes…………………	430

The Mechanics of Weight Loss & Wellness ……. 434

"How I lost it!"

Introduction

I was born Susan Ronardo Lewis, seven pounds, two ounces, and kicking my way into the cosmos on the afternoon of March 30, 1972. I was a breech birth with my feet appearing first. My mother always told me that I was unique because of the unconventional way I chose to enter the world. My dad told me I was special because despite an unusual set of circumstances, I made it here anyway. Growing up, I never thought of myself as special or unique. In fact, I spent a great deal of my life wishing I was someone else, anyone else… except me.

Along the way, I discovered a Band-Aid to soothe my internal wounds. I found something that would calm the inner torment I struggled with, and produce a feeling of satisfaction, albeit temporary. I would run to it again and again throughout my life and systematically abuse it whenever I needed to escape…

Food.

The Onset

Early Activation of an Addiction

My love affair with eating began when I was about eight years old, right around the time my parents were going through a turbulent divorce. Although my parents collectively loved me, I don't think they recognized the kind of emotional impact their clashes had on me, their only child together. I constantly felt like I was torn between the two of them. In my mind, I felt I had to choose, and that somehow one parent would think I cared less for them if I spent more time with the other.

Constantly conflicted, I internalized my confusion and guilt over my parent's splitting up. It was always in the back of my mind that somehow I was the cause of their arguing. The regular exchange of harsh words between them broke my heart. I would often eat to pacify myself. Eating served as a "getaway" from the feelings I experienced, and it worked. Soon food became my "go-to" whenever I felt upset or hurt. Many years later in my adult life, I would be embroiled in a "History Repeats Itself" chapter of my own life involving my young daughters, and a very bitter and hostile divorce from their father.

Daddy

My father was a great dad. A loving and quite peculiar kind of man, he was kindhearted, and always had some sort of philosophical anecdote to offer. I always felt we were kindred spirits; I understood him when many people could not. I was very close to my father, and in many ways related more to him than to my mother.

My father met my mother in his late forties and fell in love with her instantly. The stories he would tell me about their unique courtship let me know that despite their divorce, he was still very much in love with her. He always described her has a "fox," with a beautiful smile. Mom was a single mother with two children from a previous marriage; Dad was single with no children. The odds of my parents conceiving a child was highly unlikely. My mother, at thirty-six, had undergone a partial hysterectomy due to painful bouts of endometriosis, and my father suffered from a low sperm count—a diagnosis he received while in the Navy in his earlier years. He was told he would never be able to conceive a child, and he accepted it. God had different plans however. I was born looking exactly like a replica of him. My mother told me of the joy he experienced, and the elation she felt, giving him the child he thought he never would have.

I can recall his colorful way of describing my coming to be: "You are here for a special assignment, Susie. There is a reason why you are here. God wants you to do something amazing, that's for sure—with half of your mother's equipment missing, and my handicapped sperm, you were meant to be here, Baby!" That was my dad, through and through.

My father defined the term hardworking; he worked as a bus driver for the Chicago Transit Authority and made sure we lacked nothing. It was not unusual for him to take on double shifts to help support our family. He had one vice that kept my mother at odds with him. He was addicted to gambling. When he was not working, he spent a lot of time and money at the horse race track. His addiction to gambling caused my parents' marriage to crumble. When I was eight years old, life as I knew it changed for good. The verbal attacks between them ensued, and it did not stop. My parents divorced and became instant enemies. The stress of being in the middle of a parental warzone took its toll on me. I blamed myself and became withdrawn. Most of my time was spent wondering what I did for all of this to happen. I began over-indulging myself with anything in the house that tasted good. My self-esteem issues were born during that confusing period in my life.

After the dust settled from my parents' divorce, life was happier for me. I spent a lot of time with my father making great memories. Every weekend with him was filled with activity and a lot of bonding time, with eating being at the forefront. His priority was making sure I was happy, and nothing made me happier than eating. Our outings always included a big lunch and a huge dinner before taking me back home. The more excited I became when he took me out to eat, the more he fed me, and there was no limit, either. My dad wanted to make certain I was content for the short amount of time we spent together, so he pulled out all the parental stops to make sure that was accomplished, even if that meant allowing me to eat to excess.

By the time I was ten years old, I was eating the kind of portions that would make a grown man stuffed. My weekend outings with my dad continued in the same fashion as I grew older. There was dinner at a restaurant of my choosing, where I would order way too much. As always, my father would happily indulge my requests, no matter how much food I would ask for. After dinner we would go to have dessert; Baker's Square Restaurant was my favorite. The waitresses practically knew us by name.

Within a few minutes of browsing the various whipped cream pies, I would pick my favorite out of the bunch—French silk. When one slice of pie would not satisfy my appetite for the sugar-filled dessert, I would ask my dad for another slice, and he would always oblige. After a couple of times of giving in to my appeal for more dessert, my father would soon purchase whole pies for me to eat, by myself. Needless to say, I was thrilled.

Times were turbulent with my divorced parents, and it was not uncommon for my dad to do the opposite of what my mother asked him to spite her, even at my expense sometimes. My father adored me, but he was not the most rational parent in the world when it came to making judgment call. Purposely defiant against my mother, he'd tell me that these whole pies he purchased were just for me to eat. He instructed me to hide them in my room so no one else could have any. I did just as he said.

Soon I made a habit of hoarding food in my room—hiding whole pies and large portions of food, closing my bedroom door, and eating all of it. My mother had no idea that it was common practice for me to stockpile large amounts of food in secret and eat until I would become sick, in an attempt satisfy boredom or whenever I felt lonely or depressed. By the time I was twelve years old, I had become a full-fledged addict; I was addicted to the taste of food, even to the sensation of my stomach being overstuffed, almost to the point of vomiting. I had no limits when it came to how much I ate, and since my dad always went to great lengths to make certain I was happy when we spent weekends together, it was the perfect scenario for an already obese child. It was also the makings of a perfect storm later in my life.

For many years after, we spent our weekends and vacation time laughing, talking and…eating.

Mama

My mother Vadis was just as unique a soul as her birth name. When she said she loved you, she meant it. She put her heart and soul into everything she touched. Mama was intense and protective to a fault when it came to her children. The end of her marriage to my father made her even more resilient. My father made sure he did his part financially after they split, and my mother worked just as hard to provide for her children. She made certain I did not want for anything. When it came to my father, despite how she felt about him, she would never say a harsh word about him to me. She knew I adored him, and she made sure I knew how much my father loved me too.

My relationship with my mother was one of respect and reverence. She was the matriarch of the family, strong in every sense of the word. She worked hard for everything she acquired; and made sure that her children understood the importance of an education so we wouldn't have to beg anyone for anything. She was independent, and very proud of it. She worked hard and never complained about it.

Along with being nurturing, she ran a tight ship too. While she worked as head of security for Belscot (a popular big-box store back in the '70s, similar to a K-Mart), my brother babysat. His job, in addition to taking care of me, was to make sure the house was spotless when she came home, even down to scrubbing the floorboards with a toothbrush. Her strong work ethic was ingrained in her very being; she raised her children with those same values.

In my mind, my mother was the REAL Superwomen I had seen so many times on TV. She was fearless. I vividly remember instances of my mother's bravery. One example in particular was when she gently woke me in the wee hours of the morning, put me in the car, and drove to Belscot so she could assess a burglary that had just occurred at the store. My mother would not leave me at home during the early-morning hours, so I was also in tow. I can still remember sitting in her car with the motor running to keep me warm while my mother rushed in to evaluate the crime scene. "Stay right here baby, keep the doors locked, Mama will be right back," she whispered to me with a smile. With her hand on her gun in its holster, she fearlessly stepped through the glass doors that had been shattered and into the darkened department store, checking out the premises while waiting on the police to arrive. I still remember the mixture of pride and admiration I felt for my mom as she handled her business like the true professional she was. She was my hero.

When my Mama was not working, she always seemed to be cooking. It was her passion. Whipping up homemade dishes made her happy. I believe it was a kind of therapy for her. My mom, who was born and raised in the south, cooked the same way her mom cooked: foods rich with butter and salt, and lots of cured meat.

There was never a shortage of food on my plate for dinner, and second helpings were plentiful. When kids my age were eating happy meals, it wasn't unusual for me to devour three pieces of chicken and side dishes without batting an eyelash. Eating large amounts of my mother's meals was what I looked forward to daily. My pattern was school, homework, and anticipating dinnertime.

My Mama's meals were absolute perfection too. I mean food so good, I would actually swing my feet and hum when I ate. Savoring delicious fried chicken and mashed potatoes smothered in onions and gravy made me giddy at the dinner table as a child. I wanted the taste of the food to last as long as possible on my tongue and when it disappeared, I ate more and more to satisfy the need. By the time I left the table I was stuffed…stuffed but happy.

My Mama shopped at specific department stores for my clothes, the ones that carried "chubby" clothes for girls and boys. We'd typically shop in the specialty section of Montgomery Ward for my school clothes. Although I was heavy, my mother always made sure that I looked good in whatever I wore, always reminding me to: "tilt your head up, stop looking down all the time Baby".

I was bashful and quiet in grade school. Some of my classmates were merciless with regard to my being overweight. School became a place I hated to go. I was teased and bullied as I took the short walk home from school. I never spoke up for myself, enduring the cruel taunts as I walked as fast as I could home with tears streaming down my face.

Unlike school, home was a refuge of acceptance for me. My mother, brother and sister were always lovingly protective of me. The term "fat" was never spoken in my house or anything remotely negative in terms of my weight. My siblings were considerably older than me, (my sister by 16 years, and my brother by 14 years) due to the age difference, in many ways I felt like an only child. Lonely for companionship and friends, food remained a steadfast source of entertainment and, in a way, "company" for me. It made me feel happy; it made the loneliness disappear for a little while.

Eventually the learned behavior of "emotional eating" I established as a child would eventually take precedence over everything else in my life.

The Divorce

The gravity of my parent's divorce weighed heavily on my very young shoulders. There was always an argument brewing between them, usually about differences in parenting. I can recall when my mother discovered the food I had been hiding in my room. She was furious. When I told her my dad had instructed me to do hide it, another argument ensued. As usual, I felt torn. Within me, I knew that hiding food from my mother and siblings was wrong, yet I did it anyway when my dad instructed me to. My mother's parental rules were in direct opposition of my father's most of the time. Deciding which parent to obey was always the decision I was forced to make. I loved them both; but they seemed to hate each other. The conflict and guilt I experienced over which parent to obey grieved me relentlessly. It was just easier to blame myself for everything, so I did.

There seemed to be no limit to what my father would attempt, to get back at my mother for divorcing him. Nothing was off limits, including maligning her character to embarrass her. My father accused my mother of abusing me. He went as far as reporting her to the Department of Children and Family Services for child neglect. I remember my school day being interrupted by a caseworker who came to my classroom to question me. She even asked my fourth grade teacher a series of questions regarding her opinion on how attentive my mother was. My father was hell-bent on discrediting my mother by accusing her of being unfit so that the courts would take away her full custody of me.

I was disciplined for the normal stuff kids do, but never was I abused in any way and my father knew that. When DCFS made a visit to my house, they found a well-kept home with a loving mother in it. After questioning my teachers and even our neighbors about the kind of parent my mother was, they found nothing. The charges my father accused her of were completely unfounded. The caseworker apologized to my mother for wasting her time. Even during that mortifying experience my mother stayed on the high road, never uttering a defaming word about my father to me.

When the failed attempt at discrediting my mother did not work, my father decided he would take me away from her. I was taken by my father to his ex-wife's house for three days without my mother's consent. I was kept there on the pretense that he was "saving me" from my mother who he claimed was unfit. He did not allow me call home, and refused to contact my mother to let her know where he had taken me.

While being intent on destroying my mother, my father hadn't a clue what he was doing to me. I was petrified. Eventually, my father returned me to my mother. Whether it was out of guilt or the fear of going to jail, I'm not sure, but I had missed three days of school, and had no idea why this was happening to me. I learned early on, about the lengths to which adults will go in order to hurt one another.

Even after the abduction incident, my mother never spoke unkindly about my father in my presence. I can't imagine the agony her heart she went through during that frightening ordeal. Her strength was never more exemplified, than during that period in my young life. I loved my father, but I despised how he tried to destroy my mother.

Mr. Samuel

I find it amazing that certain childhood memories can be so ingrained in the very fiber of our being, that when I recalled, they seem to be pop with color and in some instances with pain. My self-reproach took on a different form when my mother re-married a man named Mr. Samuel.

A few years after my parents' divorce, my mother began seriously dating again. Eventually she met and married a very tall and husky man, intimidating in stature with a rather soft voice—Mr. Samuel. I can recall the way he sucked his teeth loudly after dinner, his huge fingers pressing on his stomach after polishing off one of my mother's delicious meals.

Mr. Samuel a nickname for me; he called me "Brown Eyes." He was always nice to me, and appeared to make my mother happy. Whenever I heard an ice cream truck outside, he'd always make sure I had a dollar in my hand to spend on my favorite ice cream. Mr. Samuel had a big smile for his "Brown Eyes" whenever I came from school. I totally trusted him. I didn't have a reason not to.

My mother was always on the go, and most of the time she took me along on errands with her. On the rare occasion she'd go by herself, she had a babysitter look after me. She was very protective of me. She would not let just anyone look after me, however, on this particular day; she left me with Mr. Samuel for a short period while she ran an errand.

Mr. Samuel called me into our living room, where he was sitting on the large white couch in the middle of the room. As I sat down, he smiled and asked me if I had ever seen a "buddy" before.

"Like a friend?" I asked. "Yes, like a "friend" he said, still smiling. "This is my buddy right here." Mr. Samuel then proceeded to take his penis out of his pants and rub himself. I had never even heard of a penis, much less ever seen one. All I knew was that I was scared by what I saw, and confused. I wished my mother would come home. In my adolescent mind, I knew what he was doing was wrong. I had the talk about "stranger danger" and the bad adults who try to do bad things to kids, but this was my stepdad, someone I trusted. He was supposed to be different.

As I sat on the couch I was petrified. He took my hand and placed it on his penis. He told me to rub his "buddy," and pressed my hand down on himself. I felt like I was going to throw up. I can still remember the smell of it, how disgusting it felt, and the strong cologne he wore that filled my nostrils. As suddenly as it happened, it ended. He pulled his pants up and walked away quickly before my mother returned. I felt as if I had done something horrible. I was a bad girl, and that's why that happened to me, so I thought.

I felt utterly ashamed. By the time my mother returned, I had blocked the incident out of my head. I was afraid to tell anyone. Like my parents' divorce, I blamed myself for what Mr. Samuel to me. I kept silent about it. I made certain I was always with my mother whenever she left the house from that point on. I was afraid to be alone, even for a minute. Mr. Samuel tried his hardest to get me alone again. He insisted that he pick me up from school when my mother had to work late. My mother, for some reason, never agreed to it. I was relieved.

I never told my mother about the events of the day that she left me alone with my stepfather. Being protective as she was, my mother would have never forgiven herself. I never wanted her to carry that heavy burden, so I kept my silence. Some years later, my mother divorced Mr. Samuel. I was thrilled that he was out of our lives. I never saw him again.

Silent Suffering

When my mother decided to have a babysitter watch me in the evenings, I was relieved that I didn't have to stay alone. Mrs. Jackson lived across the park from the school I attended. I went to her house, did my homework, and played with her son, Sean. Sean was a couple of years younger than me, and we got along just fine. Tracy was Mrs. Jackson teenaged daughter. Tracy was eighteen, and spent most of her time getting high with her group of friends once her mother had gone to work.

When I was in Tracy's care, things were a lot different. As soon as Mrs. Jackson left, Tracy's demeanor changed. She became a sadist, and she was especially cruel when she was high. Her brother Sean was never in her line of fire—I was. When she wanted to be entertained after smoking weed, she would order Sean to go outside and make me stay inside with her. As soon as I heard her tell Sean to go, I would get sick to my stomach. I knew what would happen next.

For laughs, Tracy and her three friends would force me to strip naked and lie down on a bed. As I reluctantly got undressed, my whole body shook with fear and embarrassment. Tears rolled down my face as she cursed at me and ordered me to lay my "fat ass" down. As I made my way to the bed, I pleaded with them not to beat me. They seemed to enjoy my begging. My legs shook so hard that I could barely walk to the other side of the room. I walked toward the bed, naked and mortified. I was beaten across the back of my legs and buttocks until I begged her to stop. Tracy put me in the closet naked and left me there in the dark for hours. When she knew her mother was due home, she let me out and barked at me to get dressed. Like most abusers, she threatened me to keep quiet.

She told me my mother would never believe me, and that she would beat me even worse if I told anyone. I believed her. Wearied from her verbal and physical abuse, I collected enough courage to tell my mother what Tracy was doing to me while her mother was away. I never went back to Mrs. Jackson's house again; but by that time, I'd already internalized Tracy's words. They became a new addition to my damaged belief system.

When I reached high school, I began to come out of my shell a little. My mother had a lot to do with that. She always knew just what to say to make me smile. She was a beautiful woman, inside and out. She had a flair for doing hair and makeup, and was very glamorous. Even going to the grocery store, she would walk out the door absolutely flawless. I would sit on the side of the bathroom tub and watch her carefully as she applied her makeup effortlessly. She taught me how to enhance my features, play up my eyes, without overdoing it. Her mantra was "Less is more." I inherited her passion for hairstyling and cosmetics, and before long, I was a pro at accentuating my own positives. I have my mother's almond-shaped eyes, and I loved to experiment with creating new looks for myself while modeling myself after her style. I decided I wanted to be a hairstylist; I liked the idea of making others beautiful.

I loved hanging out with Mama on the weekends. She owned a small shoe store, and every Saturday morning, bright and early, we would head to the flea market to sell ladies' shoes that were overstocked at her store. I LOVED the flea market! There were so many food concession stands there. As soon as you walked in, the smell of hot dogs and grilled onions seemed to smack you in the face. I'd take my allowance and run to the concession stands and buy two hot dogs with a slice of pizza on the side as soon as we arrived. That's pretty much how I would spend the day... helping my mom, but mainly eating, and drinking sugary soda.

I paid no attention to the jeans or costume jewelry that most pre-teens would beg their parents to buy. I was much more interested in the snack bar located three booths behind my mom's shoe display. Those were some of the best moments in my life, hanging out with Mother and watching her in action selling shoes. I admired her so much; I wanted to be just like her when I grew up. She was tough; she didn't let anyone walk over her. I felt so safe being with her. She kept me close and shielded me from the world's harsh realities as much she could. She kept me in a cocoon of love with my older brother and sister.

When I stepped out of the loving warmth of my home, the outside world was certainly different. Throughout grade school, I continued to deal with peer bullying, which was mostly verbal, but cruel nonetheless. A few of the nicknames I'd acquired by the time I reached 7th grade were "Moose" and "Big Sue." My tormentors held on to their desks and pretended that the ground was shaking as I walked by them to solve a problem on the chalkboard. The classroom erupted in laughter as I stood there mortified. My skin wasn't thick by any means, and I internalized every negative comment made. I often found myself wishing I could be as fearless as my mom. If I was strong like her, I wouldn't let the bad things that people say bother me so much.

Like in my favorite cartoons, I spent a lot of my time wishing I could suddenly turn into someone else…poof, like magic.

The Progression

Teen Years

Becoming a teenager can be a difficult phase for a girl. There seems to be an inner struggle taking place at lightning speed within you. There seems to be a constant state of limbo between childhood and womanhood, and an endless search to discover where you fit in between the two. It's no wonder teenage girls are so moody and temperamental. This is the point in a young girl's life where her personal values are beginning to form. She starts to discover what she knows to be true about her herself, or in some cases the internal falsehoods that she believes to be true about who she is.

I kind of tiptoed into high school. I didn't want to be seen. I flew under the radar. I was shy and had a couple of friends, but I was not popular by any means. I wanted to fit in so badly and did whatever I could to be acknowledged by my peers. I ended up joining my high school marching band, which was a great experience for me. It gave me a bit of confidence. I felt like I was a part of something. I yearned for validation from fellow bandmates, something I sought desperately.

I practiced my clarinet and strived to be the best I could be, and I was pretty good too. There were hazing rituals that seemed to be the standard; if you wanted to be a "somebody" in the band, you had to "prove" your worthiness. This was my opportunity to feel like I belonged, and to have my bandmates accept me. I eagerly went along with these "rituals" in an effort to fit into their exclusive group. From getting dirt and mud shoved down my throat, to being doused with a water hose, I endured the abuse; even being paddled so severely I had broken skin and blisters for days afterwards.

Although there were some stunts that even I wasn't crazy enough to partake in, like skin searing with hot metal forks and sex with male bandmates in exchange for acceptance, some of them I did. None of my attempts made any difference, because I wasn't accepted anyway. My esteem allowed the degradation over and over again, hoping that I could eventually belong. My grades suffered because of misplaced priorities, which ultimately made me feel not only like a social loser, but an academic one as well.

Stuffing Emotions

After I tossed my tassel and cap in the air, and the auditorium doors shut for the final time, I was excited to close the high school chapter in my life. I graduated with barely average grades, not because of a subpar intelligence, but because my grades were not a priority. My goal was a never-ending quest to find my misplaced worth. My childhood encounters with shame still burned fresh in my mind, even in my latter teen years. I taught myself to internalize rejection, and soothed my feelings with large amounts of food like I had been so accustomed to doing all my life.

By the time I was eighteen, I had the emotional eating cycle down to a science. I stuffed myself to quiet uncomfortable emotions on a regular basis. Because I was uncomfortable with confrontation, I dealt with frustrations in my personal life with a piece of cake or whatever dessert I could get my hands on. I found the taste of fried food exhilarating, so I used it as a temporary fix for anger, resentment, fear and anxiety. In other words, I ate in order to numb myself.

By the time I was twenty, my feelings of unworthiness were deeply rooted, but from all outward appearances, you couldn't tell. I was a master at hiding behind make-up and false confidence. I often found myself searching for affirmation from others, particularly men, to feel better about myself. I hid behind tight jeans and plunging necklines, to deflect the insignificance I felt within. I sought lover after lover, in an attempt to feel valued, but with each experience I was left with gaping hole of disgust. I tried drinking and smoking marijuana in an effort to create the kind of self-assurance I sought, only to come up empty each time.

In my quiet moments alone I thought about what it would be like to be someone else. I wanted so badly to look like my beautiful mother. She was so graceful, talented and strong. I wanted to be sought after like my best friend Nikki was. She was heavyset like me, but brimming with confidence. I secretly admired how she could get any guy's attention she wanted, including the ones that I was interested in.

Lies My Mirror Told Me

At twenty-one years old, I was 245 pounds and introverted. No one knew the depths of my self-degradation and the inner torment that I battled on a daily basis during that time. My lack of esteem began to affect my decisions across the board. I unconsciously punished myself with harsh self-criticism for my own perceived inadequacies. Disgusted by my own reflection, I was unable to find any redeeming qualities about myself, and made a mental checklist on how many things were wrong with me daily. When it was absolutely necessary that I attend a social event, I purposely hid in the background, hoping that no one would see the "fat girl" in the room. It unnerved me when people looked at me too long. My introversion was often mistaken for unfriendliness by others, which wasn't the case at all. Consequently, their accusations drove me further into my shell.

As a coping mechanism, I routinely ate myself happy. The taste of sugar and fried foods numbed me. I came to depend on the almost euphoric state of mind I experienced when I ate. Hunger wasn't a factor when I ate these massive amounts of food; I was hooked on the feeling eating provided. It reduced my negative feelings and enabled me to deal with daily stressors. I wasn't oblivious to what I was doing to myself either. I knew that overeating was causing my rapid weight gain, and would eventually be damaging to my health if I continued, however the immediate gratification I received was enough to outweigh any potential long-term negative consequences. Over time, my self-destructive behaviors became engrained. I no longer felt in control, and simply gave myself over to my eating impulses.

The more I ate, the more I felt badly about it. Unlike more traditional addictions where the abuse of the substance can be hidden from view, food addicts wear their addiction outwardly for the world to see. My weight began to make it difficult to walk upstairs or sit comfortably in a chair. I also found it difficult to breathe normally. I wheezed heavily from simply walking up a flight of stairs due to the excessive weight that I carried on my frame.

My poor self-image caused me to walk with my head down, never making eye contact with anyone unless it was completely necessary. My sister Brenda always made it a point to gently tilt my chin upward as a reminder to hold my head up whenever we were together, but I didn't want to be seen—I wanted to be invisible. For as long as I can remember, whenever I spoke to anyone, I shielded my mouth slightly so as not to show my crooked teeth. *"You can't open your mouth, everyone will see your teeth,"* I reminded myself whenever I began to laugh or smile.

I avoided any impending judgment by just covering my mouth altogether when I spoke. I hated taking pictures and avoided them at all costs. In the morning I spent just enough time in front of my mirror to make sure everything was buttoned correctly and that my hair was neat. Other than that, I avoided ever looking at myself for too long.

Finding My Way

My career path was strewn with disappointment after I graduated high school. I was not accepted into the university I dreamed of going to, which was devastating to me. I dreamed of becoming a broadcast journalist; in fact, I aspired to be the next Barbara Walters. When the rejection letters came from Eastern Illinois University and a few other schools I applied to, I gave up on my journalism dreams. There was one other thing that made me feel as good as writing did—creating hairstyles for others and applying cosmetics. As an alternative career choice, I decided to pursue a career as a cosmetologist. I threw myself into studying hard and applying what I learned. Doing hair and makeup gave me a sense of confidence that nothing else ever did.

I was excited when I graduated at the top of my class and earned my cosmetology license in the fall of 1991. My accomplishment gave me a new sense of pride that helped with my introversion. After graduating from cosmetology school, I immediately started working as a stylist in a salon near my home. I was thrilled that I had a job doing what I loved to do. I enjoyed creating hairstyles and building a rapport with my clients. It gave me so much satisfaction to see the smiles of appreciation from the ladies that I serviced.

Within a year, I built a solid reputation as one of the best stylists in the salon. I had regular clients from morning until night, nonstop. I was sought after for my talent, which helped to replace the negative opinions I had about myself and my abilities. No one ever told me that I was good at anything until I made it onto my salon floor. In no time at all, I was netting impressive earnings for myself as a stylist. My confidence began taking shape; however, my food addiction was still constant in the background. I celebrated a lucrative day at the salon with submarine sandwiches, bags of French fries, and pints of chocolate chip ice cream.

My happier days as a stylist came to an embarrassing halt one Saturday afternoon as I sat down for a short break between clients. As I adjusted myself in the salon chair, something about its wooden frame felt unsteady. Before I had a chance to get up, the entire chair suddenly collapsed with a loud crash beneath me. I was totally mortified. All of the salon and barber clients stared in shock as I sat helplessly in the heap of broken chair pieces on the floor; I wanted to die right there.

To make matters worse, the salon owner, who was known for her discourteous demeanor, yelled across the room at me, "you're gonna have to pay for that chair you broke!" Apologetic and embarrassed, I slowly gathered myself and walked to the restroom, my arm and shoulder still in pain from falling on the floor. I cried until my eyes burned. I left out of the back door and headed across the street to Burger King for a meal big enough to make me forget what had just happened. I sat in the back of the restaurant alone and devoured an order of chicken tenders, a double cheeseburger, and a large chocolate shake. I ate until the taste of the food granted me the level of euphoria I was looking for. After polishing off my meal and brushing the crumbs from my shirt, I returned to the salon as if nothing had happened. I felt the stares from my co-workers, but no one said a word to me about the incident. From that day on, I made it a point to stand on my breaks, or lean on my counter for needed support. My accident in the salon did not stop my eating binges, however. If anything, they became even worse.

The Dependence

Now Pronounce You…Broken

When it came to relationships with the opposite sex, my judgment was, let's say, a bit skewed. My self-esteem issues came into play overwhelmingly when it came to men. I wanted to be loved. I wanted someone to love me enough to cancel out the disdain I had for myself.

I allowed myself to become a doormat. I chose the wrong men again and again, allowing some to use me for whatever they wanted at the time. Opportunists smell insecurity. They seek out women with low self-esteem, just as lions hunt vulnerable sheep. I was the perfect target too; I was insecure and I had money. I was just happy to be with someone who paid attention to me. Even though I had a thriving career as a hairstylist, I was emotionally bankrupt and longed for a meaningful relationship with someone who genuinely cared for me.

In 1994, life as I knew it changed forever. I became a mother for the first time to a beautiful baby girl named Denai. I married Denai's father Aaron shortly after I found out I was pregnant. Aaron was not particularly ambitious, and lived with his mother. Knowing that, I didn't give it a second thought. My main concern was maintaining a relationship with someone who said they cared about me. The fact that he wasn't employed, and had no prospects of becoming employed, was of no consequence to me. *I mean, really, who was I to be that picky anyway?* I rationalized. My mother, who had an impeccable knack for discernment, warned me about getting involved with Aaron. Her maternal instinct was razor sharp when it came to advising me. Stubborn and unyielding, I refused to listen to her counsel, dismissing it for the sake of "standing by my man."

Shortly after our daughter was born, and just as my mother warned, things took a turn for the worse. Aaron was incarcerated. Because I could no longer stand for long periods of time, I quit my lucrative job as a hairstylist. My mother temporarily took on the role of provider for my newborn daughter and me without hesitation. My world began to unravel. Suddenly, I was a single mother with no income and a jailed husband, which was not my original plan after getting married. Depression set in heavily. I began to wake up in the middle of the night to fits of horrific panic—confusion, body trembling, heart palpitations, and my head pounded as if it were going to explode. The episodes became frequent and with more intensity. I was terrified of telling anyone, what was happening to me at night. I thought for certain I was losing my mind.

Meanwhile, I ate everything I could get my hands on. In the middle of eating breakfast, I would figure out what I could have for lunch, and so on. Whenever I had a few dollars to spend, I spent it on fast food. It was a regular occurrence for me to take off in my car in the middle of the night (in my pajamas) and head to a late-night McDonald's. I ordered enough food for two people and ate it in my driveway. Like a drug addict, I always binged in secret.

Hidden from view, I tore the bag open and placed the containers on the passenger's seat in the order I wanted to eat them in. The scent of the fast food seemed to intoxicate me. Whatever was going on in my life disappeared with great ease when I tasted the greasiness from a cheeseburger or the saltiness from the French fries I heaped into my mouth. The emotional crash from what I had done was the worst. When I realized how much I had eaten, I felt utterly disgusted. I despised myself for what I'd just done. I made promises to myself never to do it again, but I always did. It was a covert, vicious cycle that continued without slowing down. I kept my activities well hidden. I was a master at it. No one had a clue, but the evidence was becoming more and more obvious.

At twenty-six years old, I was tipping the scales at 300 pounds, and I started to have health issues stemming from my obesity. My back constantly ached. The pain in my knees became a problem, and although I am certain it went undetected for a long time, I began to suffer the effects from high blood pressure.

I had been experiencing symptoms for years, but never knew why I had dizzy spells and awful headaches almost daily. After a routine check-up, I was diagnosed with severe hypertension and began taking medication to control it. My doctor warned me about my excessive weight gain and was very concerned about the downward shift in my health. I have a history of hypertension, heart disease, diabetes, and stroke on both sides of my family. My mother had at least three mini-strokes before the age of fifty-five, and she had to go on dialysis for diabetes. My sister had a myriad of health issues as well, including hypertension and like my mother; she underwent weekly dialysis treatments as well for kidney disease.

I knew I needed to do something to lose weight, so I decided to go the commercial diet route. I tried just about every diet known to man, especially those that promised quick weight loss in a matter of weeks. I got the recipes for the cabbage diet, the grapefruit diet, and cayenne pepper lemonade diet…you name it, and I tried it. I bought six packs of Slim-Fast shakes, and even started getting B-12 shots mixed with some other weight loss drug injected every week by a guy named "Dr. Brown." Word had gotten around that Dr. Brown was the real deal—He had people dropping weight like crazy with these weekly weight loss shots.

Whether he was a real doctor or not didn't really matter to me at that point. He had an office that looked like a doctor's office, with the typical patient bed, and syringes for the shots on a table. I thought I would give him a try since none of the soup diets worked for me. The side effects from Dr. Brown's B-12 drug cocktail injection made me feel terrible. My heart raced uncontrollably. I felt like I was having a heart attack every time I left my appointment with him. I was dizzy and light-headed for hours afterwards. I rationalized that if I just hung in there with the injections, the side effects would subside eventually, and it would be worth it in the end if I lost weight.

The effects of Dr. Brown's weekly shots never got better. As a matter of fact, they got worse, and on top of that, I still hadn't lost a single pound. After a month of treatments, I saw no results whatsoever and got frustrated. I stopped going. I put my weight issues in the back of my mind. I quit trying to lose weight; I just dealt with it the best I could.

Being idle was never my thing. I longed to get back to what I loved, styling hair. I missed the comradery I had with my clients; I missed the salon atmosphere and the challenge of creating something beautiful for the ladies who trusted me with their tresses. After Denai grew a bit older, I made the decision to get back on my feet and start doing hair again—it was time.

I relocated to a new salon, and quickly got back into the swing of things and into my old routine. When standing became an issue while I styled hair, I sat down on a stool to do my clients. I felt like things were finally coming together. The salon I worked at was quite successful. There were lots faithful clients with money to spend each week. From opening until closing, business was booming. Eventually I saved enough money to buy my first car. A brand new, candy apple red Chevy Cavalier with vanity plates that read: SUE BABY. I was over the moon. Even though I was married with a child, in many ways, I felt as if adulthood was just beginning for me. Being able to financially take charge of my life was incredibly gratifying.

After Aaron was released from jail, his financial support for our daughter was non-existent. Still living with his mother, he had excuse after excuse as to why he could not help provide for our daughter and got angry when I would even mention his absent child support. My mother was so loving and generous to us. She made certain Denai lacked nothing. She adored her granddaughter and never asked for a dime while we lived with her. I was glad to finally be in the position to help her if she ever needed me. I filed for divorce in the spring of 1996 from Aaron. I was taking charge of my life, and felt good too. Despite my weight and health issues, I felt like my life was coming together, finally.

Searching for a Savior – Darryl

I met Darryl at the salon in the summer of 1997. He had an appointment with our barber for a haircut. Darryl was a stout, heavyset guy with a wide smile and deep dimples. I was instantly attracted to him. Always unsure of myself and painfully shy, I would have never dreamt of approaching a guy I was attracted to, much less in the crowded salon where I worked.

Over the typical salon gossip, I intently eavesdropped as he engaged in the usual barbershop banter with the other guys in the room. With curling iron in motion, I looked over my client's head and quickly glanced in the mirror next to me to make sure I looked okay, just in case he decided to say hello. Hair and beard neatly trimmed, Darryl proceeded out of the door. Just as the door shut behind him, I took an extra glance through the salon window as he walked down the sidewalk. I held my breath, still hoping he would turn around and look in my direction, but he never did.

The salon manager whom I was friends with whispered to me that she noticed me glaring at Darryl as I styled my client's hair. I giggled and confessed. Without another word, she scribbled something on a piece of paper and dashed out the door. When she returned, she was grinning from ear to ear. She literally chased Darryl down and gave him my phone number. I didn't know whether to kick her or kiss her. I dismissed her gesture and figured he would never call me anyway. *He probably just took my phone number to be nice.* I thought indifferently. I wasn't his type, I was sure of it. Much later on I would find out that I was, undoubtedly his type.

With high hopes I waited for Darryl to call me. Sure enough he did a couple of hours later. From a pay phone, he asked me if I wanted to hang out later that evening. I jumped at the chance, but casually answered, "Sure, I think I can move some things around in my schedule." I was so excited that he seemed to be interested in me. With great expectations swirling around in my head, I asked where he wanted to meet. He asked if I could come over to his house, because he didn't have a car. I didn't think twice about accepting Darryl's invitation, even though I had never driven on the expressway before. He lived on the other side of the city, which meant I would have to venture outside of my familiar terrain. Casting my fears and apprehensions aside, my new car and I headed west, via the expressway. I made it there without incident and felt pretty brave for doing so.

After finding a parking spot, I spent at least forty-five minutes assessing how I looked. I pushed and tugged on my sweater while adjusting and re-adjusting my bra so my cleavage would be visible. I wrestled with my tight girdle to make my stomach appear flatter in my jeans. By the time I was done pushing and pulling on my outfit I was out of breath and exhausted. I don't think I had ever been so nervous. My objective was to look as perfect as possible in order to gain his interest. After giving myself a final pep talk, I walked up to his apartment building. Suddenly, my head began to pound with pressure. I felt dizzy, and my heart started that racing thing it did from time to time. I stopped for a minute, took a deep breath, and remembered that in all the excitement of meeting Darryl, I hadn't taken my blood pressure meds at all that day. I dismissed the thought and began walking up the stairs with purpose.

When he opened the door and invited me in, I noticed he had minimal furniture. His living/dining room had just a couch and a table, which was fine with me. We sat and talked for a bit, just getting to know each other. When I asked him where he worked, he told me about his string of bad luck with jobs, in fact, he had just gotten fired the day before from a security guard position. I was immediately sympathetic to his plight. I told him all about my job as a hairstylist and how excited I was that I had just bought my first car, brand new. We went back and forth about our lives. He had no children; I told him I was divorced with a four-year-old daughter.

As time went on, I really began to like Darryl a lot. He was charming and said all the right things to make me smile. We shared a mutual appreciation for the same music, and he was an excellent cook too. He'd prepare great dishes every time I came over, which soon became on a regular basis. Becoming concerned about the fact that he still hadn't gotten a job after weeks turned into months, I inquired on how his job search was going. I grew worried that he would not be able to pay his rent and utilities when they were due.

He explained that his rent was not something he was overly concerned about. The apartment he lived in was owned by a good friend of his mother's, and whenever he was short, his mother would just help him out on his rent. One evening, I overheard a rather heated exchange between Darryl and his landlord concerning the non-payment of his rent. The landlord threatened to put him out if he did not become current on his bills. Apparently, this was not the first conversation they had about Darryl not paying rent. His landlord made good on his promise, and soon after, Darryl was evicted. He moved in with his mother and stepfather. I felt so badly for him. I helped him financially as much as I could with buying groceries and letting him drive my car when he wanted to.

Darryl and I became exclusive. As his girlfriend, I felt obligated to help him find a job somehow, and I did just that. I left no stone unturned in my pursuit, including asking an ex-boyfriend if he knew of any job openings for Darryl. It turned out that my ex had recently quit his job as a bouncer at a popular Chicago venue to pursue something else. As a favor to me, he was kind enough to put in a good word for Darryl with management, and just like that, Darryl was hired. I was ecstatic for him. I believed in him and knew he would do well at this job. After less than a year, he was fired for not showing up to work on time, excessively.

By this time, my mother felt compelled to let me know how she felt about my getting involved with Darryl. She cautioned me about becoming involved with a man who was not financially stable, like I did when I was with Aaron. My mother's uncanny ability to call things the way she saw them was always spot-on. I protested and rebelled against her advice. I was angry at her for not believing in my new beau like I did. Besides, she didn't know Darryl like I did. How dare she insinuate he was not good for me?

I had fallen for Darryl hard. *How could my own mother not want me to be happy?* I asked myself. Soon after, my relationship with my mother became very strained. After being fed-up with her forewarnings, I pouted and stormed out of her house and moved in with Darryl and his mother. Acknowledging my adult decision to leave, my mother's only request was that I allow Denai, who was five years old at the time, to continue to stay with her, so as not to uproot her from the pre-school she was attending. I agreed. My mother was lovingly protective of her grand-daughter. She wanted to make sure my spontaneous decisions did not affect Denai adversely. Misplaced pride sparked rebellion against my mother's advice at every turn, thus putting a strain on our relationship.

It wasn't long before Darryl was driving my car more than I was. I noticed a few dings at first in the body of the car, then dents that were more obvious. I was upset, to say the least. This was the car I had saved so long to get. I was so proud of it, and now it had been damaged, and I was still making payments on it.

The shock that I was not prepared for came in the form of a planned trip to my mother's house to pick up my Denai for the weekend. As I tried to open my car door, it wouldn't budge. The door had been dented in such a way that I had to force the car door to open. As if that weren't enough, when I did manage to force open the door, to my utter shock, I saw that the driver's seat had been completely broken back. I burst into tears immediately. I could not believe my eyes. Not only was my car destroyed inside and out, but Darryl had never even bothered to tell me. I was hurt and angry, but Darryl knew what to say to get back in my good graces. He was a charmer, if nothing else. "Oh, I meant to tell you about that, baby. I don't even know how that happened. I PROMISE I will get your car fixed. I PROMISE." I never received an apology, nor did he own up to damaging the car. I just got promises that he would make it right. I hoped with everything I had that he meant it.

Things were getting tight financially. My clientele deceased due to my sporadic work schedule at the salon; and I wasn't proactive about getting any new clients either. As long as I broke even, I was okay with that. I became too pre-occupied with making sure things were okay in my relationship with Darryl to be concerned with much else. I had become a master enabler. I did everything in my power to keep things harmonious between us. Darryl didn't seem to mind that money was tight; he knew I would take care of everything, and I did one way or the other. I went back to my coping mechanism for dealing with pressure and turmoil…eating. I spent a great deal of time stressing over bills and stuffing my face with anything that was greasy and fried.

In 1999 I found out I was pregnant. Not wanting to have my baby outside of wedlock, there was an agreement that we would get married. We set a date for the fall. My sister agreed to purchase my wedding ring, on the pretense that Darryl reimburse her. He never did. Much like the promise he made to me about getting my car fixed, it never happened. In September of that same year we got married. I was overjoyed about our new marriage, and the tiny person that would soon call me Mommy. I was confident that Darryl would become motivated to really dig his heels in and get a job, now that we were married and had a baby on the way. With our family expanding, we needed a place to call our own. I applied for an apartment close to my mother's house. We moved in, and things were okay for a while. While pregnant, I still worked as a stylist for as long as I could stand to be on my feet, counting on my faithful clients that remained with me to generate income.

Darryl, still unemployed, insisted that he was looking. My family knew we were struggling, and they did all they could to help us with things for Denai and our new baby girl we named Lanie. My mother and sister bought us a couple of pieces of furniture for our new apartment, to which I was very grateful.

We had a family friend who was like a brother to me. Chris had a thriving elevator repair company, and he was looking to hire several elevator technicians. I asked him if he would consider hiring Darryl even though he had absolutely no experience in elevator repair. Chris agreed as a favor to me. This was a great opportunity to get on our feet and not depend so much on my family. I was hopeful, and prayed that Darryl would do well, as I knew he would. I believed in him. I saw the untapped potential he had if he was only given the chance to prove himself.

Darryl started the job and was off to a flying start. Aside from his not-so-stellar attributes, Darryl was a smart man. He was adaptable, which is why I knew he would pick up on whatever Chris taught him. Anyone would have killed to be in Darryl's position. No knowledge of the elevator repair business, yet making the money of a licensed technician. Chris was so impressed with how fast Darryl learned the business that he offered to pay for him to go to trade school to become fully licensed like the other technicians. He could have potentially received a higher pay grade based on him becoming licensed. I figured that Darryl was making pretty good money working for Chris, although he never revealed to me how much. I later found out through Chris that he was making about $23.00 an hour.

Things were looking up. Darryl helped occasionally on the household bills and was enjoying spending the money he was making. He wasted no time buying new shoes, clothes and video game consoles like PlayStation and Xbox. He would hide how much he made, and would always change the subject when I brought it up. I paid the bills from my personal account. He gave me money here and there to help. We never had joint bank accounts. Darryl was unable to get his own bank account because of money he owed on past delinquent bank accounts. He asked to be added to my account, but I never did it. Deep down I loved him, but I didn't trust him. I knew if he had access to my account, he would dip into any money I had without my knowledge. After the whole car incident, I learned not to give his word much credence.

Darryl worked for Chris for almost three years. He had assigned locations that he was to go to in order to do repairs with other technicians. Chris was rarely onsite at these locations, but sometimes he would do pop-up visits to see how things were progressing with the repairs. He trusted that his crew would be at their assigned locations and not elsewhere while on the clock.

Darryl came home early from work one day looking upset. Chris had fired him. Always taking Darryl's side, my initial reaction was anger toward Chris. *"How could he just fire my husband like that? Darryl was the best tech he had!"* I griped. I soon came to find out that Darryl had been stealing time, essentially. He was clocking in, but not going to the assigned location to do the work. I also learned he had done it in the past, but Chris gave him a pass with a warning.

Darryl was banking on the fact that Chris would never fire him because of me. Chris did what he had to do. After I found out the truth, I didn't blame him. He had a business to run, and he wasn't going to allow someone to run it into the ground. Never taking responsibility for his actions, Darryl blamed everyone but himself for getting fired yet again. Some of his co-workers told Chris what he was doing, and Chris even caught Darryl not being at the location he was supposed to be at on more than one occasion. I was deeply embarrassed by his actions. There I was singing my husband's praises to Chris, telling him what an asset Darryl would be to his company, only to be made a fool of. The opportunity of a lifetime had been tossed away, along with any credibility Darryl had as far as I was concerned. The familiarity of disappointment stung within me. I was done this time, and I meant it. I made plans to end our marriage and move on with my life, my two kids and me.

During this turbulent period, my unexplained panic episodes resurfaced with a vengeance. My symptoms were the same, but more intense than before; confusion, racing heartbeat, feeling suffocated and excruciating, pounding headaches. Jolting out of the bed in complete fear, my legs buckled under me. Scanning my bedroom room to get my bearings, I couldn't figure out where I was for the first minute or so, as if my brain had short-circuited. It was completely terrifying experience. As my panic elevated, so did the intensity of the episodes.

When these unexplained episodes threatened to send me over the edge of my sanity, I called on God, the only One I knew who could relieve my tormented mind. I clutched my mother's huge white bible as I prayed repeatedly. My only source of comfort was cradling that white bible in my arms as I rocked myself back and forth, sometimes for hours at a time, repeating the Psalm 91 scripture until my eyes became heavy with fatigue: *'He who dwells in the shelter of the Most High will rest in the shadow of the Almighty. I will say of the LORD, 'He is my refuge and my fortress, in Him I will trust...'*

Those words gave me incredible solace. As I allowed each verse to deeply penetrate my thoughts, I was gently ushered into His Peace. The kind of peace that is truly indescribable. I had always heard my mother and sister talk about the power of the words in Psalm 91, but up until that point in my life, it was just meaningless chatter. Just their opinion of a scripture as it pertained to their own lives. It wasn't impactful to me until I could relate to clinging on to the words as if my survival depended on it. While going through the torment my mind created, Psalm 91 became real to me in my darkest and most distressing hours. Had it not been for the Grace of God that calmed my stormy mind, I have no idea what would have happened to me.

Home Again

It seemed as if Darryl knew I was going to end things with him, even though I hadn't announced it yet. His demeanor changed; he became helpful and was even deliberately looking for employment. I saw him searching through the paper more for jobs, which made me extremely encouraged. Deep down I still loved him and wanted our marriage to work. I hoped that perhaps this was the beginning of a shift for him.

We were over our heads between the rent at our apartment and the bills that were constantly overdue. I couldn't keep up. With no foreseeable options, I regrettably decided to ask my mother if we could move in with her on a temporary basis. I was mortified that our circumstances had declined to that point. I swallowed my pride and went to visit her to test the waters. I told her about the issues we had been going through financially, and how it was becoming impossible to keep up with the bills with just one paycheck sustaining us. "Mama, do you mind if we move in with you for a little while, just until Darryl gets a job?" I asked, looking down at the kitchen table, too ashamed to look her in the face. I hated hearing myself ask. I just hated it.

My mother took a break from cutting potatoes and turned her attention to me. "You know you and the girls are always welcome here baby, but Darryl is going to have to—"

"I know, Mama," I interrupted, anticipating her words. "He has to help out and get a job, I know. Darryl is looking Mama; he really is out there looking. We will help with the bills and stuff; I just appreciate you allowing us to stay here until we get on our feet."

"Okay, baby. Then ya'll can come on," my mother responded with a slight smile. I noticed that she looked really tired, and it appeared as if she hadn't been feeling well. "How have you been feeling, Mama? You look tired." I said, grabbing another knife and helping her chop the vegetables.

"I'm all right, got a little headache, but other than that, I'm okay." My mother never told us when she wasn't feeling well; she never complained, and she did her best to hide it. My brother, sister and I knew when something wasn't right with her even though she always denied it. "How is dialysis going?" I asked while looking into her eyes to see if I could pinpoint what was wrong. "It's going alright," she replied, as she returned to meticulously cutting the potatoes into perfect little squares.

My sister Brenda and my mother were both on dialysis, and I witnessed firsthand how physically taxing the long process was for them both. I could tell that lately my sister wasn't feeling her best either. Brenda had been through so much illness in her life. She battled with debilitating endometriosis, chronic migraines, and most recently, kidney failure. As much as she had gone through, no one would have blamed her for complaining about the constant pain she was in, but she never did. Her smile was infectious, and she had an unflappable, cheery personality that caused people to gravitate to her. Every now and then I would catch her wincing in pain when she thought no one was around, and my heart broke for her. I wished that I could alleviate her constant pain. Her strength through the adversity in her life, both physical and emotional, was nothing short of amazing.

I told Darryl about asking my mother if we could move in with her, and he was all for it. I told him about the conditions of the move-in, and that he seriously needed to find a job, any job, so that we could pay her. He promised he would, and I prayed that he would keep that promise to me.

We moved in with my mother a week after my visit with her. Darryl and I took the basement, while the kids took my old bedroom upstairs. My mother's basement was unfinished. It had no furniture, and sometimes it leaked when it rained. It was nothing fancy, but I was grateful to be somewhere where we didn't have to worry about getting kicked out because we couldn't afford the rent. Part of me was glad to be home with my mother and sister. The kids missed spending time with them, and so did I. We would have an opportunity to reconnect, and my mother could have an opportunity to bond with her son-in-law as well. I kept my fingers crossed that all would work out.

Mama's House

One of the conditions of moving in with my mother was that Darryl and I would do our part with helping to pay the household bills. The agreement was that Darryl and I split the amount my mother asked for which was $400.00 per month, equaling $200.00 from him and $200.00 from me. It was a reasonable request, and very generous considering there were four extra mouths to feed in my mother's home now.

By this time, I had been out of circulation for so long, my clientele at the salon dwindled down to just a few ladies a month. I had no time to re-build my clientele, either. I needed to generate income, and quickly. After working a few temp jobs here and there, I got a job working for Bank of America in their lockbox division. The position paid $9.50 an hour, which was a lot less than what I was making as a successful stylist, but I wasn't complaining. I was working consistently, and that's all that mattered. I accepted as much overtime as they offered on the weekends to make extra money. With me working, and Darryl still receiving unemployment, paying rent shouldn't have been an issue…but it became one—Big time.

Somehow, every month it seemed Darryl would either be late or not pay his portion of the rent at all. I began making excuses to my mother as to why Darryl was unable to pay his half. When the excuses became the same old song, I just started paying his part, or as much as I could, just to keep the peace in the house. My mother was no fool though; she knew what I was doing. She wasn't happy about Darryl not keeping up his end of our agreement, and she was quite vocal about it. The tension became almost unbearable in the house. When confronted about why he couldn't pay his part to her, his reply was always the same: "I'll have the money next month, Mama, I promise. I'm just short right now." Darryl was actually making more in unemployment than I was making working for BOA; I had no clue why he was always broke or claimed to be. I began to resent him living there, but I resented myself even more for allowing him to stay.

The arguments between Darryl and me about money were always ongoing in the house. They always ended with harsh words exchanged and Darryl slamming the door as he stormed out. I always felt guilty for causing him to leave. Maybe he was doing the best he could. I was just nagging my poor husband, I convinced myself. Just like when I was a little girl, I blamed myself for everything, constantly second-guessing my decisions. I hated when Darryl was angry with me. I would beg for his forgiveness whenever he came back home, even if he was dead wrong. I just didn't want him to leave me. I held back on asking him why he couldn't pay the rent or help out. I just did what I had to do to keep him and Mama civil toward one another.

I found myself spending my money on whatever the girls needed, and paying all of Darryl's rent on a regular basis. On the occasions when he did pay his portion, he did it begrudgingly, as if to say, "I did it, now get off my back." It didn't matter to me how he gave it, I was just overjoyed that he did. I kept hoping he would become responsible. I kept hoping that our marriage would get better, and that he would take his role of husband and father seriously. I loved him, but hated how he took me for granted. I cried myself to sleep just about every night.

When the pressure of our martial issues became too much, I'd leave the kids with my mother and drive off to a secluded area to binge eat. It was like a covert mission. I set off to find whatever my stomach demanded in order to feel better. I was particular about the location where I binged too. The area had to be secluded and well hidden. I frequented empty nearby parking lots, the back of school buildings, quiet side streets—any place away from people and traffic. When the perfect place was found, I'd park my van and turn off the ignition and wasted no time tearing open the containers. Manically, I'd begin to stuff myself with a half-gallon of chocolate ice cream, chocolate chip cookies, and boxes of crumbled ice cream cones (I liked the taste of crushed cones inside my ice cream). I'd have a liter of Pepsi nearby to wash it all down.

There was always a feeling of detachment when I mindlessly ate; almost like an out-of-body experience. I craved that feeling. It gave me the opportunity to be somewhere else in my head. I felt content in those moments; my only focus was savoring the taste of the sugar as it reached my mouth and the euphoric feeling eating it gave me. In those moments, everything was okay in my world, until I literally reached the rock bottom of whatever I was scarfing down. As I scraped the last bit of ice cream from the corner of the container with my spoon, my high began to slowly descend. As quickly as my food euphoria lifted me, it dropped me just as fast.

The evidence of my food binge was visible everywhere. My eyes began to scan over the ripped-open cookie packages, food wrappers, and containers that were scattered all over the floor and seats of the van. The sight of it made me sick to my stomach. Filled to capacity, I twisted and turned trying to get comfortable in my seat, but I couldn't. I felt tears burn in my eyes as the familiar self-imposed hate speech began. "How are you ever supposed to lose weight eating like a pig? Aren't you fat enough? No wonder your life is such a mess, you can't control anything in your life, not even your mouth! You're so stupid! You're so weak!" I scolded myself over and over again for what I had done. My binge/bliss/berate cycle was a dirty little secret that I kept well hidden from the people closest to me.

I began to dread coming home from work. Arguments erupted frequently between my mother and me whenever Darryl was not around. It grieved her to know that while I stressed over which bill would get paid, he stood and watched. Soon it became commonplace for my mother to take on Darryl's role. Whenever the kids or I needed something and I was at the end of my paycheck, my mother pitched in to help. I knew that my mother wanted more for me, like any loving parent would. No matter how she felt about my husband, she never made me feel like the girls and I were a burden. She loved us unconditionally. She was always there when we needed her, no questions asked.

In an attempt to cope, I started to sweep everything under the rug, never questioning Darryl about helping pay bills, never rocking the boat. I just became numb to it. My thoughts were constantly caught between leaving Darryl and staying with him; in the end, I always talked myself out of divorcing him. I convinced myself to be satisfied with just having a man, period. *I mean, at least he wasn't knocking my head against a wall, and beating me up, right? Things could be worse.*

My faith in God was the only thing holding me together and keeping me from falling completely apart. Desperate for a way to improve our marriage, I convinced Darryl to come to church with me, hoping that it would be a new beginning for us. We joined church together, and attended Bible class together. Things got a little better between us when I stopped inquiring about his getting a job. I just kept silent about it. I ate my way happy when all else failed. I still dealt with the awful episodes that terrorized my mind at night, with the occurrences becoming more frequent and intense than before. When my flare-ups were more than I could stand, I ran to the arms of my sister, who was now aware of what was happening to me. Her moral support was unwavering. She never turned me away. No matter what time of night, she held me until I fell asleep in her arms. I never told Darryl about my episodes, fearing that he would think I was going insane. Even I thought I was going crazy. I couldn't understand what was wrong with me, let alone trying to explain it to someone else.

Still sneaking out at night in search of food, my compulsive eating had officially become out of control. Any kind of change I discovered in my purse would be spent at the nearest fast food joint, even if I had just eaten. When the kids couldn't finish their plates, I ate whatever was left. Now weighing 320 pounds, the heaviness of my body put excessive strain on my joints, causing them to ache constantly. My blood pressure was difficult to control even with the aid of medication. I had no energy to play with my daughters, and trying to explain that "Mommy is too tired" to an eight- and five-year-old was just an excuse to children who wanted their Mom to get up and play.

Not having the physical stamina to run around with my girls made me feel like a horrible mother, and I so desperately wanted to be a good Mom to them, just like my mother was to me. My mental state was so scattered that many times it spilled over into my parenting. Putting on a happy face around the kids while in such deep despair was a tricky tightrope to walk.

When I could no longer hold my peace about Darryl's "vacation away from employment" and his lack of concern about the bills piling up, I'd blow up. I know our daughters heard Darryl and me argue on a regular basis, and no matter how hard I tried to shield them from the hostility in the household, they felt it and absorbed it. Our clashes were reminiscent of what I experienced when I was a little girl listening to my parents verbally fight and sounding like they hated each other. I remembered the guilt I felt as a child, thinking I was the reason they fought. I didn't want my daughters to go through difficult emotional changes like I did. It was our job as parents to create a harmonious atmosphere for our children, and it was anything but that.

Hope Deferred

In 2003, I became pregnant with our second child, and daughter number three for me. Like my previous pregnancies, my extreme weight caused some serious issues during my nine months. I suffered from pre-eclampsia, a condition in some pregnancies that's characterized by high blood pressure and severe fluid retention. I was so swollen; it was painful just to move my legs. Darryl was very attentive during my pregnancy, and it did prove to draw us closer. When our second daughter arrived, Darryl was thrilled about having another child.

Soon after the birth of our daughter, I began to notice more and more marked changes in his interaction with my oldest daughter from my previous marriage. Darryl had been in her life ever since she was four years old, and she adored him. Because her biological father was not around, she clung to Darryl as a daddy figure. I can recall how she would grasp his hand and wouldn't let go until she fell asleep. Those same hands that held her hand so sweetly, now seemed to let go of her without warning. Seeing the change in him towards her broke my heart. Not that he was purposely cruel to her, but there was a definite change in his attentiveness toward her as opposed to his own biological daughters. When I'd bring up how his demeanor had changed when it came to my daughter, he would completely deny it. I knew I wasn't making it up; I observed the change, and my daughter felt it. Not only did she have one father who deserted her, but now she had two. My never-ending cycle of guilt just kept revolving.

There were times when the difference Darryl made between my daughter and his own daughters was more obvious. For example, whenever Darryl and I were at odds, he'd buy his two biological children things while conveniently forgetting about my daughter, the child he had once called his. There was even an instance where the kids had a layaway that was overdue and slated to be put back. Darryl promised he would pay the final bill since I had made all the previous payments and hadn't the money to pay for the rest of it. To my surprise and utter shock, Darryl intentionally paid the final bill for our two daughters, but left my oldest daughter's clothing unpaid. With no money to pay the layaway bill, a friend offered to take care of it, so that my daughter could have the clothes she needed.

Even after that instance, I still stayed with him. Whenever the stress of being with him would become too much to bear, I would threaten to leave him, but each time his charm resurfaced. The promises, the apologies, his swearing to "do better this time," — all these pledges came out of the woodwork, and I believed it all.

Darryl said all the right things to keep me right where he wanted me. I wanted so badly to believe that he would change, that he would do all he said he would and become responsible. I believed in him, and he knew I did. He always talked me into giving him another chance, and with high hopes, I always did.

Blinded by Love or Something Like It

One particular Friday, Darryl went to visit his mother on the other end of town. He had been gone all day, which wasn't particularly unusual since he loved spending time with his mother. Around 11:00 pm., the phone rang. It was Darryl on the other end, sounding distraught. He was calling from the county jail. He had been arrested for theft. Out of my mind with worry, I asked him what happened. *How in the world could a trip to his mother's house end in his going to jail?* "I'm at the County, baby. The police arrested me. They are saying that I stole a bike—"

"What? A Bike? Stolen?" I frantically asked for more details, as my head was spinning to try to grasp what he was saying. Darryl had dropped me off at work that morning in my minivan and supposedly drove to his mother's afterward. How could he be accused of stealing a bicycle, and furthermore, where is my van? Months before, I purchased a used minivan for us to get around in right after our youngest daughter was born. My beloved Chevy Cavalier had been all but totaled after the damage Darryl did to it, not to mention the hundreds of dollars he racked up in tolls and parking tickets.

"I can't give you all the details now, baby; this is the public phone at the County, so I can't talk long. I will be okay. Call my mother to see if she can get down here and bail me out." Darryl's bail was $1,200. I immediately called his mother, who said she did not have the money to get him out. His brother was unable to get the funds either. My van had been towed by the police after Darryl's arrest. The amount to recover my car was $250.00, plus towing fees. Every dime I had went to getting my van back. I was left with nothing but my mind scrambling to figure out how I was going to get my husband out of jail. *Where would I get the $1,200 from?*

That night I was afraid to fall asleep. I did everything I could to stay up. I knew what would happen if I dared to fall asleep, so I fought it. Just when I couldn't keep myself up any longer, it started again. The blurry vision, the mental confusion; the shaking, the racing heartbeat, and the extreme pressure in my head making me feel as if I were going crazy. *"Oh my God, why is this happening to me?"* I found myself saying out loud. I needed to get out of my bedroom, fast. It felt like a torture chamber I needed to escape from.

With weak legs, I slowly steadied myself against the wall. I headed toward my sister's bedroom, attempting to calm myself down, but unable to. I tiptoed into Brenda's room and slowly crawled in her bed, my entire body shaking. She didn't ask me anything; she just held her arms out to receive me. With tears streaming down my face and my voice shaking I stammered, "I-I-I'm sorry to wake you up, Bren, but…but…but it's happening again." I broke out in loud sobs. "I'm scared, Bren, what's wrong with me?"

Still half asleep, she whispered reassuringly, "I'm here, baby. It's okay, I'm right here." My sister was a very small-framed woman, five feet five inches tall and about 120 pounds. I was three times as big as she was, but that never stopped her from wrapping her tiny arms around me so tightly that I could feel her heart beating. In that moment I felt safe, protected. The soft sound of her voice praying for me as she held me was like a beautiful melody that lulled me to sleep. Like I did so many nights before, I finally fell asleep in my big sister's loving arms.

The next morning, I woke up brainstorming on how I could get Darryl out of jail. I did the only thing I could think of to do. I asked my family to help with Darryl's situation…again. I went to my brother Wayne to see if he had the money or at least a portion of it for Darryl's bail as a favor to me. Darryl was not on my brother's favorite person list, not in the least. Much like my mother, Wayne knew that Darryl was manipulating me, and simply tolerated him for my sake. Wayne agreed to let Darryl borrow $600.00, but made it clear that the money was a loan. I frantically called the only other person I knew would have the money to possibly help…Chris, Darryl's ex-boss. I told Chris about the situation, and as a favor to me, again he agreed to help Darryl by allowing him to borrow the other $600.00.

I called off work immediately that morning and waited for Darryl's call. When he called, I was excited to tell him the news about my getting the money together for his bail. I gathered the cash from both Wayne and Chris, put it in an envelope, and in a rush, took off for the County Jail to bail Darryl out. When I got to the jail, there was another roadblock that prevented me from getting Darryl out. There were other miscellaneous charges associated with the theft that needed to be taken care of. Darryl would need a lawyer to represent him. Not wanting to take a chance on a public defender, I called on Chris yet again for a favor. He was able to get a colleague of his, who happened to be an attorney to represent Darryl at his first hearing.

I was sitting in the first row in court, waiting on the edge of my seat to see Darryl's face when the guard brought him out. I was so worried about him, I didn't care anymore about the details of the case, guilty or not, it didn't matter. I just wanted my husband back home. The attorney was able to convince the judge to drop the other charges, but not the theft. After paying the bail, Darryl was released, and I breathed a sigh of relief.

There was large amount of paperwork that needed to be verified and signed off by the sheriff before Darryl could officially be released. For six hours I waited for him in my car. The day had turned into night, and the temperature dropped significantly. I turned the car on periodically to warm up when the windows began to get icy. All I could think about was Darryl coming home to me. It didn't matter how long I had to wait or what I had to do to get him out. At around 2 a.m., Darryl was finally released, carrying a plastic bag with his belongings in it. He smiled broadly as he walked quickly to the van. The ride home was quiet as I held his hand tightly. I had no questions for him. Nothing mattered anymore. I turned up the radio and drove hastily back home. In my mind, all was now right with the world.

My time at Bank of America had run its course. I needed something that paid more money, so I decided to look for another job. Not too long after, I was hired as a receptionist at a law firm in downtown Chicago. It was making a bit more than what I was making at BOA, and despite being happy about my new position; things were still a mess at home. Besides a few day-labor jobs, Darryl still hadn't found a job. The worst part was, I knew in my heart he wasn't even trying to get one. I suggested that he fill out job applications for some fast food places, just until he got something better, but he didn't want to go that route. In fact, he had become totally comfortable with not working. He depended on his unemployment checks, which I reminded him, were just temporary and wouldn't last forever. Resentment was setting in fast. His days now included taking care of the baby, eating, and playing PlayStation all day while my mother, sister, and I went to work. I was still paying rent; meanwhile he spent his money on whatever he wanted to. I went to work with a smile on my face, but behind it was anguish and frustration. I hid it well from my co-workers—they never suspected how jacked up my home life was. I felt trapped, and sunk deeper into depression, all along self-medicating with food.

Many evenings when the kids would be put down for the night, I'd drive off and wonder if my life was worth all of the stress I was going through. I hated myself for allowing my husband to run over me. I hated myself for not having self-control and allowing myself to let my weight get so out of hand. I hated…me.

My self-esteem was in the gutter. I couldn't even make eye contact with people anymore. I was certain that if I looked at someone directly, they could see through my thin facade and recognize what a weak person I was, and how completely pathetic I was. Convinced that I was slowly losing my mind, I'd stay up all night, petrified to fall asleep for even a minute. My "terror episodes" were like spending ten minutes in complete mental torment. *"God must have forgotten about me…Where was He when I needed Him? Maybe He just gave up on me... who would blame Him?"* These were the conversations that went on in my head as I drove aimlessly in the night. When the tears in my eyes clouded my vision, I stopped and sobbed endlessly, my wailing echoing through my van.

I felt like I was in a deep pit of quicksand slowly descending into darkness. I was devoid of hope. I had no faith in myself anymore, not as a mother, not as a person. I began to contemplate ending my life. I began to strategize how I would do it so it could be quick. I felt powerless over my life. I had allowed everything to get so out of control. I wanted to end my marriage, but did not have the courage to. I was afraid of everything—afraid that God would hate me if I divorced, afraid that if I stayed with Darryl my mother would be angry with me, afraid that I would never be the kind of strong mother to my daughters that my mother was. She was strong, self-assured, and beautiful—in my mind, everything I wasn't. My destructive thoughts taunted me relentlessly: *My kids don't need a weak, spineless mother; they would be better off without me.*

I critically laughed at myself when I realized that I didn't even have enough courage to go through with my plan to end my life. I banged my fists on the steering wheel in frustration. Tears filled my eyes and ran down my cheeks like a flood. I screamed and cried until I lost my voice and my eyes burned. I squeezed my eyes tightly, begging for God to just let my heart stop, to just let me die. My emotional state was so extreme that I became dizzy and disoriented. I closed my eyes, hoping they would never open again.

Suddenly, I felt calmness throughout my body. My tense fingers loosened around the steering wheel. The tears stopped, and a warm sensation came over my body—not at all like the scary episodes I was so familiar with—no, this was quite different, the total opposite, in fact. It was almost as if I were somehow being wrapped in a blanket. I felt my body go limp, and my heart beat slowed to an even pace. I didn't feel afraid, just at peace. I slumped down in my seat and allowed whatever I was experiencing to sweep over me.

Staring out my window, my eyes became fixated on the depth of the sky, and all the stars surrounding it. My mouth dropped open with awe. Slowly my eyes closed as I fell into a deep-sleep state. I am not sure how long I was out, but when I woke up, I didn't feel the same way. Something was different. I wasn't thinking about taking my life anymore. What I experienced was my first close encounter with the Spirit of God. That night He granted me the rest I so desperately needed in my restless mind. He granted me the kind of Peace that I had never experienced before. I wasn't sure of what the future held, but I knew that God wanted me to stay put. He wrapped the magnitude of His love around me that night, and saved me from myself. After that, I never had another thought about committing suicide again.

A couple of weeks after the whole jail situation, I asked Darryl when he planned on giving Chris and Wayne at least a down payment on the money he had borrowed from them. In a dismissive manner he replied, "I'm gonna pay them, come on now Sue, don't start."

That was a song I had become so familiar with. It's the same song he would sing to my mother and me whenever he owed money toward the rent or any bills we had. A month turned into six months—still not a dime paid to my brother or Chris. When he began to receive calls about the money he owed, he became indignant, vowing not to pay anybody anything if they didn't get off his back about it. Even for Darryl, this shocked me. Here they were, going out of their way to help bail his butt out of jail, and he has the audacity to get angry because they asked for the money he promised to pay them. Once again, his refusal to honor his word incensed me. I don't know why I was so surprised at his behavior; Darryl was running true to form. Eventually, Chris got a portion of his $600.00 back from Darryl, and my brother may have gotten $100.00 back, but by that time, Darryl had already burned his bridges with my family.

I told Darryl he needed to move out. When it came to my mother, he had already overstayed his welcome at her house, so she was eager to see him leave. So was I. He protested, but reluctantly went back to his mother's house. After his latest stunt of snubbing Chris and Wayne over the money he owed them, he was done. I researched divorce attorneys and made up my mind to end things with my husband. I wasn't going to fall for the "baby please" routine anymore. I thought of my car he had single-handedly destroyed, the lies, the false promises, and the arguments. I was done with it all, or so I said. He went back to his mother's house, and I eventually followed him back there.

The foundation of our relationship was built on a toxic co-dependency. I needed him because I didn't want to be alone. He depended on me because he needed someone to make sure his needs were met. He needed a woman who didn't mind footing the bill, and I fit the bill.

When it came to intimacy, I really didn't feel desired by Darryl. I longed to experience what it felt like to be truly loved and not taken for granted. I didn't feel attractive, especially after I had gained so much weight. I was depressed most of the time, and except for interaction with the kids, I felt miserable most of the time. Darryl would often leave the house for hours at a time, so our interaction was minimal most times. I had a confidant who I would talk to every now and then, my ex-boyfriend Phillip.

I dated Phillip back in my twenties, and he was still a good friend of mine. He was always available to me whenever I needed a sympathetic ear. Phillip knew about Darryl. In fact, he was the one who got Darryl the job at the nightclub when I first met him. Phillip was also the person who paid for my oldest daughter's layaway, the one that Darryl neglected to pay for. Phillip was kind in that way. He genuinely cared about me, no strings attached, and I appreciated that. Our conversations made me feel so much better.

I always thought that Phillip and I would get married, but he was a workaholic and didn't have much time to spend with me. He was always working long hours as a support technician for the fire department, and that bothered me. He was ambitious, but I was too immature to see that as an asset. I ended our relationship because he... worked too much. The irony would be laughable if it weren't so ridiculous. I ended things with a great guy who had an obvious strong work ethic; to marry a man who seemed allergic to work. Go figure.

Phillip never made any moves on me, but always made it clear that he still had feelings for me. I was flattered at the thought of him still caring for me. He would mention the fact that he was still waiting for me, whenever I decided to come back to him. He always added a chuckle when he said it, as if he was joking about it. But his words stayed on my mind, and I wondered if he was actually serious about his invitation. The more Darryl and I argued, the more time I'd spend with Phillip, just to decompress from the madness. We'd go to the movies, a ballgame or sometimes just a walk along the lakefront. He treated me as if I was significant, worth listening to. He often told me I was beautiful to look at, just out of the blue. I hadn't heard my husband utter a flattering remark to me since we dated. As a matter of fact, the only time Darryl touched me was to have sex. There was no affection or kissing attached to our encounters. It was just...sex.

I began to rely on Phillip as an escape from my life. He was a big guy, around 450 pounds, so we had a common interest in eating—and lots of it. He didn't mind that I was over 300 pounds, and he never made me feel less than desired when we were out. I became more and more attracted to Phillip, or maybe it was the way he made me feel when we hung out together. When I came home from one of our outings, Darryl would always be out, playing PlayStation video games with one of his friends who did the same thing Darryl did. I hated that video console; I even hid it out in the garage so that he wouldn't be so engulfed in it twenty-four hours a day. We had huge arguments about his abnormal fixation to gaming; which kept him from any productivity around the house or outside of it. The respect I had for my husband slowly began to deteriorate, and my actions began to show signs of the decay.

My thoughts always seemed shift to Phillip somehow. Guilt consumed me each time I thought of him and smiled. I knew in my heart it was wrong to be fascinated with another man to that degree, but I couldn't help the feelings that were mounting for Phillip. I was hooked on the connection that we shared, the comfortability, and the reverence he freely showed me. It was an odd mixture of happiness and regret that left me in a state of confusion.

During this time, my night terrors escalated even further. I began to experience them not only at night, but also during the day out of nowhere. One particular episode was so intense; I was convinced that I on the verge of either a stroke or heart attack at any moment. Scared senseless, I finally made an appointment to see my doctor. I had to find out what was wrong with me; these unexplained episodes were now frequent and twice as frightening. I couldn't put it off any longer.

Going for a doctor's visit can be an annoying experience... I mean, who really wants to spend hours upon end, at the doctor's office with other annoyed patients, while flipping through old issues of *People Magazine* on a Saturday morning? Like most doctors' offices, my doctor always seemed to have a thousand people ahead of me, no matter how early I got there for my visit. Despite the wait, Dr. Thomas was a really great doctor. He had been my ob-gyn since the birth of my first daughter. He had a down-to-earth demeanor that really made me comfortable with him. He was professional, but not stuffy, and always had a funny joke or some crazy nickname he would give me. Several years prior, Dr. Thomas dubbed me "Mary, Mary, Quite Contrary" because of my unwillingness to abide by the healthy eating regime he gave me to lose weight. He really was something else.

As soon as Dr. Thomas came into the examining room, he'd always recite the same thing as he closed the door: "Wellllll...how's it going Mary-Mary? I see that you STILL aren't following my instructions, huh? Do you know HOW I know?" He would ask sarcastically while looking at my chart. "According to your chart, the scale is moving in the wrong direction...so either I need a new scale, or you ain't doing what I instructed." Even when he fussed at me, he always made me giggle.

"Seriously, Mary, we've talked about this before. You gotta start doing something to lose this weight." His tone becoming more serious.

"I will, Dr. Thomas, I know…I know," I sheepishly replied with a half-smile.

I didn't go to see Dr. Thomas as regularly as I should have. I'd purposely reschedule my appointments until I needed to see him for my blood pressure meds to be re-filled. I didn't want to hear what I already knew…I was gaining weight. When getting on the scale, I'd squeeze my eyes shut and turn my head so as not to see the number. I hurried off the scale as soon as the nurse was done, and quickly changed the subject to something else when I thought she would mention my weight aloud.

Having my blood pressure taken was just as embarrassing. Every visit, the nurse had to search for a cuff big enough to accommodate my large arm. Before Dr. Thomas completed my exam, he'd reiterate about my weight gain. He didn't treat his patients like an assembly line, he took time with them—he genuinely cared. As my physician, he was concerned about me and the state of my health. I knew that, and despite being in denial, I appreciated it.

"I don't like your blood pressure reading. It's way too high, one fifty-six over ninety-nine. I am going to write a prescription for hydrochlorothiazide. Take that with the one you are already taking, and we'll see if we can get your pressure leveled off. He briefly looked up at me as he scribbled out the new prescription and a refill for the other. "When I see you next time—"

I interrupted him before he could finish round two of his weight loss reprimand. "Before you leave, Dr. Thomas, I wanted to talk to you about something else. Something weird has been happening to me for the past several months. I am having these...I don't really know how to describe them...I'm having these episodes in the middle of the night." My eyes began to fill with tears just talking about it.

"What kind of episodes? What's going on?" Looking interested, he put down his prescription pad and folded his arms.

I made an attempt to explain the unexplainable. "For the past several weeks, I wake up in the middle of the night in a complete panic for no reason at all. When I wake up it's like...I'm outside of myself. I'm confused, and sometimes I have to figure out where I am. For a few minutes, it's like can't get my mind together or something. As soon as my eyes open, I'm scared to death for no apparent reason. My heart race, my vision is clouded, and my whole body shakes and trembles so uncontrollably, I feel like I'm on the verge of a nervous breakdown. These horrible episodes go on for about ten to fifteen minutes, sometimes longer. I can't seem to calm my body down afterwards; I feel like I am losing my mind or something. What's wrong with me, Dr. Thomas?" I held my breath and waited for his response to all that I said. I tried in vain to suck my tears back in, but they rolled down my cheeks anyway and onto the paper gown I had on.

"I will prescribe you some Xanax; it sounds like you are experiencing some sort of anxiety attacks." He said it so matter-of-factly that it didn't seem too bad. "Take the Xanax whenever you feel the symptoms coming on, and it should relax you..."

I had heard of Xanax before, but never knew of anyone who took it. I had always heard it was addictive too, which made me leery about taking it. Despite my uneasiness, I trusted Dr. Thomas. Anything would be worth trying if it would eliminate the awful attacks I was experiencing. I prayed that the meds Dr. Thomas gave me would cure the fits of anxiety, as he called them. Between going through changes with Darryl, my Phillip guilt-trip, and trying to make ends meet, I had too much on my mental plate to be sick.

Addiction and Disorder

Even with the doses of Xanax I was taking, the attacks seemed to worsen at times. I refused to request a higher dosage from Dr. Thomas for fear of addiction to them. Eventually, I was diagnosed with a mental disorder called Generalized Anxiety Disorder, or GAD. Generalized Anxiety Disorder is a neurological disorder that is characterized by excessive, uncontrollable, and often irrational worry. During a GAD attack, the fear response is taken to extremes without reason or warning. Over time, a person with Generalized Anxiety Disorder develops a constant fear of having another panic attack, which can affect daily functioning and general quality of life.

Looking back, I can remember all the signs that pointed to this diagnosis. There were bits and pieces of it that began to surface when I was younger, right after the turmoil of my parents' divorce and the incidents of abuse at the hands of my neighbor and stepfather. Now it was made clear what was going on with me. The binge eating and the self-loathing that followed were all relative to what had now been revealed.

I found temporary relief from taking my "happy pill," as the kids called it. I went from taking a half dosage to a full pill quickly. Addiction really wasn't my main concern anymore; I just wanted to feel "normal." By this time, feeling very comfortable in his unemployed status, Darryl was officially a full-time video gamer. That was all he did from morning until evening. When he wasn't playing with his cohorts, he was gone. I worked, came home, made sure the kids ate and were content, and talked to Phillip on the phone. I looked forward to the times when I could see him.

It became easier not to argue with Darryl anymore. I didn't have the energy. Our verbal fights began to affect me physically. Upon Dr. Thomas's suggestion to check my blood pressure from time to time, I bought an at-home blood pressure monitor. Whenever the heated exchanges between Darryl and me would ensue, I'd almost black out. My blood pressure escalated to stroke-level numbers. Petrified, I'd use the Xanax to calm my body down. It became my immediate go-to for relief. I was now co-dependent on my "happy pills" and food; I did both in excess whenever I couldn't cope with my life.

I began to feel more and more guilty about my ongoing affair with Phillip. I lied and did what I had to do to be with him. He continually gave me the validation I desperately wanted. With him, I didn't feel manipulated, I didn't feel used. He made me feel special. He treated me better than any man ever had. He gave, and never took from me, whether it was his time or his affection. He spared no expense to make me smile. He was everything I wanted and didn't have. On the flip side, my secret rendezvous with Phillip were eating me alive on the inside. It seemed every time I left Phillip, by the time I got home, I was in full fledge GAD mode. My attacks were becoming too intense for me to even hide them from my children anymore. Many times they witnessed me rocking myself and crying uncontrollably while in the midst of an attack.

To make matters worse, due my level of panic, my blood pressure was constantly dangerously high. In those moments, I prayed for relief, I didn't want to die in the middle of one of my attacks. I was convinced that this was God punishing me for my infidelity. Thank God for my mother and sister, who encircled me with prayer through those very difficult nights.

I decided to end things with Phillip. I couldn't take the guilt anymore. I told him how badly I felt, and that we couldn't communicate anymore. He understood, and kept his distance from me as requested. He told me if the girls or I ever needed anything, he'd still always be there for us, no matter what. Phillip was someone who I could depend on, with no questions asked unlike my husband. As difficult as it was, I broke all communication with Phillip. I prayed that God would forgive me for the inappropriate feelings I had for another man, but I already convinced myself a long time ago that God was just as disgusted with me as I was with myself.

I worked hard to push Phillip to the back of my mind and shifted my focus solely on Darryl. I was determined to do what I had to do in order to make our marriage work, even if I had to do it alone. The shame of my affair with Phillip made it palatable for me to become timid—a doormat for Darryl to walk all over.

I allowed Darryl to do as he pleased, with no mention of his finding a job or his playing PlayStation while I went to work. I rarely asked him to do anything. I took care of the kids and made sure they had what they needed. I took out the garbage, cleaned, cooked dinner, and did what I had to do to keep things harmonious while bottling up any reaction or emotion. I became quite proficient with not expecting anything from my husband. If I didn't have expectations, then I couldn't be disappointed. I adopted the prospective of just being grateful that I had a husband at all. My justification was: *A little bit of a husband is better than none at all.* It was a pretty sweet deal for Darryl too.

My husband was content with no responsibilities and doing the bare minimum just to keep my mother off his back. Meanwhile, I resumed self-medicating, alternating food and Xanax whenever I began to think too much about my situation.

The Mission

The Paradigm Shift

At some point in our lives, though the Grace of God, He allows us to experience rare episodes of clarity that can change our lives for the better. My paradigm shift arrived in 2006 via a discussion with Dr. Thomas.

It was March 2006, and I was eagerly anticipating my thirty-second birthday later on that week. My mother always made these extravagant birthday meals for everyone's birthday each year. I had put in my request for my favorite meal: fried shrimp, steak, garlic mashed potatoes, and chocolate cake and ice cream for dessert. I could taste the meal already.

My thoughts veered away when I turned into the parking lot at Dr. Thomas's office. I was running late for a follow-up appointment for my high blood pressure issues. He kept a close eye on my numbers, which were still in the very high range. I was always nervous for my appointments with him. Even the scent of disinfectant in the doctor's office made my palms sweat. I took several deep breaths as I tried taking my mind off the appointment.

"If you're a bundle of nerves, Sue, your pressure is really gonna shoot up once you get in the office. You gotta calm down," I told myself. I heard the soft rumble of my two-year-old snoring in the backseat; I smiled as I unbuckled her car seat carefully as not to wake her. She looked perfectly precious when she slept. "Gosh, you look so much like

your Daddy when you sleep, you even snore like him too, sweetie." I chuckled.

Dr. Thomas requested that I bring my daughter with me whenever I came back for my next appointment. He hadn't seen her since he delivered her two years ago; I loved to show off my beautiful daughters. I loved them with everything in me. They were my reason for waking up in the morning with purpose, the reason why I worked so hard, the reason why I smiled. All I wanted was to see them happy and emotionally stable, unlike like their mother who was a basket case most of the time. I tried everything I could to keep them from being affected by the turbulence and chaos that went on with their father and me.

With baby bag in hand and sleeping daughter on my hip, I made my way into the doctor's office. My name was called unusually quickly, to my surprise. The nurse ushered me in and did the normal routine of taking my pressure and weighing me. "Dr. Thomas will be in shortly Sue; your daughter is adorable!" I smiled with pride as I began taking off my jacket and getting comfortable on the examining table, or as comfortable as I could. It seemed like that damn table got smaller and smaller every time I sat on it for my checkups. I did my usual routine of grasping the sides of the table and did my best to raise my body enough to be seated.

Slightly out of breath I asked, "I don't need to take everything off, do I?" I hoped the nurse would say no.

"Nah, he is just going to go over your chart with you this time and re-fill your meds."

"Okay, thanks." I got situated on the table and swung my feet while thinking about which fast food restaurant my daughter and I would visit when I left my appointment with Dr. Thomas.

Not long after, I heard Dr. Thomas's voice down the hall coming toward my room. I was glad that for once I would get out of the doctor's office before noon. Opening the door, he immediately turned his attention to my daughter, now awake and digging around in my purse. "Welllll…hello Lil' Mary-Mary! Aren't you a cutie! How are you, sweetie?"

She looked up from the tube of lip gloss she was attempting to put on her lips and smiled. "Mommy's purse!" she exclaimed as she offered my bag to Dr. Thomas, I guess so he could go digging through it too.

"Yes, I see, sweetie. I'm going to talk to Mommy for a minute, okay? Can you go with Shauna for a little while? Shauna, can you take the baby with you for a minute? I want to talk to Sue." Dr. Thomas motioned to his nurse to take my daughter into the reception area.

"Sure can, Dr. Thomas. Come on, little pumpkin. Let's see if I have some crayons and paper for you in the front."

Shauna held out her hand for my daughter to hold as they both walked out, closing the door behind them. I wondered what Dr. Thomas wanted to talk about. I really just wanted to get my prescription and go. I convinced myself it was nothing, probably just another finger-wagging session about my weight, or maybe even congratulating me because I had lost a couple of pounds somehow. I grabbed the baby bag and my coat off the chair and waited to find out what he had to say. "Let's talk a walk back to my office. We can talk there."

His office? Okay…what was this really about? I thought to myself as we made our way there. I placed my bag and coat down, eager to find out what was going on.

I stood by the door, as if in a rush, but it was really just nervous energy at that point. "Hey, Dr. Thomas, what's up? You wanted to talk to me about something?" I said with an uneasiness that I was sure he probably picked up on."

"Well, I was looking over your chart just now, and your blood pressure is still very high Sue."

"How high?" I asked.

"It's one sixty-eight over one hundred. Are you taking your blood pressure medicine, both of them?"

"Yes," I answered, growing worried. "Maybe it's because I was nervous when Shauna took it. I hate getting my blood pressure checked. The cuff is so tight and—"

"Sue, I'm gonna get right to the point." Dr. Thomas interrupted my excuse session in mid-sentence before I could finish. While he was usually upbeat with his brand of sarcastic humor when I'd go for my routine visits, this time his demeanor as he sat down was different, almost somber. A look of concern washed across his face as he motioned for me to sit. "I am worried about you. I am worried about the state of your health." I sat straight up in the chair and thought, *if he is calling me by my name and not "Mary-Mary," something has got to be wrong here.*

My heart seemed to sink to my feet as he began to explain. "Let me tell you how serious this situation is, Sue. You are in your early thirties, and three hundred forty-eight pounds. Even with medication, your blood pressure is consistently at stroke level, and you are borderline diabetic. I'm going to be honest with you. At the rate you are gaining weight, coupled with your family history of hypertension, stroke, and heart disease, you are a prime candidate for a stroke. If you don't make a serious decision about getting your health in order and losing weight, you are on the fast track to dying an early death."

He continued, "Now, if are okay with someone else raising your beautiful daughters, then proceed down the path that you are going. If not, you need to make a decision to lose weight much sooner than later. The choice is yours, Sue. I have given you the information; it's up to you what you will do with it. Do you have any questions for me?"

It was as if someone had thrown an ice bucket full of cold water on me. I was so stunned that I couldn't open my mouth to respond to what I had just heard. I swallowed hard as tears stung my eyes. After a few moments, I managed to gather enough words in my mouth to mumble softly. "Okay, thank you Doctor. No questions."

I couldn't even look him in the face when I said it. I was too embarrassed. He squeezed my shoulder gently as he walked out of the door. I sat there for a minute, trying to process what Dr. Thomas said to me. In those moments, a million thoughts dashed through my mind. I thought about what he said about my being a prime candidate for a stroke. My birthday was in two weeks. I would be turning thirty-two years old.

Historically, as my doctor indicated, my genetics did make me a prime candidate for own health crisis in the not too distant future. My mother was heavy, not as much as I was, but she had weight issues as well, she suffered with diabetes and chronic gout. She was also prone to strokes, experiencing three mini-strokes by the time she was in her early fifties. Dr. Thomas was right; I was following in her footsteps.

There I was, confronted with the harsh truth about my obesity and the dire state of my health. I knew undoubtedly that the straightforward commentary from my doctor was not coming from a place of cruelty, but rather concern for me as his patient. I walked out of his office in a daze. No one had ever spoken to me so bluntly about my weight before. My family had always tiptoed around the fact that I was extremely overweight. No one addressed it. It was just accepted.

Dr. Thomas's words rang in my ears as I walked to my car and slowly drove out of the parking lot; attempting to digest the information I had just been given. He was right. The truth had been laid plainly before me. I was a mother of three in my early thirties and well over 300 pounds. To make matters worse, I was on multiple blood pressure medications, and reliant on Xanax to help me cope with debilitating anxiety attacks. My obsession with food was at an apex, and I was on the fast track to eating myself to death, literally. My life seemed to have spun out of control without me even realizing the severity of it. My stomach churned with distress as I made my way down the street, my hands clutching the wheel. I needed to make some hard decisions. All I knew was I NEEDED to be there for my children. I didn't want someone else raising them because I was no longer able to.

Doubt began to flood my thoughts. "You can't do this...you tried so many times in the past to lose weight, and it never worked. *What makes you think this time will be different? Just deal with the way things are now. You'll be all right... Dr. Thomas was just going overboard, and being dramatic,"* I silently reasoned. Self-doubt was a demon I struggled with all my life. It was natural to talk myself out of trying. It was just as normal as breathing. I never thought I had the capacity to be truly successful in any area of my life, much less losing weight. I could see all the potential in in everyone else, but never in myself. I gave myself over to the idea that I was "too" everything—too weak, too tired, too busy to lose weight. Over the years I convinced myself that nothing would work, so I simply stopped trying. The mind is such a powerful tool. We can either arm it for self-construction, or self-destruction. When we convince ourselves that we are not equipped to accomplish something in our lives, eventually we will begin to believe it. Essentially, failure became my personal truth.

I stopped at a red light and glanced in the rearview mirror. I watched for a moment as my cheerful two-year-old daughter played in the backseat with her doll, softly humming a little tune to herself. Looking at her sweet little face created a whirlwind of emotion within me, both happy and sad. In an instant, I thought of her and my other two daughters not having me around anymore. I thought about my children not having a Mommy to protect and take care of them as they grew older, not being there to give them advice about choosing friends wisely and the dangers of peer pressure. I thought about not being there to wrap my arms around them when they were heartbroken over a boy, or some other painful loss they might experience in their lifetime.

Dr. Thomas's words kept playing over and over again like a skipped record. The blare of the car horn behind me snapped me out of my trance as I realized the light had turned green. I needed to escape from my thoughts. I needed to feel better, even if it was momentarily. I followed suit with what I normally did to ease my troubled mind. I searched for a place to turn in to so I could eat. Almost robotically, I drove into a Wendy's that was not too far from the doctor's office. I needed to taste something good. I lustfully craved to feel the euphoria that eating something fried or sugary offered my senses; whether I was physically hungry or not didn't really matter. In that moment, I just needed to feel something other than disappointment and disgust for myself.

I got to the drive-through window and ordered quickly. "May I have a large frosty, large Pepsi, double cheeseburger, two orders of chicken nuggets, and a large order of fries please?" I reached in haste for my wallet to pay for the food, never making eye contact with the cashier. I never made eye contact when ordering food. I always chose the drive-through instead of going in. Everything was covert and secret. Looking at the fast food cashier would somehow serve as a cue to me that I shouldn't have been there in the first place ordering such a massive amount of food to eat. I didn't want to be judged as "the fat woman ordering all of that food" by the person taking my order. If I didn't look at the cashier, then he/she couldn't see my eyes either, thus making me "invisible." Bottom line, I didn't want any personal connections when I binged always wanted the money/food transaction to be quick. No small talk—I just wanted my food quickly so I could hide and eat it… Alone.

As I reached over to give the money to the Wendy's cashier at the drive-through window, my chest suddenly began to tighten as if in a vice grip. The intense pain caused me to drop the money out of my hand and grab hold of my chest. As I struggled to catch my breath, I began to feel a sensation of intense pressure in my head so painful that it was like someone had dropped a cinder block on it. I squeezed my eyes shut, praying it would go away.

"Are you okay? Miss?" the girl at the window asked me, or at least that's what I thought she said. I was too preoccupied with the rush of pain from my chest and head to hear anything clearly. "Ma'am? Are you okay?" The cashier insisted, evidently noticing something wasn't right with me.

As I took slow, deep breaths, my symptoms subsided long enough for me to answer. Oh, I'm…I'm okay. Just a little tired I guess. Thanks." Embarrassed, I nervously laughed the situation off, my eyes focusing downward so as not to look at her. I quickly handed her my money as the discomfort slowly subsided.

The sensation I experienced lasted for a minute or so…but God, it felt longer. I had become familiar with the onset of my awful anxiety attacks, but this was different; I never felt my chest tighten up like that before. Grateful for relief, I grabbed the bags and drinks and handed one order of chicken nuggets to my daughter while keeping the other order for me, along with the huge amount of food I got for myself. "Shicken, yay! Tank chu, Mommy!" Jo happily chirped as she reached for the box of nuggets.

"You're welcome, sweetie," I replied, still trying to get my wits about me.

I made my way to the parking space farthest from the restaurant. I felt so sick, unlike I had ever felt before. *Is my pressure up? Is my anxiety flaring up again?* Instinctively, I reached in my purse for my Xanax and realized I was out. My breathing was labored and heavy. My heart began to palpitate. I don't think I'd ever been so afraid in my life. As I leaned back in the driver's seat, I closed my eyes as tears burned within them. God, please help me; please don't let me die. My babies need me. I looked in the rearview mirror and caught a glimpse of my happy, munching toddler. "Hey Jo-Jo Bean, Mommy loves you, sweetie pie!" I called out as tears streamed down my face.

"I wuf you too, Mommy!" Her beautiful big brown eyes had such an amazing way of smiling when she spoke, and her dimpled smile always made me putty in her hands. In that moment, it was as if something "clicked" on in my brain. Something shifted within me…I can only describe it as an "awareness" that took place inside of me, like I had just been roused from sleep.

I looked at the bags of food on the passenger seat. My eyes scanned across the pieces of paper with the prescriptions on it from Dr. Thomas, ready to be re-filled for my blood pressure meds and Xanax. *"What am I doing?...What am I doing?"* I whispered to myself in anguish. No longer able to hold back the flood of tears that filled my eyes, I turned the radio up to drown out the sound of my crying.

Like never before, I came to grips with what my doctor told me in his office that day. I couldn't turn a defiant ear to it anymore. The consequences of what I had been doing to my body would come to pass if I didn't do something about my weight. What was cloudy had become clear, and my reason was right there in the back seat of the car. I slowly became repulsed by the smell of the food I had just bought. For the first time in my life, the thought of eating the kind of food I had craved for so long literally made me sick to my stomach. Totally disgusted, I tossed everything out of the car in one fell swoop. I wiped my face and cranked up the car to drive home with my baby.

As I drove, my only thoughts were of my children. As if I were having a board meeting with myself, I presented the facts as they were with conviction. *Your babies need you...what would happen to them if you were no longer able to take care of them? Who can love them like you do?* The internal conversation continued: *What would happen to them if you were suddenly incapacitated due to a heart attack, stroke, or some ailment that could have been prevented had you taken your obesity seriously? You can't just abandon your kids and leave them without a mother to love and raise them.* I rationalized to myself as I traveled down the street.

God must have navigated my car, because I have no clue how I got home. My thoughts were so deep. All I could think about was my own survival for the sake of the little ones who depended on me. Everything became illuminated enough for me to really see what was important, and who was worth changing my mind for.

In that short drive home from Dr. Thomas's office, all those years of pre-conceived notions about what I couldn't do were forced silent. I decided all that mattered was making sure I didn't succumb to the fate Dr. Thomas talked about. I was going to do what I had to do to reverse the physical condition of my body, and all the harm I'd done as a result of my slavery to food. It didn't matter what sacrifices I had to make in the process either.

Right there in my car, with my beautiful Jo-Jo in the backseat sleeping soundly, I pledged to surrender anything that kept me from living the full life God intended for me. I finally discovered something that was stronger than my own insecurity, my will to survive.

 It was then, in the spring of 2006, that I opted to make a U-Turn, not in my car...but in my life.

The Launch of a Journey

Now that I had made my mind up to lose weight, I had no earthly clue where to begin. All I knew was that turning back was not an option, but the how's were not worked out yet. I started by telling my family about my decision to lose weight. I did not receive an overwhelming amount of support at first, mainly because I had cried wolf so many times about losing weight, no one really took me seriously.

"Really? Oh, okay, that's good, baby," was the initial response I got from my mom when I told her of my decision. The rest of my family followed suit with lackluster responses. The reaction I received made me more purposeful with regard to my pursuit.

Determined, but still shaky in the confidence department, I walked into the room where Darryl was watching TV, hoping I could find some reassurance in talking over my decision with my husband. He had been with me while I was overweight; in fact, he hadn't seen me any other way. By this time in our marriage, he knew of my GAD attacks and my critical hypertension issues. I was hopeful that I would get his support for this new phase of my life.

"Darryl, remember when I went to see Dr. Thomas recently? I received some troubling news that I couldn't even bring myself to tell anyone at the time because I was so upset about it," I said as I sat down beside him on the couch.

"What did he say? Are you all right?" he said as he briefly turned away from the football game he was watching.

"He told me basically that I had to lose weight because my health was suffering. I'm steadily gaining weight, and with the stress I'm under—"

"Stress?" he interrupted, looking confused his face in a frown. "What's wrong? What Stress?" He said it as if he had no earthly clue what I had to be worried about. Never mind that our bills were due, that he and my mother were constantly at odds because of his lack of help around the house. Never mind that I had three kids we were struggling to provide for on my one paycheck, and it had been for well over a year, and he still didn't have a job. I would have laughed if it wasn't so pitiful that he was oblivious to what was going on with me. I went on like I hadn't heard him ask the "stress" question.

Thinking back, it was typical that Darryl would think there was nothing to stress over, because in his case, there wasn't. I was making sure everything ran as well as it did. I took care of the car payment, any repairs and upkeep that needed to be done, paying my mother rent for us, and making certain the kids had what they needed. Throughout our courtship and marriage, Darryl consistently dismissed himself of any real responsibility with regard to the children and me. But alas, it was what I allowed to happen. When you make allowance for anyone to treat you in a manner that is less than what you deserve, that person will make certain to take full advantage of the opportunity, and won't think twice about it.

I continued my explanation: "To make a long story short, baby, I need to lose weight, get off all these pills, and get my health in order. Otherwise I may not be here, at least that is what Dr. Thomas said to me. I have made a decision to get into a gym and start working toward losing weight. I am tired of living like this, I am tired of feeling like this, and I am sick and tired of being sick and tired." I waited for Darryl's reaction. I wanted my husband to take me in his arms and tell me that I can do it, and that he would stand behind me one hundred percent.

"Man, well...yeah. I mean go for it, then. What gym are you gonna join?" It wasn't the rousing show of support I desired from my husband, but I took what I could get.

"I don't know yet. I have to do some research I guess," I said, getting up from the couch and heading upstairs where the kids were.

"Okay," he said, returning his focus to the game he was watching. Darryl was never big on displays of affection, but I would have loved for him to notice the tears in my eyes when I told him about what Dr. Thomas said. I wanted him to have some sort of physical connection with me that didn't involve sex sometimes. I needed his arms around me. I needed to feel his support for what I was about to embark upon. Deep down, he probably felt like my mother did, and the rest of my family. Like this was just another "I gotta lose weight" phase I was going through. I just needed someone to stand with me in my decision. I felt like I needed someone to push me in the right direction so I could do what I had to do. My faith in myself waivered so much, Like the wind, one minute it was there, and I could feel it, the next minute…nothing but stillness, as if it were never there.

The next day I talked over my decision with my best friend Nicole, who worked with me at the bank. Nicole and I had been best friends since we were little kids. She also had weight issues. Like me, she had struggled with her weight all her life. Over lunch I began my campaign for a joint venture to lose weight.

"Nicole, I have been thinking a lot…girl, I am so tired of this weight, I am going to seriously do something about it. You want to go in with me to lose weight, for real this time?" I put my sandwich down and eagerly awaited her response.

"You know what, Sue? I was actually thinking about the very same thing the other day! I'm sick and tired of being fat too. Actually, I'm considering weight loss surgery, stomach stapling. You know the kind that Carnie Wilson had? It's called bariatric surgery. I was thinking that you and I could do it together. You know everyone always says that we do everything together anyway; we might as well do this together too! What do you think? I have an appointment next week for a seminar about the surgery... ya know, how much it would cost, what the procedure entails, etcetera, etcetera."

I sat there for a minute and just kind of looked at her, perplexed. "Surgery? Girl, that sounds serious. In fact, I know a girl I graduated from high school with who had weight loss surgery, and she died on the table from complications. I don't know, Nikki, it's...risky. I—"

Before I could finish my thought, Nikki began a campaign of her own for the surgery.

"Aw girl, it's not as dangerous as you think it is. There are lots of folks who have had bariatric surgery, and everything goes well. With technology the way it is, it's a lot safer now. It's practically outpatient. You just stay in the hospital for a couple of days, and BAM! You're out with your new improved smaller stomach!" Nikki really should have been a car salesman; she had a knack for making everything sound so appealing. I swear that girl could sell sand at the beach.

"Nik, to be honest, I'm just scared. Even if it's a small risk, I am just not willing to take it." Nikki tilted her head and let out a long sigh as if my reasons for not wanting to go under the knife were unfounded. The reason why I had decided to get my health in order by losing weight was for my kids, and I didn't want to take a chance on being a statistic and leaving them motherless. For me, it wasn't worth the gamble.

"Nikki, I will support you and be with you every step of the way if this is what you decide to do…it just isn't for me, that's all. I think I will try to lose weight on my own," I told her.

"Okay. That's fine. If all goes well, I'm thinking I will go in for the surgery next month," Nikki said while thumbing through a magazine, never looking up once.

"Let me know, and I'll be there." I was happy for her. She felt as disgusted with her weight as I was with mine. Over the years, we compared countless war stories about everything from tight pinching girdles to the uncomfortable friction experienced from big thighs rubbing together. Nikki could relate to all the "big girl" issues I encountered all my life. We laughed about them together, all while despising the experience.

Although I opted out of having bariatric surgery, I would not discourage anyone else for choosing that route. It's a personal choice. In the end, we have to be happy with the choices that we make. For me, my choice was clear, and my work was cut out for me. I had a long road ahead of me, but for the first time in my life, I was really ready to do something about how I looked and how I felt. Not just on the outside, but on the inside as well. My weight loss journey was on the horizon, and it was full steam ahead.

Everything was a go for Nikki's Lap-Band surgery. She was more excited than I had ever seen her. She had a right to be—her life was about to change forever. I was happy for her too. The dream we had fantasized about for so long was about to become a reality for her. I began to wonder if I made the right decision about not having the surgery along with her. To be honest, I became a little jealous. The "what ifs" came out of the woodwork: *What if Nikki lost weight and I didn't? Maybe going the diet and exercise route wouldn't work for me...what if I couldn't do it?* The negative voices in my mind taunted me: *"You actually think you can do this on your own? Please! You can't do it; you love to eat too much.* My mental mockery was like a played out record that I was determined to pull the plug on. My mind was made up. I would lose the weight, get off these pills, or die trying.

The doctor had given Nikki the green light for surgery with one exception; she needed to lose at least fifteen pounds before she could have the surgery. For various reasons, insurance companies or the patient's doctor will require that the patient lose a percentage of weight before surgery. Reasons can range from improving safety and access for the surgeon, to getting the patient acclimated to a healthier lifestyle in terms of proper diet and exercise. Either way, Nikki had homework before her surgery could take place.

She asked me if I would come along with her to a new gym she had heard about not too far from where we lived. I figured I would go and see what it was about. It couldn't hurt; besides, I needed to find a gym anyway to get started on my own weight loss program.

Shelly's Great Shape

Before we got to the doors of the gym, I heard music pumping and lots of activity going on inside. A tall blond lady met us at the door. She sported yoga pants and a blue T-shirt that read, "It's great to be at Shapes." Her smile was as wide as any I'd ever seen, almost infectious; even her blue eyes looked as if they were smiling. I greeted her grin with my own as Nikki rifled through her purse for the Shapes brochure with the owner's name on it.

"Hi. Welcome to Shapes! What can I do for you ladies?" I had to read the blond lady's lips, due to the blaring 80's music that filled the room. I took a quick glance around the room while Nikki searched in vain for the illusive brochure. Some of members seemed to be doing more chatting with each other than working out. They appeared to be middle-aged women, happily jabbering on about the latest season of *"Dancing with the Stars"* and who got booted off, while others were noticeably focused on their workout, sweating and panting and pushing themselves to the limit on the exercise machines. This place was full of liveliness and activity if nothing else.

"Hi, we had an appointment with…I believe her name was Shelly. My friend and I are considering joining Shapes," Nikki loudly explained while closing her purse and ending her fruitless brochure search.

"Oh sure, that's me, I'm Shelly!" the tall blonde lady squealed with loud enthusiasm. "I think I spoke to you earlier over the phone. You gals wanna take a quick tour of our facility? You will LOVE it! Follow me gals!"

"Boy, this lady is a real cuckoo," I whispered to Nikki. "Either she is off her rocker, hyped up on some serious caffeine, or maybe both." We both giggled under our breath. As we followed close behind, Shelly explained in detail what we could expect from a workout at Shapes, and the unique equipment set up. Her blue eyes widened and her voice went up a couple of octaves every time she spoke about the benefits of a Shapes workout as opposed to any other gym, and how working out at Shapes was the answer to losing the weight and feeling great. Shelly was one heck of a saleswoman. I was ready to sign on the dotted line after the first ten minutes of her convincing narrative about all the benefits of becoming a "Shapes Sister."

"Our culture is quite different than your traditional gym setting," Shelly explained. "As you can see, we are a 'women only' facility, so there is not that awkwardness you might experience with a co-ed gym. We're working on our lumps, bumps and sagging tushies together! HAHAHHAAA!" Shelly cackled.

"Yikes," I heard myself saying.

"No, seriously, ladies," Shelly continued, "for beginners or those that want to lose a significant amount of weight; sometimes there is a tendency to feel self-conscious. The members here share a huge support system with one another as well as our trainers. Everyone is heading toward the same goal—fitness and better health. Exceptionally busy women also enjoy our circuit-style gym, which allows you to get a full-body workout in and feel in the best shape of your life with as little as three thirty-minute sessions a week. Our thirty-minute circuit has a very simple premise: you do an exercise on a particular machine, then dance, lightly jog, or simply walk in place on a step pad, then immediately follow it with another exercise on a different machine that doesn't directly affect the muscles you just worked."

As Shelly continued on with her explanation of the Shapes culture, I was even more impressed. I took a glance over at Nikki, who looked as if she was ready to go to sleep at any moment. I could tell by her nonchalant body language that she was clearly not as impressed as I was with Shelly and Shapes. Nikki's main focus was on her weight loss procedure. Working out at a gym temporarily to lose the fifteen or so pounds she needed for her stomach stapling surgery was just a means to an end with her.

"Well gals! Are you ready to do a REAL Shapes circuit workout right now?" Shelly said giddily, her voice screeching and her eyes doing that wide, animated thing again. She had mentioned when we made the appointment initially that we would get a complimentary thirty-minute workout just to see how we liked it, so Nikki and I came prepared with gym shoes and workout gear on, all ready for our first Shapes session. Shelly introduced her Shapes crew to Nikki and me. Three ladies who had on the same Shapes gear as Shelly.

They all seemed very nice, cordial, and excited to see us, but without that over-the-top-hyper-puppy enthusiasm Shelly had going on. "Hello ladies, my name is Toni, and I will be showing you how to do your first Shapes workout!" Toni was a cute little dark-haired young lady, probably in her mid-thirties. She was fit, but not skinny, which appealed to me. She looked to be a size 14, stocky, with warm eyes and a friendly voice. I wouldn't mind being her size, I thought to myself, sneaking glances at her, careful not to stare.

I hated when people stared at me. I always felt judged when folks did that. For the most part, people look at other people because it's human nature to do so. When I noticed someone looking at me, it made me extremely self-conscious, which is why I rarely went to heavily populated places like malls and such. I would imagine what people were thinking as soon as they noticed how overweight I was. When I did go to the grocery store or a department store, I'd look downward most of the time, only looking up to see which direction I needed to go in.

As Toni demonstrated how the various machines worked to Nikki and me, I stole quick glances and admired her physique when I thought she wasn't paying attention.

As I looked around, I noticed there were about five ladies working out at the time, sizes ranging from very heavy to very thin. Just like in any situation where new people join a group, there were some members who stared at Nikki and me as we approached the circuit some cordially smiled and others simply were too focused on working out to care who we were. True to form, I became very uncomfortable when I noticed the faces who stared at us. Without my even realizing it, my body language mimicked my feelings of awkwardness. In response, I hid myself behind a larger machine so I wouldn't be seen by onlookers while I watched Toni work with Nikki on the abs machine. Out of view, I intently paid attention to Toni's instructions on how operate the machine correctly to get the optimum benefit.

Now available to join Toni in helping explain each machine and how it worked, Shelly arrived back on the circuit grinning from ear to ear. Narrowing her eyes, she detected me over at my temporary hideout behind the shoulder press machine. "Hey Sue!" She beckoned. "What the heck are you doing back there? Join the party! Front and center, girly!" She screeched with that high-pitched tone of hers.

"I'm back now. I apologize disappearing on you gals just now...but whew, this joint is jumping tonight! I had to get a couple of folks manually checked in so they could start their workouts because our swipe card system is down, and then phones started ringing off the hook with appointments, and then...blah, blah, BLAH, BLAH..."

Good grief, Shelly's mouth moved faster than the speed of light, I thought in amazement. When she stopped to take a breath, I took full advantage of the moment. "That's okay. I'm ready when you are, Shelly." I was eager to get started, and I didn't want to waste another minute with small talk. Nikki was halfway through with her workout with Toni, and I was raring to get busy burning calories too.

Shelly walked me over to the circuit by the first step pad. It looked so small; I hoped I wouldn't fall off of it. As *The Best of Kool and the Gang* blasted from the speakers perched high on shelves on both sides of the room, I tried my best to read Shelly's lips for further instructions. "Just step on the pad like this and start moving. You can dance, walk in place, whatever you feel, as long as you are moving at a good steady pace." Shelly demonstrated on the pad a few paces down from me. As she did a high-stepping march to the beat of the music, I couldn't help but notice her thighs jiggle just a bit in her not-so-snug yoga pants. Her arms, although toned, had looser skin underneath that swayed to the beat of *"Celebration"* as she marched on the pad. Shelly was by no means your average fitness trainer like the ones you see on those late-night infomercials touting weight loss DVDs. She was an older lady, I figured in her late fifties or even early sixties with a short and sassy haircut, and she was quite attractive.

I eyeballed Shelly's frame with a mixture of admiration mingled with a teeny bit of jealousy. *I bet she has never been fat a day in her life*, I thought. *What does she know about losing the kind of weight I need to lose anyway?* My skepticism meter engaged as I walked on the pad next to Shelly's.

"Come on, girly! Get those legs moving! Up…up!" she commanded as I tried to get my legs to move faster and higher, but getting really winded in the process.

"Shoot, lady, in case you haven't noticed, I'm FAT over here! I can only move so fast!" I silently protested with a frown. Deciding to ignore my own whining and give it a go, I tried to move as fast as Shelly did, my massive thighs jiggling, my large arms wobbling to and fro. I only stayed on the pad moving in place for about three minutes, but it felt longer than that. By the time I changed to the next station, I felt as if I had run a marathon. The first actual machine I attempted was the high press machine. The seat looked so narrow, I thought twice about sitting down on it, and I think Shelly knew it too.

Just before my attempt to sit down, Shelly gently squeezed my shoulder and led me to the gym's stretching area, where it was quieter, and no one happened to be the immediate area. I had no clue why she was taking me over there, perhaps to tell me I wasn't trying hard enough on the step pad. I tried to prepare myself for whatever she was going to tell me. Shelly looked at me with compassion in her blue eyes as she took my hand in hers. She began to speak, but not with the overzealous pitchy voice that I had gotten used to. This time her voice was soft and assured as she spoke.

"Sue, I am picking up on a few things with you. You are afraid. You are so afraid this won't work that you are on the verge of not even trying. You are afraid you may be judged by other members here if you do make an effort to try to exercise. You don't want others looking at you negatively. I know I'm right because I saw how you tried to hide yourself when you first got out there. Am I right, Sue?" Shelly tilted my head upward, forcing me to look in her eyes, something which usually petrified me to do with any stranger. Her demeanor was comforting and warm. It didn't feel like I was talking to stranger at all. She spoke as if she was a concerned friend, someone who really cared.

As I was forced to look at her, tears welled up in my eyes. I tried to suck them back in, but couldn't. As tears rolled down my cheeks and onto her hand, her blue eyes smiled, and without another word, she hugged me tightly, just like my mother did when I needed encouragement. Even though I didn't know Shelly for more than a couple of hours, it was as if she knew my story, or at least

Digging Deep For Change

part of it. I stayed in her arms for a couple of moments, my tears dampening the sleeve of her blue Shapes t-shirt.

"Yes, you are right, Shelly. I feel like part of me doesn't belong here with these women. I don't think I can hack it. I see how they are looking at me, and I know what they are thinking, too. They see a fat woman who looks stupid trying to hop up and down on these pads, and they are waiting for me to sit down and break one of these machines with all this weight on me. I've broken chairs before, you know."

Shelly interrupted my tearful confession. "Sue, first of all, you are just like any other woman that is in this gym right now. You are looking to change your life, you are looking to lose weight and get your health in order. They are too." Shelly pointed toward the circuit. "Have you ever stopped to think that when people are looking at you, they are looking at you because you are so beautiful? Look at yourself." She pointed over to a nearby mirror, and I immediately turned away from it. "No, look at yourself, you are one gorgeous chick! Whether you are in this body or a smaller one, you are still worthy and still beautiful. I can see it, even if you don't, and so can the members here. If you give us a chance, you will see that we are a huge network of women with a variety of issues, not just weight-related. We have women here who are battling everything from alcohol abuse and troubled marriages, to illnesses like breast cancer and yes, severe obesity. You are not alone. All of us, we are all battling something in our personal lives.

That's why our members come here to work out faithfully each week. It's therapy. Some are here to work on the inside, while others come here to work on the outside. We talk, we laugh, and sometimes we cry too. We support one another here, and if you'll have us, we want to support whatever you are working on."

Shelly's genuine kindness is something I would never forget. Her words of support touched me so very deeply, in a place that perhaps hadn't been reached before, with regard to her steadfast belief in me.

"I have tried everything to lose weight before, and nothing ever works. I just keep getting bigger and bigger. I want to stop eating, but sometimes I just can't. When I am stressed, it's the first thing I turn to. When my husband is—"

I stopped short of telling Shelly the sordid details of my tumultuous marriage to Darryl. I was already emotional, no sense in making more tear puddles on her sleeve. "I just can't do it, but I need to. The whole reason why I am here is because of what my doctor told me last week. He told me that if I didn't lose weight, I…I…I just have to."

I couldn't bring myself to tell her the words Dr. Thomas said to me.

"Shelly, this is serious for me. I have to do something about my weight. I have children, who need me, and I want them to have a mother who can care for them properly, they deserve that. Here is the deal. I was about three hundred and sixty pounds the last time I weighed myself. This is a literal do-or-die situation I'm facing. I don't want to have surgery to lose the weight because I am scared, and part of me-a tiny part of me—believes I can do this thing on my own. I know what I am up against. I have a long road ahead of me, but I promised myself that I'd sacrifice what I had to in order for this weight loss journey to become a reality. I have to save my life, but I don't know how.

I don't know the first thing about losing weight. I...I...don't...know...what...to do." The tears began to flow again. "I'm here, Shelly. I believe that Shapes is the place where it can happen for me. But I need your help. Will you please help me? Will you please help me save my life?"

I was so overcome with emotion that my hands began to shake. I had laid it out there. Bared my soul to this lady whom I barely knew, but I somehow felt so comfortable talking to. She saw the potential in me that no one else did. Not even my closest relatives. She believed in me. She said it, and I felt her sincerity.

"Of course I will help you, sweetheart. I will help you in any way that I can. If you are willing to learn, then I will teach you how to lose weight, and not only that...but I'll teach you how to maintain the weight you have lost. I'm not going to sell you a fairy tale, and I won't lie to you, it won't be a walk in the park. It won't be easy, and it won't happen tomorrow, but it WILL happen. If you don't have enough belief in yourself right now, that's okay. I have enough belief in you to tide you over until you catch up with me," she said with a confident tone.

"You can do it," she continued. "And you will do it. If you are ready to put in the work that it takes, then I can promise you it will pay off. I will let you know one thing about me upfront," she said, her voice escalating with enthusiasm, "I am not accepting any excuses. Excuses are for those who don't want to achieve their goals. I won't kill you out there on the circuit, but you will feel your workouts at the end of the day. I'm tough enough to remind you of why you came here in the first place—to change your life, to feel better, to look better, and to prolong your life and feel good while living it. You got it, Chickie?"

Her voice had returned to the old Shelly I was familiar with—screechy, loud, and full of excitement. "Yep, I got it, and I am on board, Shelly. I am looking forward to making myself proud and you too," I said though my sniffles. I hadn't realized that my nose was running from my sobbing, and I quickly tried to suck up any mucus remnants before it hit my lip.

"Well then...let's get to work! Let's get started on the brand new you, Sue!" She laughed as if she was tickled by her own rhyming skills. "But before we get to work, you'd better make a trip to the ladies' room before you sling that snot that's hanging off the tip of your nose all over the machines!" We both roared into laughter so loud that the other ladies in the gym turned around to see what was so funny. I ran to get the tissue and came back, and just doubled over with laughter again. I really needed that release of pent-up emotion that had been there for so long; I needed a good dose of hearty, belly-aching laughter, and I think Shelly knew it too. We both laughed hysterically for a few minutes...and boy, it felt so good.

After our little chat in the stretching area, I had a renewed sense of confidence. I went back to the circuit feeling triumphant and hadn't touched one machine yet. Nikki, on the other hand, was done with her complimentary workout and had her coat on, looking anxious and ready to go. I walked over to Nikki. "Girl, how did it go? How do you feel? Was it hard?" I piled on inquires, eager to know what I was in for.

"Um, it was okay," Nikki said in a rather monotone voice. "The machines are okay, and I am a little tired, but it was alright. The music was corny though, come on now...Kool and the Gang? Really?" Nikki rolled her eyes upward in blasé fashion as she stood by the door. It was pretty obvious she wasn't exactly blown away with Shapes or their choice of retro music.

"Well, Nik, as you probably noticed, their member base appears to be middle-aged women; maybe they are just appealing to their audience. The music was pretty cool to me. I love 'Ceeeel-laa-bration!' I nudged Nikki with a slight chuckle. She gave me a halfhearted grin in return, not amused by my cornball rendition of the tune. Nikki sounded so indifferent that I wondered if she liked her gym experience even in the slightest bit. I was really hoping she did. I figured I would wait until we got out of there to chat about her opinion of Shapes and if she was interested in joining. I already knew I was, and I was hoping that I could have a buddy to workout with.

"You disappeared all of a sudden when that Toni lady was showing me how to do the machines. I looked around and you were gone. Where did you run off to? Did you even finish the workout?" Nikki asked, still standing by the gym door as if she was either guarding it or trying to escape.

"I was actually talking to Shelly in the stretching area." I already knew what her next question would be, and I tried to think of something quick as I anticipated it.

"Oh, what about?" Nikki inquired while digging for her car keys in her purse.

"Oh, nothing really...she was just reiterating all the benefits of the gym, the culture, yadda, yadda, yadda; just basic stuff, ya know?"

Truth be told, I didn't want to reveal the true nature of my conversation with Shelly to Nikki. It was private, just between me and her. The feelings I revealed to Shelly were very personal, how I felt about myself and my failings. Even though Nikki was my best friend, a part of me wasn't comfortable with letting her into the realm of how I truly felt about myself. Maybe part of me felt that Nikki might have viewed me in a different light had she known what a low opinion I had of myself. I just didn't want to reveal how ashamed I was to her.

"Well, why did she have to take you in the back to tell you that stuff?" Nikki probed as her interrogation became full throttle. I had just about run out of viable explanations to give Nikki when Shelly appeared from around the reception desk.

"So, are you gals ready to sign up? Did you enjoy your workout?" Shelly chirped while holding two Shapes applications in her hand. There was a pen behind her ear, and she was smiling broadly as usual.

"You have a really nice gym here, Shelly, and Toni was very patient in assisting me with the equipment and explaining what machines worked what muscle groups. I enjoyed the workout, but would like to sleep on it before I make my decision to join or not," Nikki explained to Shelly. She damn near had one foot out of the door while talking. "I'll definitely let you know by the end of the week. Thanks, and it was really nice meeting you, Shelly."

"Good enough. Think it over and we will have the paperwork ready when you come back to sign up," Shelly said while shaking Nikki's hand, obviously very confident that Nikki would return to join. Quickly spinning around to my direction, Shelly smiled. "Sue, you really didn't get an opportunity to work out this evening, did ya? I'm sorry about that. I'll tell ya what, come back later on this week to complete your complimentary workout. If you can come on Thursday, that would be great. Thursday is game night here at Shapes. Its LOADS of fun I tell ya. We have a good time while we burn calories...all the gals here love Thursday game night...think you can make it?" Shelly's eyes lit up like a Las Vegas slot machine as she waited for my response.

"Okay...sure. I think I can make it. Sounds like a good time!" I replied, Shelly's contagious smile rubbing off on me and causing me to grin too. Meanwhile, Nikki had already gone out of the door and was waiting for me with the car running. "Thanks Shelly, it was a pleasure. See you on Thursday," I said while moving quickly out of the door, hoping Nikki hadn't left me for taking so long.

"It was a pleasure meeting you. Looking forward to seeing you on a regular basis here!" Shelly winked as she waved goodbye.

"Bye, Sue! Hope to see you back with us soon!" I heard the other trainers yell from the circuit while waving and smiling. Even some of the members took a moment from their huffing and puffing to bid me goodbye. Some of them even called me by my name, as if they knew me already. It felt good to be acknowledged so warmly. It felt really good.

I hopped in the car with Nikki, who appeared a bit annoyed and ready to go. "Hey, girl. Sorry for the wait. Why did you leave out? Never mind...so, what did you think about Shapes?" I said, hoping for a bit of positivity now that she had rested a little bit.

"It's cool. I will probably join. I do need to lose these fifteen pounds. Yeah, I will go in tomorrow and sign up...what about you, with your CELLL-LAA-BRATION-singing butt!" Nikki said, inserting a bit of cornball humor herself finally, and I was happy about it too.

"Yeah," I said as I tried to downplay my excitement as much as I could. "I probably will too. I really like the gym's circuit layout, and Shelly kind of grew on me after a while. I still think she's a bit looney, but not in a 'make a reservation for a padded cell and straitjacket' kinda way." We both simultaneously burst into giggles. "She's just super eccentric and perhaps a bit stuck in a time warp, but aside from that, I can tell she knows her stuff. She knows about fitness, and I think we can learn a lot from her about losing weight. And I'm ready for my new body. This one has run its course." I looked down at my belly that sat on my lap.

"Nikki, I swear there is a little man that shrinks your seat belt every time I get in your car. This thing is so tight it's cutting off the blood supply to boobs!" I said as I wrestled with the seat belt for breathing room. We both laughed hysterically as I squirmed and wiggled in vain to get comfortable the entire way home in her two-seater car whose manufacturer obviously did not have "fluffy" people in mind when constructing it.

The Dawning of a New Day

I was pumped as I jumped out of Nikki's car, still reflecting on my experience at Shapes. Putting my key in the door, I excitedly ran upstairs to check on the girls. "Hi, Mommy…shhh, don't wake up Jo, she just fell asleep." There they were, all huddled in my oldest daughter Denai's bed while my middle daughter Lanie sat crossed-legged rocking little Johanna in her arms.

"Okay, I'll be verrry quiet," I whispered, over-exaggerating my tiptoeing over to where they were sitting just to make them laugh. Denai and Lanie erupted in giggles.

"Shhhh," they both turned to say to one another, each one holding up their little finger against their lips.

"I just wanted to say I love you before you guys went to sleep," I said as I gently kissed each of the girls on their foreheads.

"We love you too, Mommy, and guess what? Ma-Ma made us some gooooood chicken and macaroni and cheese tonight. You missed it!" Denai whispered, over-exaggerating her words as if she could still taste how delicious her dinner was.

My mother had a very loving relationship with her grandchildren; they were her joy, next to cooking. She loved spoiling them rotten, and they loved every minute of it too. Whatever they requested to eat, she'd happily prepare it, no questions asked. My girls affectionately called my mother "Ma-Ma." Denai pinned the nickname when she was just learning to talk, and "Mommy" came out as "Ma-Ma" when she referred to my mother. As far as my daughters were concerned, the hierarchy in the house was very clear. I was "Mommy," but my mother was the "The head Mommy" in their world.

My girls gravitated toward her, and sometimes it made me a little jealous. When my answer of "no" was not received very well, Denai would go seek the "higher authority" for an overruled decision in her favor. My mother spent more time nurturing them than I did at that time. Even when her health began to decline, sickness never kept her from tending to them. She always made time for them, even if it was just cuddle time while she watched *General Hospital* or some game show in her bedroom. Although I loved my three daughters with all my heart, I wasn't as available as I should have been to them, in particular to my oldest daughter, Denai. When she was a toddler, my mother practically took care of her full-time. After my divorce from her father, I threw myself into working long hours at the hair salon. When I wasn't working, I was too busy seeking validation in relationships; looking for confirmation of worthiness wherever I could find it.

"Sweet dreams, see you in the morning," I whispered as I blew kisses and turned off their bedroom light. Looking at them made it clear who I was fighting my battle for. My babies deserve a mom they can be proud of, I reiterated to myself as I proceeded to my bedroom to tell my husband all about my evening at Shapes.

When I got to the bottom of the basement stairs, I saw Darryl in his normal spot on the couch, engrossed in the latest version of *Madden* on PlayStation. "Oh hey, baby, you're home late tonight," he said, never looking away from the screen.

"Yeah, I wanted to tell you about where I went today. Remember I told you I was planning on joining a gym? I think I found one; it's not too far from us, on 95th Street. It's called Shapes. I was really impressed with the place, and the owner Shelly is a little nutty, but really nice," I told him while gushing with excitement. I wanted so badly for Darryl's reaction to mirror my own enthusiasm. I wanted him to be excited for me just as I was when something good was on the horizon for him.

"Oh, okay…cool. Did you eat yet? Mama made some good chicken tonight. Me and the kids are stuffed," he said with a slight bit of eye contact in my direction.

Darryl was too pre-occupied with what he was engaged in to really hear what I said. His response was a typical canned reply to make it appear as if he had been listening. His halfhearted responses were a pretty normal occurrence. When it came to something that involved my gratification on just about any level, it was really low on his priority list. I accepted his lackluster response, but unlike so many times before when I would beg for his attention, I didn't this time. I walked away in silence, but with a feeling of determination.

I had made my decision that evening at Shapes. I would do what I had to do, what I needed to do, even without a cheering section. Besides, at least I had Nikki in the trenches with me. We would do this thing together, side by side like we always did. I was so ready to get started at the gym with her. I went to sleep that night with a smile on my face, anticipating getting started at Shapes with Nikki later on that week.

Step 1...Step 2... (349.2)

Maybe it was just me, but I could have sworn that I felt a little lighter. Since my talk with Dr. Thomas I started cutting back on the junk I ate. I started drinking less Pepsi and more water. The pep talk with Shelly was exactly what I needed to help me over my self-confidence hump. I was looking forward to for my first official workout at a gym.

Step 1...Step 2...

Nikki and I agreed that we were to meet up at Shapes at 6 p.m. on Thursday. I was at Shapes by 5:00 p.m. in my workout gear and gym shoes. While I waited, I scanned the gym for Shelly to greet her. Shelly was out on the circuit doing her thing, yapping about something while making sure each member was operating the equipment efficiently. I happened to catch her attention, which caused her to stop mid-sentence and head in my direction, almost as if she had forgotten she was just in a conversation with someone else mere seconds before.

"Hey there, Susie. Glad to see you back, girlie," she said, her eyes twinkling. "Have you made your mind up? Are you going to join the ranks of the Shaper elite?" She folded her arms and smiled.

"Yep, I'm joining today both me and Nikki are, whenever she gets here. But I'm ready to complete the process now." I didn't want to wait; I didn't want to give my decision a second thought.

"Fantastic! That's great, Sue!" Shelly said with that familiar loud and screechy tone that caused the entire circuit to turn around to see what her cheering was about.

With pen in hand, I glanced over the Shapes application and the health-related questionnaire, all the while looking over my shoulder to see if Nikki had arrived yet. My eyes stopped at one question in particular. *How much do you weigh now?* I stared at the question as if I could somehow will it to disappear from the paper. I hadn't been on a scale since I last saw Dr. Thomas. I had no clue how much I weighed, and honestly, I didn't want to know. My thoughts drifted as I turned away from the application momentarily and stared down at my thighs, which were spilling off the side of the folding chair I was in, causing me a lot of discomfort. It snapped me from my trance and made me remember why I was at Shapes in the first place.

"Shelly, I don't know how much I weigh, and the application states my answer must be accurate," I said, looking for an excuse to maybe come back later. "No problem, just step right here on the scale. We can weigh you right now; just take your shoes off." I shuddered at her invitation. The truth was, I didn't want anyone to see how big I had gotten and how much I really weighed. I didn't even want to see it myself, let alone have Shelly see. I knew I weighed somewhere around 330, but that number always fluctuated.

I should have just put 330 on the dang paper, I thought, chastising myself for being honest. Maybe since my shoes were off, the number on the scale would be more forgiving. I wished for a fleeting, ridiculous moment I could strip down to my underwear just to give myself a fighting chance with the number on the scale.

I had hoped Nikki would come in so that Shelly would be distracted for a minute, but to no avail. Shelly was right there, pen in one hand, my member profile folder in the other. "Step right up,

Sue," Shelly beckoned as she held my hand to help me balance on the see-through digital Shapes scale. I closed my eyes tight as I waited for the results. My paranoia kicked in as the after-work crowd started trickling in to the gym. I just knew they were standing behind me to see how much I weighed too. The scale seemed like it took forever to calculate my weight...240...255...280—the numbers continued to go up—300...315...336.8...349.2. At last, the scale made its final stop at 349.2 pounds. I wanted to get off the scale, but my feet felt heavy like lead. My eyes were fixated on the scale in disbelief: 349 pounds.

I'd never weighed that much before in my life. I tried so hard not to cry in front of Shelly and the rest of the members that were around, but everything in me wanted to sob like a baby right then and there. My heart sank to my feet. My eyes burned from an influx of tears that were ready to fall. Dazed and frozen to the spot I was in, I felt Shelly's hand squeeze mine. "That number will change. Don't get used to it," she whispered in my ear. I managed to give Shelly my best halfhearted smile. I stepped off the scale and returned to my seat slowly, still reeling from what I had just seen.

Not long after, Nikki finally showed up. I overheard Shelly asking her to fill out similar paperwork so that we could get started. I noticed that Nikki never stepped on the scale, probably for the same reasons I didn't want to. I wished I hadn't either. Facing the truth about our condition is not always pretty, sometimes it's downright ugly. There only two roads to take: either we admit and correct, or deny and dwell in a lie. As much as it hurts our pride, the truth has to be confronted if real transformation is ever going to begin in our lives.

Looking at that number coupled with the Dr. Thomas's conversation made everything real to me. It was the gut-punch I needed. After filling out the necessary paperwork, the final phase of the membership process was a short Q and A session with Shelly concerning my long-and short-term goals with regard to fitness and improving my health.

"Why are you here, Sue? What made you want to come through our doors? What are your goals, and what do you want to accomplish here at Shapes? Please be as specific as you can with your answers, take your time," Shelly said with a seriousness I hadn't seen in her demeanor before. It was evident that she loved what she did for a living. Her compassion and attentiveness to her members were qualities that overflowed with a sincerity and authenticity that made women like me gravitate toward her facility. It's no wonder Shapes had such a thriving membership.

I thought about the questions she asked me for several minutes. No one had ever asked me those questions before. I wanted my answers to reflect my true intentions, my true feelings. After giving it some thought, I told Shelly exactly why I was there:

"I'm here because I don't want to die earlier than I am supposed to because I can't stop eating. I want to lose weight, because wishing it away is not an option anymore. My goal is to lose about one hundred pounds, maybe even more, although that might be too much to shoot for. Right now I am on multiple medications to control my high blood pressure, and Xanax to cope with a panic disorder. I am sick of taking medicine. I want my children to be proud of me—what they have come to expect is a Mom who is always too tired to play with them. I want my daughters to know that they are capable of doing whatever they set their minds to do, no matter how difficult it may seem. I want more than anything to be that kind of example for them. If Shapes can help me achieve that, I'm in the right place."

Saying that to Shelly felt incredibly good. I visualized everything I spoke about coming to pass. I even found myself smiling afterwards. I wondered what Shelly was thinking as she jotted down notes in my file. When she was done, she looked up with tears in her blue eyes, as if she had followed me on that destination trip.

"I will keep the notes I have taken in your file, Sue. We will look back at them together when you reach all your goals, which you will. You have everything you need right now to make all the things you told me a reality. So let's get to it. Welcome aboard, Sue!"

Just like that, I was an official member and was ready to get going with my first official workout. Just around that time, Nikki had finished her profile and Shapes application. I greeted her with a wide smile as she walked over to the circuit.

I don't know how those sixty-something-year-old ladies did it. My first workout kicked my butt. Here I was in my early thirties, watching the "Grey-haired Golden Girl Wrecking Crew" whip around the gym circuit like it was nothing, while I was breathless, battered, and barely making it on those damn machines. I rolled my eyes at them as they effortlessly jumped off one machine to hop the next, skipping over me in the circuit rotation. I felt like I needed one of those orange "slow moving vehicle" triangle stickers on my butt. Nikki wasn't much better, which was my only saving grace that first day. I managed to get close enough to Nikki to tap her on the shoulder by the bicep curl machine. "Hey…do you see these old ladies?" I said while resting briefly on the wall, being careful not to be spotted by Shelly.

"Yeah, I know…the one over there almost ran me over by the squat machine," Nikki said, pointing at a senior citizen in amazement.

By the time I reached the twenty-minute mark of my thirty-minute workout at Shapes, I was done, and by done I mean leaning over, exhausted, and drenched with sweat. My body wasn't used to vigorous moving, and it was letting me know it too. I looked over at Nikki, who was still hanging in, but I could see she was on her last leg, too. I had just enough energy to drag myself to the bench to sit down. I really wasn't in the mood to chit-chat, especially since I had been run off the circuit by a group of grannies. In her usual animated style, Shelly came running up to me as I was putting on my coat. "How was your first workout, kiddo?"

"I feel like an eighty-year-old woman right about now, Shelly." (Well, not any of the eighty-year-old ladies at Shapes, but I think she got my point.) "I couldn't even finish the whole circuit."

"Good! You will fit right in, then!" she said as she roared with laughter. "Tomorrow will be better; your body is not used to movement like this, it's totally normal. Shake it off, girlie; you can make it up tomorrow. Take a hot bath and that will relax your muscles and help you recover...I will see you tomorrow, right?"

"Uh...Yeah. Tomorrow," I said, not certain if I could make it through to the next hour, let alone the next day.

"You did well today, Sue, one day at a time. I promise it gets better. Just keep coming. Tomorrow I would really love for you to take advantage of my healthy eating class. The new cycle has just started, so you are joining us at just the right time."

In addition to fitness training, Shelly taught a class on proper diet, based on a book that Shapes had recently published in conjunction with their exercise program. Upon my joining the gym, one of the main talking points she discussed was the importance of not only exercising, but also eating properly, something I knew nothing about. I was eager to learn anything she could teach me, and I made plans to be there for every class. Because of my life-long struggle with food addiction, this proved to be the greatest challenge I had ever faced. But I refused to let that stop me. I remembered the promise I made to sacrifice for the sake of changing my life. Ever since I was a child, food was my lifeline; it was my key to coping. Eating is was what calmed me, what made me happy, and comforted me throughout my life. I would have to learn how to detach those emotions and put them in their proper places. I had my work cut out for me.

Wendy's was not too far down the street. I had already passed it when I was going to the gym and made a mental note…just in case. I thought of how great a chocolate frosty would be, but I didn't go. I had things to accomplish. Ruining my first workout just wasn't worth it, not even for a frosty. I knew that my next test would be learning how to eat to lose weight, which was more of a challenge than working out. I would have to literally learn how to eat all over again. I dismissed the frosty notion and began to think of how good my size-14 jeans would feel as opposed to the 26-28 plus-size ones I had in my closet now.

The following day was brutal; my body never knew what hit it. The whole hot shower, muscle relaxing thing Shelly told me about? Yeah, that didn't work for me. I felt as if I had been in a boxing

Step 1...Step 2...

match with Mike Tyson AND Muhammad Ali back in his prime. My body was racked with soreness of every variety. Even my eyelashes hurt. Despite the discomfort, I felt proud of myself. That next morning after my shower, I looked at myself in my mirror while getting dressed for the first time in a very long time. Talking out loud, I told myself that every ache and pain was moving me closer to my goal. I made those words my morning affirmation every day after that.

The Pursuit

Learning to Fly Solo

The following weeks would include many physical and mental challenges like I had never encountered in my life. As the weeks went on, I started seeing less and less of Nikki at the gym. There would always be some reason why she couldn't make it. Soon she stopped coming altogether and cancelled her membership. She told Shelly that Shapes wasn't for her.

For a brief moment I thought about quitting too. I was used to giving up—it's what I knew. My first reaction was: "I CAN'T do this by myself…who would make sure I got to the gym on time? Who would remind me to go at all? Who would tell me not throw in the towel when I contemplated going back to my old ways?" Nikki was the one who had introduced me to Shapes in the first place. From day one, my weight loss journey included her. It was OUR journey that we would carry out together, just like everything else we did in our lives. Sue and Nikki were a packaged deal. Now I would be by myself, without my best friend by my side to share the ups and downs of this difficult weight loss battle.

As the days went on, I thought about all the reservations I had about staying on at Shapes without Nikki, weighing out the pros and cons. After going for a few weeks, I concluded that I actually liked being at Shapes. I liked the comradery of the staff and the friendly ladies I worked out with. I didn't feel like I thought I would, going into a place where I didn't know anyone. I didn't feel judged, I felt welcomed. When Nikki asked me if I was going to stay on at Shapes with that crazy Shelly, I told her yes without a second thought.

Nikki went on to have her Lap-Band surgery, and just as I promised, I was there at the hospital the day after her surgery to help her in any way I could, even if it was just for moral support.

I realized just because someone begins on a journey with you, they may not necessarily stay the course with you throughout it. Sometimes you have to go it alone, and maybe that's how God intended it to be in the first place. We cannot realize our own capabilities if we are constantly using others as a crutch to hold us up. It was during that time, very early in my journey, that I learned how to fly solo when I was pushed out of the nest. I used my own wings to sustain flight, as scary as it was to do by myself.

In the coming weeks and months, God showed me I was a lot stronger than I thought I was. Each time I stepped on the gym circuit, He taught me something new about myself, something I didn't know I had the capacity to do before. I learned that I needed to hold myself accountable and not depend on others to do the job for me. I also came to grips with the fact that although Nikki and I sought the same destination, our chosen paths to get there were completely different. I'd had my first experience with getting acclimated to change during my weight loss experience—I accepted it and made the necessary adjustments. Nikki's season at Shapes, however short-lived, had ended. But mine had just begun.

Now that Nikki had officially cancelled her membership, I wondered how I would feel going to the gym without my best friend by my side. The truth is; it wasn't bad at all. Nikki had stopped coming a while before she officially quit, so nothing really changed. I just continued as I normally would, slowly and deliberately working through the routines on the machines while trying to increase my endurance in the process. I really wanted to get in there and whip through my workouts, but that first week was more than I bargained for. I had such high expectations that when I couldn't make it through the thirty minutes, I was ready to throw in the towel. I was completely frustrated with my body, which seemed to be working against me every time I stepped on the circuit. Patience was never my strong suit, and trying to get into the swing of things was taking way too long for me. Some evenings I would walk up to the reception area where Shelly usually sat with the intention of telling her to cancel my membership too. Just as soon as I would get enough nerve to tell her that I just wasn't cut out for all this exercise business, something made me stop short and go back to give it another try. I was constantly tired, sore, and cranky. I'm sure it was a result of not giving my body what it craved, which was sugar and fat. As soon as I stepped foot out of the gym, I wanted have something I had no business eating. Every day, it was a constant relentless battle for control over my urges to eat. When I fed the girls, I hoped they would leave food on their plates, just so I could eat the rest.

I combated my thoughts of unhealthy food with thoughts of the consequences I'd pay for indulging in it. I had to make a change. If I didn't change now, I may not ever have the opportunity again. I kept thoughts of my transformation in my mind's eye constantly. How it would feel to walk without being winded, and how it would feel to not have to squeeze into chairs and airplane seats and constantly be in state of discomfort. I kept my mind on my children and how much I loved them, and I kept going to Shapes. I just refused to give up, no matter how I felt. I held on to what Shelly said, about the workouts getting easier once my body became acclimated to the change. On the days when I became frustrated with myself, downright defiant and wanting to quit, I instantly rebuked the notion of going backwards as soon as I recognized its emergence. I told myself, even out loud sometimes, that quitting wasn't an option that was available to me, ever again.

Someone once said, anything foreign to you gets harder before it gets easier. I can attest that it's totally true. Through battling thoughts of defeat and telling myself I couldn't make it, I continued to make an effort anyway, constantly confronting my negative thinking about what I couldn't accomplish out there on that circuit. I talked to myself constantly, but I talked to God even more. I wasn't a Bible scholar, but I knew one verse that got me through those tough times: "The Joy of the Lord is my Strength" (Nehemiah 8:10). Perhaps the term "strength" might not have signified physical strength in the Bible, but I certainly used it in that context whenever I felt like I couldn't make one more step. I believed it, and indeed received strength every time.

The members of Shapes were a sight to see in action. Granted, some were there for companionship and conversation, but most were there to work on themselves, improving and sustaining their health. Sometimes while pausing to rest momentarily, I'd just observe all the women around me. Some were old enough to be my grandmother, but you can bet they were giving it all they had and they weren't complaining. Not working out at a rapid pace necessarily, but the tenacity was clear and their commitment was evident. They never knew it, but those women began to serve as my fuel. The more I looked at them go, the more I figured that if these ladies who were considerably older than me could work out three days a week for thirty minutes, then so could I if I just kept going. Those "Golden Girls," as I affectionately called them, motivated me probably more than anyone else did those first weeks at Shapes.

Looking at them also helped me realize that once I took my thoughts off my temporary fatigue and focused that energy in other places, like moving my legs a bit faster, lifting my arms a little higher, and stretching faith in myself a bit wider, I would find momentum. I would discover my "groove," and that's exactly what I did. When I got winded, I learned to pause briefly, and then keep going. When I felt like I could go a little further than I did the last time, I went for it. Every so often I'd hear Shelly yell out of nowhere, "Go, Sue go!" Her cheer would incite some of the other members of the "Golden Girl Crew" to follow suit with shouts of encouragement and barrages of high fives for my efforts.

Right there in that moment, for the first time in my life, I didn't want to be invisible. I didn't want to hide behind something like I did when I first arrived at Shapes. Their praise made me feel just like a little kid in school who got a gold star from the principal and teachers for some great achievement. I felt so proud.

Caution: Incentive Engaged (332.0)

Two weeks into my membership at Shapes gym and I was in full throttle. The soreness I had been experiencing was slowly diminishing with every workout I did, just as Shelly told me it would. I wasn't sure if I had lost any weight yet, but I was feeling better than ever. I noticed my jeans felt looser on me too, the same jeans I had to pour myself into and pry my way out of weeks ago.

Today would be my first official weigh-in day, and I was anxious about it. It had been fourteen days since I had joined Shapes, and I had no idea if I lost two pounds or gained five. This would be the test to see if my diligence on the exercise circuit and abiding by what I was learning in Shelly's healthy eating classes was paying off.

Going to Shapes no longer felt like a sacrifice. When I first began, I could only complete twenty minutes of my thirty-minute workout two days a week. Now I could finish the entire thirty-minute workout, and I moved up to three times a week. And I didn't feel like I was going to die when I got done. I was making small strides in the right direction, and it was really good.

I had always had an issue with punctuality, but not when it came to going to Shapes. You could practically set your watch to the time I would walk through the doors. Now that I was capable of doing three days a week, I scheduled myself to work out on Tuesdays, Thursdays, and Fridays. At exactly 5:17 p.m. on those days, you could find me swiping in at the gym like clockwork. After work, I'd go straight from the Metra to the gym, which was a half a block away from the train station, so I couldn't conjure up an excuse not to go.

My mother gladly babysat the girls for about forty-five minutes on those evenings when I was scheduled to work out. She was onboard with my new attitude, and she was a big factor in helping me stay on track. I was now able to keep up with the "Golden Girls" on the circuit. The ladies who used to bypass me because I couldn't keep up were now slapping me high fives when they began to see how much I had improved on the gym circuit. Shelly always had the biggest pom-poms though; she made sure I knew how proud she was of me.

In my heart, I felt like I had already achieved my goal and hadn't even weighed in for the first time yet. From the members to the trainers, I had stumbled across a network of people who believed in me and in what I could accomplish, and they had only known me for a short amount of time. Their confidence in me made me confident in myself—a feeling that was totally foreign to me before now. That felt incredible. I didn't want to let my Shapes alliance down. I tried as hard as I could from that point on. Every workout wasn't always a home run for me, and some days were better than others, but I vowed to always give my all when I was there. I wanted to show Shelly and the rest that their faith in me wasn't a waste of time.

After two weeks of pain in places I didn't even know I had, combined with sweat and determination had all come down to this. My very first weigh-in since I started at Shapes. Did I work as hard as I thought I did on the step pad and machines? Was the fact that my clothes zipped up a little easier than before just a figment of my wishful thinking? I would certainly find out after I finished my last set of side crunches on the ab machine.

As if I didn't already know, Shelly strolled over to where I was to remind me that my first weigh-in was that evening. Shoot, I had marked this day down on my calendar at work. I KNEW what today was. I couldn't help but feel scared though, I didn't want to disappoint Shelly if I hadn't lost any weight or, God forbid, gained any. More than that, I was afraid of disappointing myself —again. I had been through this hopeful stage before in my life when I had trotted down the "fad diet/weight loss shots" avenue, only to be let down when my efforts proved unsuccessful. I was nervous.

After my last set was done, I slowly made my way down to the weigh-in area. "Are you excited, Sue? It's your first weigh-in, Mama!" Sasha enthusiastically chirped as she came by and held me around my waist. Sasha was the younger and way more hip Shapes trainer who had been cheering for me since day one. Sasha was in her early thirties, drop dead beautiful with a figure to match. You would think she'd be vain, but her personality was just the opposite. She was kind, sweet, and very helpful whenever I needed assistance on how to perform on one of the exercise machines in proper form.

Sasha never made me feel like I was a nuisance, no matter how many times I asked her how to do something. We talked beyond the typical Shapes chatter when my workouts were finished. We'd talk about our lives outside of the gym as well. She had an autistic son whom she adored, and a vindictive ex-husband who sounded like the devil himself. I talked about my drama with Darryl and the new things the girls were doing in school. Turns out, Sasha needed a listening ear just as much as I did. She was easy to talk to, and always kept me laughing with her hilarious but harmless impressions of Shelly in action.

The moment I was anticipating was finally here. I waited for Shelly to finish talking to a member so that she could grab my chart to write down the particulars. I would be weighed and measured just like I had when I officially became a member. The weigh-ins for members were every one to two weeks. Shelly's preference was two weeks, so I went with that. She explained how weighing ourselves too often can lead to disappointment. Our bodies fluctuate from day to day, and the weight reading may be off due to menstrual cycle, retaining water, etc. The best timetable for monitoring weight loss when you are actively seeking to lose weight is from weekly to bi-weekly.

Shelly came barreling down the circuit with my folder tucked under her arm. "Sorry for the delay, Sue, I was trying to get someone's new checking information for her membership fee to come directly from her account. Do you know this lady has changed banks at least—"

I smelled the makings of a classic Shelly tangent coming on about this lady and her desire to frequently change banking institutions, none of which I gave a flying monkey about. I stopped her before her motor started going:

"Shelly, my weigh-in? I gotta get home to the girls."

"Oh yeah, let's get you started here, girlie," Shelly said absentmindedly as if she just remembered why she was standing by the scale in the first place. I happened to look out of the corner of my eye to see Sasha doing her best impression of Shelly's blabber mouth. I almost bit my tongue trying to hold back the laughter that was just itching to come forth. I was glad that Sasha was there to take the edge off with her silliness; it made me forget how nervous I was at that moment.

Shelly flipped through my folder and pulled out my weight and measurements progress sheet. Ready with pen in hand and eyeglasses resting on the tip of her nose, she was prepared to record my first weigh-in results as she and Sasha stood beside me. With shoes off and shaky confidence, I stepped on the scale and waited for the numbers with bated breath: 340…328…330………..332.0. The scale stopped and remained at 332 pounds.

I couldn't believe what I was looking at. Just to be sure there wasn't some sort of scale malfunction the first time, I got off and got back on. It was the same number, 332.0 pounds. I just stared at the scale in disbelief for a few seconds. There was silence briefly, then a shout of joy from all three of us. In two weeks I managed to lose 17 pounds. I thought of those nights when I wanted to quit, the frustration of not being as agile as the other members, the first workouts when I had to go into the bathroom and cry because I was upset with myself that I couldn't finish a complete thirty-minute workout because of the pain in my legs. I recalled those nights that I had to rub my sore body with alcohol, all the times I opted to drive past Wendy's to go home and make a salad with lots of vegetables and broiled chicken, the two-liter bottles of Pepsi that I swapped for glasses of water instead. All of the strides I was making paid off in the number that was before me. I had never in my life been so proud of what I had accomplished. I closed my eyes and whispered a prayer of thanks to God, who gave me the strength to do what I thought I could not. He showed me I didn't need a workout partner, all I needed was Him, and that was enough.

I had renewed confidence like I never had before standing on that scale. With a loud war cry I yelled as loud as I could without caring who heard me just three words, "YES, YES, and YES!" I drove home and simply floated on an imaginary cloud into my house. I decided not tell anyone about my 17-pound weight loss. Although my mother had mentioned that my face looked slimmer, that was about it. No real wow factor yet. But it was coming; I would make sure of it. The 17-pound loss was all I needed to jumpstart my determination. I vowed to remain tight-lipped. I would let my weight loss speak for itself.

Darryl asked me what I was smiling so hard about when I went into our bedroom. "Nothing. Just had a great workout, that's all," I said as I jumped in the shower still grinning from ear to ear. For the first time in a very long time, I went to bed without having to pop my Xanax pill. I snuggled up, warm and toasty with my secret. My only thoughts were of my accomplishment, the pride I felt when I stepped on the scale that evening, and the mini celebration Shelly and Sasha enjoyed with me. I kept replaying that triumphant movie in my mind and freeze-framing it until I fell into a deep, peaceful, wonderful sleep.

Earning my Wings

Not only was I learning how to exercise different muscle groups for weight loss at Shapes, I was also learning how to eat properly. Shelly's healthy eating classes were so interesting to me. I sucked up the knowledge like a sponge. Not only did I attend her weekly classes every Tuesday evening, I was the first one there. I became interested in the mechanics of losing weight. I not only wanted to learn what I should be eating, but more importantly what I shouldn't be. The more I learned, the more curious I became about the foods that caused me to gain weight in the first place. There were so many unanswered questions I had swirling around in my head at the end of class: *What in the world are carbs? Why are "complex carbs" better for me than "simple carbs?"* Shelly was teaching me how and what to eat, but I wanted to know WHY I should eat it.

When my queries went beyond the scope of Shelly's classes, I went on a hunt for answers. I found myself picking up everything I could get my hands on about weight loss and weight management. From books, to magazines on fitness and proper diet, I absorbed it all. When taking the girls to the library, we would all be reading and learning something. I spent hours reading and educating myself about my body and what I had been doing to it with my poor diet all these years. The knowledge I obtained blew my mind. I never knew that eating certain foods on a consistent basis could cause so much potential illness and even damage organs like the heart and clog arteries in the body. By the same token, I also learned that certain foods could revitalize the body, give it strength, energy, and even aid in weight loss. I felt like I had just stepped into a whole new realm. I slowly started to put into practice all I had learned, making changes in the food selections that I had been choosing for years.

I passed along my newfound information to my mother, the matriarch of the household. Since she prepared meals for the girls, Darryl, and me, I thought that she would be interested in the things I was learning about the food that had made me so heavy over the years. My mother, who loved cooking more than just about anything in the world, was very polite when I informed her of my findings, yet it didn't make much of a difference. My mother was born and raised in the deep south—Moultrie, Georgia to be exact. My mother grew up on southern style meals that were prepared with lots of butter, salt, sugar, and cured meat. She was accustomed to cooking in that same fashion.

Aside from the high carb content, her meals were always decadent. I would have to adjust to a completely different way of eating, which was a challenge, but a necessary one. I no longer had the excuse that I didn't know how and what to eat. Even when I reminded my mother that I was weaning myself off of certain foods like mac and cheese or fried chicken, she gave the infamous retort: "A little won't hurt you." But it would.

I know her intention was not to cause me to slip up and return to my old habits; she had no idea how serious I was about this journey I was on. I had to focus on changing my lifestyle, and just like a drug addict, I couldn't afford to slip up and have "just a little" anymore. I know what my "little" was like, and I wasn't willing to sacrifice all the strides I had been making in the gym to revert back to binge eating…even for my mother's signature baked macaroni and cheese and fried chicken. I realized the payoff in eating those foods wasn't worth it anymore. I was on a mission, and I just refused to let my penchant for the kind of food I had grown up on rule my life anymore.

Darryl didn't mind my decision to convert to a healthier eating lifestyle, but he didn't want any part of it. At close to 400 pounds and hooked up to a breathing machine at night due to sleep apnea, he needed to lose a significant amount of weight as well. I talked about what I had learned about the benefits of certain foods, and he would listen, but that was about it.

When I explained how I felt to my mother, she eventually began to take me seriously and respected my stance, but it didn't stop her from cooking the meals that she loved to prepare. I really didn't expect her to, even though with her myriad of health problems like diabetes, heart issues, and high cholesterol, I was hoping she would jump on board too.

She was swayed into cooking a bit healthier, and even cooked separate meals for me on special occasions like Thanksgiving when there would be calorie-rich foods everywhere. She'd set aside the gravy and high-carb foods and prepare healthier versions for me. My mother admired my commitment and helped me as much as possible with babysitting the girls while I worked out, as well as taking the time to prepare healthier versions of the meals that I loved. She even did some experimenting with healthy recipes she saw on TV, and surprised me with them when I got home from the gym. I loved her even more for that.

Butt-Kicking Mode (312.7)

The days seemed to go by so fast. I had gotten acclimated to my new lifestyle and was actually looking forward to going to the gym on my three days each week. My body was getting stronger, and my energy level increased. Soon I noticed that at the end of my thirty minutes, I was no longer winded, and actually had a boost of "get-up-and-go," so I went. I increased my gym workouts from thirty minutes to forty-five, and sometimes even an hour. I had such an incredible rush when I was done. It was like nothing I had ever felt before. Shelly explained to me that it was an adrenaline rush, when my endorphins really went into full "butt-kicking" mode. Whatever it was, I was hooked on it!

I fell off the wagon a few times, eating things I wouldn't normally eat, but I refused eat like I had in the past, gorging until I felt like vomiting. I ate an occasional cheeseburger or an order of fries, but kept in mind all the hard work I was putting in at the gym. There was no way in the world I was going to gain back the pounds I had lost. So when I ate outside of my healthy diet, I would beat myself up a bit, but then I would jump back into the groove of things and remind myself I had goals to meet.

Those cheat meals became few and far between, especially when I noticed how baggy my tight jeans were getting. I had never owned a belt in my life, and I had the best time shopping for one. Three months into working out consistently, I had lost 37 pounds. I was officially in the lower 300's, and weighed in at a hard-earned 312 pounds. I felt like a little kid at Christmas-time anticipating the weigh-ins. I even began to sneak in extra weigh-ins before my time was scheduled. Shelly warned me about weighing too frequently, but I had become addicted to seeing those numbers drop. I began to weigh in weekly just to see my progression. With every pound lost, I was motivated to push harder at the gym and be even more vigilant with regard to my carb and calorie intake. My eating regime was based on the information I received from Shelly's classes, coupled with guidelines I put into practice while researching healthy eating practices for weight loss. I adhered to a low-carb lifestyle that included vegetables, fruit, and baked or broiled chicken, fish, and beef. I cut out white carbs and swapped them for whole-wheat products. I traded my two-liter-a-day Pepsi habit for 64 ounces or more of water a day. I didn't snack on anything but fresh vegetables or fruit in-between my meals. I formed a new way of eating, and I stuck to it religiously.

The hardest part of sticking to my new lifestyle was when I became stressed about my husband and his being so comfortable with being unemployed. Nothing had changed in our situation at home. He was still fascinated by video games and enjoying the luxury of food and shelter without having to work for it. The excuses were getting so old that I just didn't want to hear them anymore. The girls were ecstatic that they had Daddy in the house full-time; he was their playmate, while Mommy, Auntie, and Grandma went to work every day. I would occasionally vent to my sister Brenda, which helped a bit. She understood my frustration, but wasn't as vocal about it as my mother was. I would overhear Brenda and my mother discussing what a poor excuse he was for a husband, which made me incredibly embarrassed. This was my husband, the man who promised to help provide for our children and me when we got married. And now I felt more like I was his meal ticket than his wife, and I knew for sure that my family concurred with that line of thinking.

I stopped asking Darryl about finding a job. I don't think I really cared anymore. I just conceded for the sake of peace. Whenever I got fed up with his lies about trying to find work, it was always the same scenario. I would threaten to divorce him, and he would promise to do better. He would find a couple of day labor jobs for a couple of weeks, give me some "good faith" money, then slowly go back to doing nothing again. It was a manipulative cycle that he had down to a science. "If you kick me out, where will I go? The kids need me here...so you are just going to snatch their father away from them, just like that?"

The truth of the matter was, Darryl wasn't alone in the world like he would have me believe. Aside from me and the kids, he had a solid family foundation that included his mother, step-father, and an ambitious younger brother who was the polar opposite of him. His brother was hard-working and held down three jobs to support his wife and kids. Darryl's family loved him, but would not allow him to live rent free with them for any extended amount of time; over time, he had simply worn out his welcome with them. Darryl had found a good thing with me, and he knew it. He played on my sympathy like a mastermind and fought like everything to keep his "good thing" secure. Guilt tripping me into staying with him was his number one tool.

I hated myself for falling for his manipulation when his false promises came up empty. I hated my blind optimism where he was concerned. I wanted the overheard whispers of my family to be about what a hardworking husband Darryl was, and how well he provided for his children and wife. When it all became too much to bear, I simply gave myself permission to forget about the fact that Darryl had not found a job and had no intention of doing so. Our marriage became the "lump in the rug" that I didn't even bother to try to straighten out anymore; I just stepped over it and kept moving.

Shapes became my oasis away from it all. I was a different person when I stepped through those doors. I wasn't a meek and chunky wife who couldn't stand up for herself; at the gym I was a fearless warrior. I began to love the feeling of sore muscles, and sweat pouring from my face—it meant that I was burning fat and heading toward my goals. My enthusiasm for the gym became infectious to the newer members that were coming in. I would stay a bit longer to encourage those who were just beginning their journey to keep going. I stayed longer at the gym to help Shelly and her staff prep for game night on Thursdays. I'd stay late just to talk to Shelly and Sasha about the newest Shapes products and classes. I simply adored being there. For me it had become more than just a place to exercise—it became my home away from home.

The icing on the cake was when the members began to notice my weight loss and comment about it. "Sue, how much have you lost, girl? You look great! Keep up the good work." I could barely believe what I was hearing, and in many respects, I didn't. I wasn't used to people telling me I had lost weight. I was polite and very gracious when I received the compliments, but in the back of my mind I figured they were just being nice. My mind would not allow me to accept that I really was dropping pounds and that it was indeed noticeable. Even at the bank where I worked, my bosses and co-workers were commenting as well. "What are you doing to lose weight, Sue? Whatever you are doing, it's working. Keep it up, you are looking good!"

My family began to chime in about my weight reduction as well. My sister, who was my biggest supporter, was the most vocal regarding the physical change that was becoming apparent, and her encouragement meant the world to me. She was my big sister, and to see how proud she was of me made all the sacrifices worth it. Equally proud were my parents. My mother, who noticed I was losing weight before anyone else did, took it upon herself to alter my pants and skirts when she saw that they were getting too big for me without my even asking. On more than one occasion, she'd take the pants right off me and stitch them up as I sat on her bed.

My dad was elated as well. Even though he did his fair share of contributing to the cause when I was younger by indulging my every whim when it came to food, my obesity became a real concern for him as I became heavier and heavier. During my teen years, he would drop not-so-subtle hints about my losing weight, and even had discussions about his concerns with my mother on a regular basis. When I started losing, he couldn't have been happier for me. Darryl wasn't as vocal as everyone else in my family. He made very little mention of my accomplishments, and when he did, it was just to save face when someone else took notice in his presence. His indifference about my weight loss didn't faze me much at that point. Gradually my impression of him was shifting. I still loved him, but I was beginning to feel very differently about him because of his apathetic attitude toward our marriage and his longstanding unemployment status. I coped with the situation by ignoring it. I was so tired of the excuses; I just didn't want to hear them anymore, so I kept my distance from him while in the house. I shifted gears toward areas of my life that made me fulfilled and happy. I spent more time with my girls and getting acquainted with a new body that was surfacing.

Whose Body is this Anyway? (276.8)

They say time flies when you are having fun, and nothing could be truer. I had become a regular fixture at Shapes; so much so that some of the newer members thought I was a part of the staff. I added more days to my workout schedule because of my increased endurance and energy, but besides that, I just missed being there on my days off. I felt so out of sorts when I wasn't there in the evenings, so I started going five days a week. The extra time I put in really paid off on the scale too. I was already down to 276 pounds, breaking free from the 300's. My thigh, arm, and waist measurements were dropping significantly, and my size 42 DD bra looked like a droopy slingshot whenever I attempted to put it on. I found myself looking down at my nakedness every morning and asking, "*Whose body is this, anyway?*"

Seven months into my healthier lifestyle and I was completely awestruck by the new me that was emerging. It was all so strange and exciting at the same time. I felt as if I had to learn about my body parts all over again like I had in kindergarten. Up until this point, my frame was shrouded in folds of skin from my shoulders to my ankles. My large stomach had always blocked my view of anything past it. There were places on my body that I hadn't seen in so long, it was a pleasure just to stand in the mirror to take a gander at them. Bath time had become a world of wonderment. In the shower while I lathered up, I'd snicker to myself when I felt the evidence of muscles actually forming on my arms and thighs. I could actually see them sticking out a bit. I'm sure that Darryl probably heard me in the bathroom each time I hollered out phrases like: "*Whoa! Wow,* and *would ya take a look at that?*"

The amazement went on when I looked in the mirror and noticed my collar bones begin to emerge from my shoulders Randomly, I would just rub them at work, just to make sure I wasn't dreaming or something. My weight loss had even affected my feet as well. I went from a ladies size 12 shoe to a size 11. I felt like kicking myself for waiting all that time to finally feel the things that most people take for granted, like sitting down without fear of breaking a chair, or simply walking down the street and not feeling winded after the first couple of steps.

While I was becoming increasingly aware of the difference in my body, others were too. It was difficult to absorb at first, and I had a difficult time taking the compliments to heart. Even with the accolades I was receiving from co-workers and familiar commuters I rode the train with, it still didn't really register that my 60-pound weight loss was substantial. I had been so conditioned to seeing my heavier body when I looked in the mirror, and I still saw myself as I always did—300 plus pounds. The clothes I owned were practically falling off me, so to save money I shopped at thrift stores frequently and bought smaller sizes to accommodate my shrinking body. Yet my mind still wasn't up to speed with all that was taking place.

I noticed other perks that came with my loss. Physically I felt stronger than ever. My workout schedule included intense cardio on the step pads and strength training on the gym equipment for forty-five minutes to an hour. From my biceps to my triceps, from my abs to my quads, and from my calves to my glutes, everything was being tightened and strengthened. I was on such an adrenaline high that when I left Shapes, I didn't simply walk to my car, I jogged there.

The Woe of the Plateau (277.1)

It was December 5 and my nine-month milestone at Shapes. It was officially freezing in Chicago, and getting around from place to place was like an arctic adventure. If the wind didn't slice you like a knife across your face, the sub-zero temperatures would give you hypothermia in twenty seconds flat. Bitterly cold as it was, it didn't stop me from my workouts. I arrived bundled up with gym shoes and towel in hand when no one except the staff was there. They called me crazy for coming in as they were leaving due to the extreme weather conditions. "It's my weigh-in day, guys, and I didn't want to miss it," I said through my scarf as I rushed in, trying to shake the cold air off me.

"Girl, you have got to be kidding...what are you doing here in this blizzard? Who else do you see here besides you're crazy behind? Hmph, I was gonna call off today, but I knew there would be one nut who would still want to work out, and how did I know that nut would be you?" Sasha exclaimed as we both burst into laughter.

"Yep, I'm here, so take that coat off and work out with me!" I demanded. Sasha took off her coat and exchanged her boots for gym shoes to join me on the circuit.

Each time I took to the exercise area, I gave it my all and then some. I worked hard, as if I saw my 100-pound goal in the rearview mirror of my mind and it was getting closer every minute. Tonight was the night I would be weighed in. I had waited an entire month to weigh myself on purpose. I wanted to see a huge drop in my numbers, so I reasoned that I would skip a weigh-in for that sole purpose. The last time I had weighed in I was 276 pounds; I was looking forward to a number somewhere in the mid-260s or even lower if I was lucky. I made sure I followed my eating regime to a T, taking my vitamins and not giving in to any of my mother's mouthwatering meals. I made sure my water intake was where it needed to be, and even drank more than my 64 ounces daily.

I was beyond eager to see how much I had lost. I rushed Sasha off the circuit the same way I demanded that she get on it so we could get started. This particular weigh-in was different from the others though—there would be none of the usual celebratory shouting going on when the numbers on the scale stopped rolling. Just as the arctic conditions of the weather outside were bone-chilling that night, I was slapped hard in the face by a bitterly cold response from my friend the scale.

Since it was Shelly's day off, Sasha would be the one who would document my progress in my folder. I waited with bated breath as always for Sasha to pull my file and get her pen out. I stepped on the clear scale with a smile and watched the numbers: 269…271…I frowned as I mentally commanded the numbers to go down instead of up...275...275.9...277. The scale reached its destination at 277.1.

"What?" I heard myself say in disbelief. I jumped off the scale and got back on—same result on the scale, and the same reaction from me. I was devastated. Sasha looked at me with a smile and rubbed my shoulder as I was preparing to throw the biggest pity party the world had ever seen, complete with gold-embossed invitations and everything. I didn't understand it. At my last weigh-in, a whole thirty days ago, I was 276 pounds, and now the scale was informing me that not only had I not lost any weight, but I GAINED a pound? In a flash I reviewed everything I had done in that months' time. I combed over my diet to see where I had messed up. I became infuriated with myself, and Sasha could sense it.

"Sue, have you ever heard of a weight loss plateau?" she asked me softly.

I had no idea what Sasha was talking about, and furthermore, I was pissed that she would be asking me about something completely irrelevant to what was going on right at the moment, which was my impending nervous breakdown. I turned my frustration and directed it toward Sasha, since she was the only one there. I knew it was completely irrational, but I just didn't care at the moment. I was so upset; I could feel the tears welling up in my eyes. "No, I have never heard of waiting for a plateau or whatever you just said," I retorted, obviously very irritated.

"I just want to figure out where I went wrong. At this rate, I will never get to where I want to be. I thought I was doing so good, too," I whined as I started piling on my layers of clothes to go out into the weather that had now turned into a full-fledged blizzard.

"Sue, you're doing everything right, keeping track of your carb intake, eating right, and doing huge amounts of cardio and strength training on the machines. You are an inspiration to the women here when they see how much you have progressed. There is no reason to beat yourself up like this. Let me explain to you what a WEIGHT LOSS PLATEAU is," Sasha said, saying the phrase slow enough for me to hear it correctly.

Although I understand the physical dynamics of occasional "plateauing" now, it was not something I was thrilled about upon my initial introduction to it. Basically, a weight loss plateau is a temporary pause in weight loss as our bodies get acclimated to a healthier more active lifestyle.

One of the most common frustrations in weight loss is when all progress stops despite the fact that you are diligently following your plan. It's a normal occurrence that comes with any weight loss journey, but temporary. Essentially, your body has gotten used to your routine. You're consuming fewer calories than you used to, so your metabolism has slowed down to conserve them. As long as exercise routines and healthy eating regimes are adhered to, weight loss typically resumes in a few weeks. It's also important to note that while weight loss may be temporarily stalled; experiencing positive changes to the body like a smaller waist, more toned stomach, and stronger arms will still take place.

With all that being said, I understood Sasha's explanation, but I still didn't feel any better about this little unauthorized vacation my body apparently decided to take from losing weight. I worked so hard and followed my routine religiously only to feel cheated after I stepped off the scale. I licked my wounds and prepared to leave the gym disheartened but determined to turn things around. The great part about plateaus is that they are temporary, and with a few tweaks, like shaking up my exercise routine with more challenging workouts and adding a few more healthy calories to my diet, I would be able to break through the stall and get back to the business of realizing my goal. "One monkey don't stop no show," as my mother always said, and I wasn't about to give up now.

I had come too far and had too much invested in my dream. After I calmed down, I realized that I wasn't very nice to Sasha when I was going through my mini-breakdown on the scale. I lashed out at her and felt awful about it. I apologized for my tantrum and gave her a tight hug; she returned it with an even tighter one and a smile. "I'm so proud of you, girl. You are a fighter, I know you won't let some silly plateau stop you from where you are trying to go…keep going and kick this plateau's butt!" I thanked God for Sasha, Shelly, and the community of Shapes members that were the greatest group of women I have ever had the pleasure to know.

Suddenly, I was reminded of when I had the inclination to quit when my friend Nikki told me that she wasn't coming back to Shapes. That was nine months ago. I am so glad I didn't give in to that impulse. I was so grateful God had me stay there to work out alongside women who, just like me, weren't just talking about changing their lives anymore, but putting those words into action every day. We were pressing toward the mark, no matter how difficult it seemed.

We oftentimes underestimate the power that words have. The Bible says in Proverbs 18:21: "Life and death lie in the power of the tongue," and nothing could be truer. Sasha called me a "fighter" that night. She said I was fighting for what I wanted. I never thought of myself as a fighter for anything, in fact, it was completely contrary to what I thought of myself my entire life…but for the first time ever, I gave myself permission to embrace that title.

Even with my bout of disappointment that night, Sasha's edifying words gave me hope. She never knew it, but her words breathed life into my resolve. One thing is for certain: when we make a decision to embark on a life journey for the sole purpose of creating change in our lives, setbacks come with the territory, but it is how we bounce back from them that say a lot about how desperate we are for transformation. When obstacles emerge, or we fall off the proverbial wagon, do we shake it off and pursue a plan B," or do we waste time wallowing in the regrets of our plan A? My typical response would have been the latter, but not this time. I was like a dog with a bone; I wasn't letting go. Plateau or not.

"Well, I'm guessing you're gonna rent a dogsled to get you here tomorrow night, if I know you. You ain't letting this blizzard stop your workout," Sasha quipped with her usual brand of humor.

I just smiled and nodded. "Yep, you know I'll be here. Just bring some treats for the dogs though, they are gonna be hungry after hauling my big butt all the way over here," I retorted as we both giggled.

"Maybe I am a fighter after all," I said to myself as I bundled up and prepared to go out into the polar vortex outside. "Maybe I am a fighter."

The Setback

Hey Friend, Where Ya Been?

Christmas was a couple of days away and I was excited. I couldn't wait for the girls to see what Santa had for them. As usual, I spent every last dime I had to make Christmas special for Denai, Lanie, and my little sweetie Johanna. I had just a few more gifts to buy, and to my surprise, I received a call from Nikki. She suggested that we go shopping together, and I was elated by the invitation, especially since I hadn't really seen much of her since her surgery. We talked on the phone every now and then getting caught up with each other, but we didn't hang out like we used to. Her life was busy, and on a really good upswing. She sounded happier than ever.

So much had taken place in her life in a relatively short amount of time. Her biggest dreams had been realized. She underwent successful Lap-Band surgery, which was something she desperately wanted, left the bank after she landed a better paying job, and was engaged to be married to the love of her life. Nikki had been through the ringer with her daughter's father, and she deserved to be happy with someone who'd appreciate her. Many times we would compare notes about relationships and the toll it can take when you feel trapped in them. I wished her and her fiancé nothing but the best, but couldn't help but wonder what it felt like to be in a fifty-fifty relationship where both people seek to give to one another and not constantly take. To be honest, part of me was envious of her happiness. Not that I didn't want Nikki to be happy, because I truly did, I just wanted to know what it felt like to be loved unconditionally by a man. Now that I was moving in the right direction where my physical health was concerned, my emotional and mental state was still a mess.

We decided to do lunch before the shopping to chat a bit. I drove up and noticed Nikki pulling up almost at the same time. I laughed to myself because that was so typical of our friendship that spanned over twenty years. Planned or unplanned, we always managed to do things in sequence. It was like we were twins separated at birth. Nikki stepped out of the car and I did a double take. I couldn't believe it was her. I looked at the woman who was coming toward my car, only to find out it was indeed Nikki. She had lost so much weight that I hardly recognized her. She was slimmed down and beautiful as she walked over to me with a huge grin and outstretched arms. "Hey, Susie Bell!" Nikki called out as she hugged me tight. I hated that stupid nickname she gave me. I know she only called me that because she knew darn well I hated it with a passion.

"Hey, girl! Boy…I ain't seen you in a month of Sundays!" I replied, returning her hug using an old southern adage I borrowed from my mother.

It was so odd hugging such a small-framed Nikki. As heavy as she was prior to the surgery, Nikki always had a beautiful figure—a smaller waist and a huge, rounded butt. She was the typical Coca-

Cola bottle shape, and now it was more pronounced than ever before. She looked absolutely fantastic. "Girl, you look HOT! How much weight have you lost already, Nik?" I asked, very curious as I eyed her snug jeans and trying to figure out in my head what size they were.

"Thanks, girl. I don't really weigh myself, so I'm not sure how much," she said matter-of-factly. Throughout our friendship, Nikki never gave full disclosure about herself, unlike me. I figured since we were best friends, we could share things that other people weren't privy to. I blabbed all my dirty laundry, while she always held back, giving me just enough insight into her private life, to keep the conversation going, and not an ounce more. She always spoke on the positive side of her life, while she kept the darker side to herself. It was always on the upswing with Nik; very rarely would she talk to me about issues that bothered her. Through the years I always felt a bit hurt by her actions. I never revealed any secrets she had told me, yet it seemed as if she didn't feel comfortable telling me anything too revealing about herself for some reason. Her response to my question about her weight loss wasn't surprising to me. I should have expected it.

"Well, what size jeans are those? They look great on you!" I said, still prying and curious.

"I dunno, girl, a 10 or 12? I don't really know, I just threw 'em on." I decided to silence my interrogation, seeing that it would apparently lead to several others "I don't knows." I knew by then what the deal was—she just didn't want to tell me for some odd reason. She looked great, so *why not tell your best friend about your transformation?* I thought to myself. I decided to shrug it off as typical Nikki behavior and move on. The annoying dinging of my open car door reminded me that we had better get inside the restaurant before I would need a jump to get my van started. "Let's go, I'm starving." I said, slamming the door and following Nikki up the parking lot.

"Girrrl, you gotta catch me up. What have you been up to?" Nikki asked as we waited in line at the sandwich shop.

"Well, I've been working really hard at Shapes. I've lost some weight too. Not as much as you, but I have lost some, can you tell?" I said proudly, doing a slow twirl in line to show Nikki my own budding transformation after losing 60 pounds so far.

"Yeah, I was about to tell you that you look like you lost a little. That's good, girl." It wasn't exactly the glowing endorsement I was eager to hear from my best friend. It was actually a bit of a stale response. She didn't have to be as exuberant as I was about her loss, but I was disappointed to hear the ho-hum tone of her answer, and it really hurt my feelings. "So, you are STILL at Shapes, huh?" Nikki said with a little bit of a twist in her lip.

"Yep, I am. I have learned so much, and the staff is really great. Shelly has helped me so much with my eating, and I feel better than I ever have physically, and the sweat is paying off. Girl, the way I feel when I leave is amazing. I wish you had given it a shot. I think you would have liked it a lot," I said, finding myself defending Shapes and my decision to stick with it.

"That's really good. So, what are you gonna order?" Nikki replied as she sailed past my endorsement of Shapes, leaving it DOA right there on the sandwich shop floor. It was strange even for Nikki; I thought this meeting would be about us living out our dreams when we finally got to our weight loss goals—the anticipation of being able to shop at regular women's clothing stores and not at the few plus size stores that sold those ugly mu-mu dresses.

I hoped we could chat about the ups and downs of losing weight…the good, the bad, and the ugly of it. I didn't have anyone else that could relate to some of the issues I had begun to experience—like the saggy skin, the floppy boobs, and my deflating butt—as a result of losing a great deal of weight. No one else could understand, and I wouldn't be comfortable talking to anyone but her about those very personal details, at least not yet anyway. All our lives, we were so relatable in every sense, but now there seemed to be a distance between us. I decided to turn the tables and find out what was going on in her life. Maybe she was preoccupied with something that was bothering her. I wanted to find out so that we could go on as usual not have this weird vibe between us. I wanted my old Nikki back.

We got our sandwiches and sat down. At first I shuddered when she suggested a sandwich shop. I had taken myself off bread. Even though I knew that I would be okay eating whole grain bread, I still didn't want to chance it so early on in my journey while I was diligently losing weight. Surprisingly enough, I didn't even miss it like I thought I would.

I opted for a salad with chicken breast and almonds with vinaigrette dressing on the side, and no croutons. Nikki ordered half of a sandwich and soup. When we got back to the table, Nikki went to work on immediately cutting her half sandwich into a smaller third and wrapping the other part up in a take-home container. Actually, she could have taken it home in the foil from a chewing gum wrapper because that's how small it was. By the time she got done dissecting the poor sandwich, it looked to be the size of a small Post-it note. I looked up at her from my salad in disbelief. "Who is that piece of a sandwich for? The bird outside this window? I know that's not all you are gonna eat, Nik," I teased, almost choking on the forkful of salad I had just put in my mouth while trying to suppress a runaway giggle.

"This is how I eat now since my Lap-Band surgery. Girl, as soon as I eat this little piece of sandwich and this soup I will be stuffed. That's how I have been able to drop the weight so quickly, from the decrease of food that I eat. Less food, less calories. I can only eat a half of a chicken wing now, not like the days when I could dust off six wings with mild sauce, fries, and the white bread without batting an eyelash," Nikki joked as she sipped her broccoli and cheese soup.

"Yeah, that white bread and those wings with that addictive mild sauce," I said, thinking back on it rather fondly. "I think we made that chicken joint rich, Nik…shoot, with all the money we spent there, we should have our names embossed in gold somewhere on their wall, right next to the 'Our Sauce is the Boss' sign." I hoped to rekindle our lighthearted banter that I missed so much. We slapped each other a high five and laughed so loud that the obviously annoyed couple sitting at the table next to us turned around to give us the evil eye. I was glad my attempt to lift the heavy aura seemed to have worked.

"So, you can't eat, like, an entire plate of food anymore?" I asked, getting back to the sparrow-sized portion of nourishment on Nikki's plate.

"Nope. Maybe a saucer, but certainly not a plate." Nikki explained that the gastric sleeve surgery involves shrinking the size of the stomach, which makes the person feel full faster and eat less food. It's the restrictive nature of a smaller stomach that leads to weight loss.

Although the surgery is intended to promote weight loss in an obese person, if the person overeats consistently, the results can lead to a stretched stomach, which means that the person can regain the weight they've lost and then some.

Whatever the case, the results were amazing. I couldn't help but stare at Nikki's great-looking body. When we finally prepared to leave the restaurant, I followed her outside on purpose just to get another glance at her. I still couldn't believe that within a couple of months she had dropped the weight so quickly. I had an urge to pull the back of her pants just to see what the tag said. Why did it matter so much to me at that time? I was admittedly jealous of my best friend, plain and simple. My feelings did not derive from hateful envy toward my friend, but rather admiration. I marveled at her obvious success in shedding her weight. Nikki was way ahead of my progress and looked fantastic.

I shouldn't have compared myself to her, but in my fragility, I did. In my mind, I came up miserably short. To add insult to injury, I didn't feel her support for me, and it crushed me. There I was, beckoning for her encouragement, just as I had when we first stepped into Shapes together. I got into the car feeling just like I did when I heard that she wasn't coming back to Shapes—abandoned without her advocacy. Only this time I added a new sentiment to the list—envious of her progression. We still had Christmas shopping to do, so I sucked up my emotions and went on with the business at hand. After licking my wounds a bit on the drive to the mall, I shook off my misplaced envy for my friend and reminded myself out loud that I was on a mission, that I would not be deterred by the negative thoughts that have made themselves at home in my mind for way too many years.

I decided that if no else celebrated me, well, I would just have to learn how to be my own cheering section. I wish I could say it was as easy as simply declaring that to myself, but the fact of matter was it would take considerable time to break some really old habits concerning my self-esteem. Perhaps Nikki had her own esteem issues too, which is why she rarely felt persuaded to congratulate me in terms of any achievements I had during our long friendship. Be that as it may, I wouldn't let that stop me from letting her know how great she looked now and congratulating her jaw-dropping weight loss.

Make Way for Mama

Christmas was finally here. I tried my hardest to be happy for the kids' sake, but it wasn't easy. There were so many things going on that had my mind in a perpetual state of disquiet.

My mother, who always hid the dire state of her health from us for years, could no longer hide it. One week before Christmas, her favorite holiday, she was rushed to the emergency room for chest pains so severe that we all thought for certain she had suffered a heart attack. She was immediately admitted to the hospital where Wayne, Brenda, and I held vigil to hear what her diagnosis was. Her doctor determined that she had several blocked arties that were keeping blood from her heart. Over the years, calcium deposits had built up inside of these clogged arteries. Decades of heavy smoking was the likely culprit, according to her longtime physician.

During her hospitalization, it was determined that she would receive minor surgery to get an Implantable Cardioverter Defibrillator (ICD), a small device which is placed in the chest, just underneath the skin. After performing stress tests on her heart, Mama's physician made the decision to implant the device to help treat the arrhythmias, commonly known as irregular heartbeats. We couldn't have asked for a more attentive and conscientious doctor for my mother than Dr. Varghese, in spite of the fact that my mother was stubborn and flat out refused to abide by some of the doctor's orders. Warned about her heavy smoking, she still continued to sneak cigarettes, and she was still eating stuff she had no business eating, which contributed to her high cholesterol and increased hypertension.

After much pleading from us, and promises that we would keep Mama on the straight and narrow with regard to her diet and her smoking, her doctor allowed her to come home on Christmas Eve. Mama would have to be closely monitored, making certain she had lots of bed rest and only light activity. We were elated that she would be home to celebrate Christmas; it wouldn't have been the same without her at home. Knowing that our beloved Mama would be there to share in the holiday joy was the best gift anyone could have given us.

We made all the preparations to make certain that Mama would be comfortable at home. In those few days she spent at the hospital, we could tell that she had lost weight, evening appearing a bit gaunt. My mother had always been a strikingly beautiful woman, and not even this recent turn of events with her health dulled her beauty in my eyes. Seeing her so obviously weakened made me start to think about what I would do if I lost her. My mother was my Superwoman; she was a prime example of strength under pressure. She showed me that no matter how many blows life hits you with; you can still remain strong and assured that God will see you through them when you trust Him.

 I never could figure out how she did it. She had been through it all: bad marriages, financial crisis, and health issues that were becoming very concerning. Yet she kept going without complaint. I saw her cry sometimes, but not for long. Her resilience was amazing to me, and I wanted to be just like her in that respect. From time to time, my mother and I bumped heads, but regardless of our fall-outs with each other, I loved and respected her greatly. Despite the missteps she took along the way in her own life, she was still my hero. Just the thought of her not being around anymore grieved my heart.

It was Christmas day, and in spite of just being discharged from the hospital, my mother was in the kitchen doing what made her happiest—cooking her famous holiday dishes for her family. She just couldn't be still and rest like her doctor advised; she had to be moving and making things happen. That was just Mama's way. Making certain everything was properly in order was her role, especially during the holidays. Even with her ongoing illness, she couldn't turn off her maternal instinct. Tending to her family was simply in her DNA.

We left her alone to do what she was determined to do anyway. For us, it was a losing battle. We just made sure that she rested periodically and didn't overexert herself in the kitchen. Trying to stop Mama from doing something she was bound and determined to do was like trying to keep a bull from charging at a red flag—it just ain't gonna happen.

This is Only a Test (271)

Christmas dinner preparations were always like a comedy show at Mama's house. Besides the delicious and plentiful dishes that were made, the kitchen area was like a 'battle of the Iron Chefs' starring my mother and my brother. My brother Wayne, who previously owned a restaurant, inherited his fondness for cooking from my mother. His attempt at hijacking a dish Mama prepared, to add his own touches when she wasn't looking was hilarious. When the jig was up and Wayne was caught attempting to alter her recipe, it was comedy at its finest. The comical way those two went at it in the kitchen was the stuff reality shows are made of. Out of the three of us, Wayne was the one who inherited Mama's quick, hilarious wit and her prowess in the kitchen.

Wayne was a big ham when he had an audience, but when you got all of us got together; it was better than any comedy stand-up show you could go to. That's what made each Christmas so special for our family. Getting together, laughing and just being silly with one another. Presents didn't matter. You could not place a price tag on the kind of joy that was experienced when we all gathered together during the holidays.

My first real challenge of will power would be at the Christmas dinner table. I had followed my newly adopted healthier lifestyle religiously, not giving in to as much as a crouton. I played it by the book and omitted all high-starch white carbs out of my diet thus far. I switched up my routine at the gym, adding more cardio for longer amounts of time, and just like Sasha predicted, I broke through my plateau and lost seven additional pounds. I was in it to win it, but my mother's famous Christmas meal would be the real test for me.

It was amazing how my Mama prepared her traditional feast with its usual flair and elegance without skipping a beat after being in the hospital. Her kitchen smelled absolutely amazing. Although slowly recovering, I was still a food addict with the same tendencies and self-control issues when it came to food as before. I wasn't tremendously hungry at the time, yet I felt a growing urge that I was so familiar with to gorge on the food that I was looking at. While preparing plates for my daughters, without warning, familiar impulses started to emerge. The aromas excited my senses and drove a desire to quickly heap the food in my mouth without stopping. I thought for sure I had conquered my demons when it came to binge eating, but with every whiff I inhaled, I felt my restraint getting shakier.

Even with my new mindset, my old habits were not going down without a fight. Prior to the conversion of my diet, I would polish off three helpings of everything on the table with extra gravy on it without batting an eyelash. Traditionally, my mother set her dinner table family style, with all the dishes on the table at once for everyone to pass around. I always liked the set-up because it was an opportunity for me to get as much as I wanted as many times as I wanted while we all laughed and talked. My mother always prepared enough food for an army, and I took full advantage of it. Most times I was the first at the table and one of the last to leave it, and when I did I was stuffed so tight I could barely move, only to return a few hours later. When everyone gathered to chat in the living room, I was back in the kitchen, eating again.

Like always, it was a packed house for Christmas dinner at my mother's place, just the way she liked it. She was over the moon that all of her children and grandchildren were there to celebrate

Christmas in the house that we all grew up in. Close friends of the family showed up too, just to get a taste of some of my mother's delicious fare. Because of our growing extended family, we started a tradition of eating in shifts to accommodate everyone in attendance, making certain that everyone had a chance to sit at the table to eat.

This year I was on the first dinner shift. I purposely made my way to the dinner table last, hoping that there wouldn't be enough room at the table and that I would have to stand by the kitchen island to eat. "Sue, you don't have to stand over there. Here's a seat, right here by me. Come sit down so we can say grace and eat." My mother waved me over like she was directing a 747 to come down a landing strip.

"Oh, okay. I didn't see that empty chair over there," I said, lying through my teeth.

I sat down and began to survey the table for all the healthier dishes like collard greens, string beans, and the sweet potatoes that my mother so thoughtfully made just for me, with Splenda instead of regular sugar. Yet just like that forbidden delicious red apple in the Garden of Eden that Eve could not resist, sitting right in front of me and at my easier disposal was my Mama's famous melt-in-your mouth macaroni and cheese. It was fresh out of the oven and so hot that I could still see the melted butter sizzling on the sides of the casserole dish. Her mac and cheese wasn't your typical mac and cheese, either. She layered the macaroni with heaps of butter, whole milk, and three kinds of cheeses layered on super thick. The amazing aroma that exuded from the oven when it was baking made your mouth water. Unless you were dead, you simply couldn't resist it. I don't know anyone who has ever tasted it being satisfied with just one helping of it either. It just wasn't possible…and here it was, sitting front and center…Taunting me.

These are the moments in the life of a food addict which shine the brightest. Here was a table of great food, virtually limitless. I had come to a crossroads of sorts—saying no to a fast food restaurant was easy because I didn't have the food right in front of me. I could just choose to drive past it, unlike the situation I was in at that moment where everyone was laughing, talking, and getting spoonfuls of the foods they wanted. No one had a clue as to what I was going through, and what a pinnacle this chapter in my life had become for me. To some, I know it may sound trivial to say this was a huge decision that I had to give great deliberation while at the Christmas dinner table. I mean, it's just a meal, right? What's the big deal?

As an addict, my whole life essentially revolved around where, when, and how I could get to my drug of choice. Because my obesity was accepted by my family, it was no big deal that I had two or three plates of food, because it was the norm for me. Now, with no one to remind me how far I had come, how much I had lost, and how hard I worked to get there, I had a decision to make on my own. Would it be business as usual or would I put the knowledge I had acquired about healthy eating into practice? For me, it was now or never.

"Aren't you gonna eat, Sue?" my mother asked, eyeing my empty plate with a frown. "Girl, you better eat before it's gone." Everyone except me had already filled their plates to capacity, and some were already heading for seconds. I looked at my mother for a long time after she spoke, her beautiful eyes now puffy from all the medication she had to take. I observed the loving arms that used to hold me, forever scarred from the painful insertion and re-insertion of stents for the four-hour-long dialysis treatments she had to endure three days a week. I surveyed the patch of gauze on the left side of her chest which covered her fresh surgical scar from her defibrillator implant to sustain her life in case of possible cardiac arrest. My mom had just come home from the hospital after being diagnosed with not one, but several clogged arties due to years of smoking, and the damage was deemed irreversible. She suffered three mini strokes within a five year span, and the odds of her suffering a major one were imminent.

I realized I could lose my mother soon. I grieved for the state of her health. In a split second, my next thought was, this could be me in a few years. My mother started her life the same way, not eating properly when she was a child, and she grew into adulthood the same way. The result of years of not taking proper care of herself was finally catching up to her, and there it was, laid out in plain view. It hit me like a bolt of thunder and put things in perspective. If I didn't stick to my plan to reverse the state of my own health, I may not ever get a chance to later.

"I'm about to eat right now Mama, just trying to figure out what I want." I bypassed the mac and cheese, cornbread dressing, rolls, and gravy. I filled my plate with greens, my special sweet potatoes, turkey, and a few slices of ham.

"Is that ALL you're eating, Mommy?" My Denai asked me, looking rather puzzled. "You didn't get any dressing or mac and cheese. It's really good," she said, recognizing that this was completely out of character for her mother.

"I know it is, Denai, but I'm not gonna eat any of that stuff for a while," I said, feeling rather proud of myself.

"Oh Sue…its Christmas. You can have a little bit. A couple of bites ain't gonna hurt you," Mama insisted, sounding a bit offended that I didn't taste her signature dishes.

"Thanks, Mama. It looks good, but I'm gonna stick to what's on my plate, and it looks just as good. You guys enjoy the rest for me. I'm on a mission!" Out the corner of my eye, I saw Brenda smile at me and nod her head in approval, understanding what I meant. I smiled right back, even harder.

I do believe that was the best Christmas meal I ever had. Sitting at the same table, where eating until I literally became sick was the norm each year, my decision to eat in moderation and keep my diet regime intact, despite temptation felt incredibly gratifying. That night, I refused what I thought I never could: my mother's great Christmas carb fest. If this was a test…I had passed it with flying Christmas colors.

Love Don't Leave Here Anymore

Coming off my victory, I went downstairs to talk to Darryl; he already had eaten and disappeared to the basement bedroom. I asked Darryl if he liked his meal. "Yep it was good. Mama threw down as always."

I smiled, trying to spark a bit of conversation. "The girls really loved the stuff we bought them, didn't they? Especially the new bunk bed for Lanie and Johanna. I'm glad they had a great Christmas."

I always used the term "we bought," I guess because it sounded better. The truth was, when it came to buying the girls what they needed and wanted for occasions like birthdays and Christmas, it was rarely ever "we." It was always "me" who bought things for them. Darryl was still getting unemployment, but his contributions to the household were consistently absent. He held on to his money, and was very content making sure I spent mine. The bunk bed for the girls was supposed to be a joint effort at $450.00; however, I never saw a dime of that "joint" money. "If you pay for it now, I will give it back to you, baby." The line was so old I could almost repeat it with him verbatim. My hope was fading that my marriage would last through the end of the following year. I was sick and tired of feeling like I was carrying my husband while he sat on my back comfortably.

Since we were in a conversation, I decided that I would cross my fingers and ask my husband that age old question: "So, how's the job search going? Have you tried any of the fast food places? Didn't you say you have a cousin or something who was a manager at McDonald's? He could probably get you in there for sure." I turned over in the bed to look at him directly in the eyes, hoping he could feel my frustration and could sense my being ready to throw in the towel on our one-sided marriage. If I had to financially struggle, there was no sense in having someone happily sit by and watch me do it, least of all my husband. I was busy making preparations for a better life, not only personally, but professionally as well. I couldn't afford to let any grass grow under my feet. The girls were growing out of shoes and clothes so fast I could barely keep up, and what I was making at my job at the bank would no longer cut it. I began interviewing for jobs during my lunch hour at the bank and using my vacation time to job hunt.

"No, nothing has come up yet; my cousin said she would get back to me about the job at McDonald's." Instead of a response, I didn't say a word. There was nothing to say. I chided myself for even asking. I was losing respect for him, and I felt it. I felt Darryl's hand brush across my shoulder as I lay in our bed, his indication for intimacy. I felt instantly disgusted by his nonverbal proposition.

"The kids are upstairs…" His whispering repelled me even further. I responded by gathering my blanket and heading toward the couch, my own nonverbal language being communicated loud and clear. That night I didn't give in to being his source of sexual release like I had done so many times before. The thought of it repulsed me.

Upstairs, the Christmas spirit was going strong. The kids were running back and forth playing with their new toys and the sound of laughter filled the air as everyone celebrated Mama's return home. I hated the darkness I felt inside that kept me from celebrating with everyone else upstairs. I should have been up there with my family and kids, but I felt too hollow inside. I kept going over in my head the pros and cons of my marriage to Darryl, trying to pull out any redeeming factors, any at all.

I had slowly witnessed the changes in him, or perhaps not changes at all. My eyes were beginning to see what I was blinded to when I met him seven years ago. At the heart of him, he was a decent person. The type of guy who would help an elderly lady with her bags, or assist a stranded person on the side of the road. But I also knew the side of him that was a manipulator and a charmer, the side that used his dimpled smile to get whatever he wanted, especially out of me, and I am sure others before me. That Casanova fairy dust had all but rubbed off by this time; left in its place were feelings of distress, discontent, but mainly disappointment. We were on the heels of yet another year and, there was still no progress on the job front with my husband, and no sense of urgency to help me provide for our family.

By this time, I was all but convinced I was an object simply to be used as a means to an end for Darryl. I began to recall certain conversations that I didn't pick up on at first with regard to his previous relationships with women. I was too blind to see and too deaf to hear his format of how he chose the women he dated. Just like a flashback in a movie, I suddenly began to hear things he said in the beginning of our courtship. "You're the only women I have ever done this much for," he would almost arrogantly tell me, as if that was some huge testament of his love. Given the facts I now knew, his statement at that time spoke volumes about the kind of women he sought.

In my moments alone, I began thinking of the state of my life outside of the gym. The gym had become my source of refuge from my life. Outside of it, I was miserable and depressed. Even interacting with my daughters, whom I loved with all my soul, became a strain. I tried desperately to put on a "happy mom" face when I was playing with them, but they always seemed to see through my attempts to hide my misery, especially my oldest daughter Denai, who was now thirteen. She'd become especially intuitive when it came to me, and always picked up on my emotional state, no matter how hard I tried to mask it.

Denai had already been experiencing the distance between her stepfather and her, the subtle way Darryl would favor his birth daughters in certain situations. There was a distance there, and she felt it, as did I. At that point, Denai had become accustomed to having an absentee father, since Aaron barely called her to check on her, most likely for fear that I would ask him for child support money. She knew that I was unhappy. She would often ask, "Mommy, are you okay?" Even with my "I'm fine" response, she'd always shake her head and say, "No you aren't." I was so ashamed that I couldn't be the kind of mother I desperately wanted to be. I wanted so badly to interact with them with laughter in my voice, and the silliness they had come to expect from me when we would all play together. But my mind was so heavy, and my thoughts were forever consumed with bills and the guilt from having to depend on my mother so much. Without any financial support from Darryl, and a tiny paycheck from my job at the bank, I barely made ends meet. With no foreseeable options, I signed up for public assistance so that the state could provide my daughters and me with insurance.

A Crisis of Christian Conscious (256)

My mind raced so fast sometimes, I'd become dizzy. I was conflicted with thoughts of divorcing Darryl and the possibility of my daughters not having their father in the household anymore. To further add to my internal turmoil, I was a Christian who was considering divorcing my husband, which is an abomination in Christian culture. Darryl and I both joined church together a few years ago. I was saved, and trying my best to live my life in accordance to the way God wanted me to. Darryl and I attended church regularly with our kids, and were involved in various activities within the congregation. I wanted to please God with my every action; I owed Him my loyalty and obedience.

The battle within me lit a firestorm of guilt and shame every time I would even consider leaving Darryl. How could I even think about divorcing my husband? God would never forgive me if I did that. He wouldn't love me anymore if I disobeyed what He clearly said in His Word, "God hates divorce." I had read it over and over again in the Old Testament. My pastor spoke against it in sermons. My primary focus was on the words "God" and "hate," and what that meant in terms of my relationship with God. Those two words scared me. I didn't want God to hate me, and I didn't want to be a disappointment to Him. To me, that verse meant that not only did God hate the action of divorce, but also the one who pursued it.

On rare occasions, I would confide in some of the women I served with on church projects. My contemplation of divorce would be met with immediate scrutiny and judgment, thus adding to my feelings of shame. "How could you even consider divorce? It can't be that bad…no, you have to stick in there, sweetheart, no matter what. God said in His Word that He hates divorce." After hearing the older women of the church spiritually chastise me, I knew that I would just have to "stick in there" no matter what.

I put aside my feelings, opting to not to anger God with my decision. Each day, I felt more and more trapped in a lifeless situation. Desperate to hold on, I sought marriage counseling at our church. Darryl agreed to go with me, which did make me feel a glimmer of hope about us. But within a couple of weeks of going to counseling, things just reverted back to business as usual in our marriage. I worked and looked for a better job, and he was at home playing video games while enjoying his "extended vacation" from employment. He'd occasionally get day labor jobs when he got tired of my insisting that he find long-term work, but other than that, just more of the same… excuses. I continued to "stick in there," hoping that with enough church, he would begin to realize how burdened I'd become.

Stress began to make its appearance physically again. I began to experience skin reactions, complete with pimples and blemishes the likes of which I hadn't seen since my adolescent days. The severe headaches and high blood pressure that had subsided as I lost weight were making a vengeful comeback. More alarming than anything was the re-emergence of my horrendous panic attacks. The attacks that had been kept at bay were beginning to happen at night again, as well as in the daytime.

On several occasions I had to take off early from work due to panic attacks that were striking in the middle of the day, which was mortifying. Try explaining to your boss that you have to leave midday because you feel like you are going crazy…literally.

Every night I felt a sickness in the pit of my stomach as my mind would race with thoughts of God, divorce, guilt, and disgust toward myself for the state my life was in. Consistently doing well with the mini-goals I set each month at the gym, aside from a few plateaus here and there, my objectives for my health were on target. My goal of a 100-pound weight loss was almost within reach, but what good would it do me if I was in a psychiatric ward from suffering a nervous breakdown? What good would it do to lose weight in order to save my life, only for me to lose it from stroking out due to stress, or locked up and declared mentally unfit?

For me, it wasn't a notion that was too far off. My father's family tree had branches of mental illness attached to it; my uncle was institutionalized for many years after being diagnosed with a mental illness that kept him from living a normal life. With my panic attacks now more frequent and intense, I was worried all the more of what might happen to me, and more importantly, how it would affect my children.

Every night it seemed, I'd find my thoughts constantly being bombarded with the knowledge that although I was freeing myself of weight that was slated to kill me, I had nothing to really be happy about—my personal life was a pathetic mess, and I had myself to blame. I reverted back to what I knew…self-criticism. My displeasure with myself grew, and my comrades at Shapes recognized it immediately. My demeanor had become subdued and distant. I went from encouraging others to being the one in need of encouragement. I felt like a pitiful basket-case most of the time.

Instead of using food to soothe myself, I threw myself into my workouts to combat the negative noise in my head. The sweat that poured from my body was like a healing waterfall that washed away my anxieties and replaced them with assuredness. The adrenaline rush that accompanied my movements relieved my pent-up frustration. Shapes became my refuge; it was the only place where I truly felt like I was in the driver's seat of my reality. The only place in the world where I felt like I had complete control of my destiny was on the gym circuit, unlike my marriage where I felt as if I was trapped and bound by guilt. When I decided to consistently exercise and fuel my body with healthy foods that would transform it, the results translated in pounds lost—simple as that. For the first time in my life, gluttony wasn't in control…I was. Strangely enough, the command I had over a lifelong battle with food addiction did not translate over to other areas in my life—my problematic marriage in particular. I felt powerful and powerless at the same time.

The Comeback

Happy NEW Year! (231)

The bright sun from the window above my head slightly warmed my face and slowly brought me out of a hard-fought slumber. Still feeling the zoned-out effects of the dose and a half of Xanax I took the night before, I lazily opened my eyes to the dawn of a brand new year, 2009.

New Year's Eve wasn't exactly party central in my house. My mom and sister turned in early upstairs, and my girls had a sleepover at Darryl's mother's house. That night, as Dick Clark counted down the clock in Time's square on his televised *"New Year's Rocking Eve"* broadcast, I was popping pills to ward off one of my nightly panic attacks. I was all too familiar with the signs of a looming attack, so as a preventive measure I'd take a pill and a half before one would hit me full throttle. I had become dependent on the feeling that the pills gave me; it was like being in hell one minute, and drifting to heaven the next. I woke up feeling renewed and oblivious to the events of the night before, just the way I preferred. I was grateful for the times when my mother-in-law requested that the girls come over to spend time with her. It allowed me to just "zone out" from everything.

Drowsily I rolled over in my bed with ease, simply delighted with fact that I was able to twist and turn my body without the familiar struggle it took to shift my 300-plus-pound frame from side to side. It felt so good that I decided to do it again and again, tossing and turning my body around in the bed like a little kid hyped on sugar. It's amazing how the things that seem so insignificant to some can be so incredibly impactful to others who have never experienced it. The fact that I could get out of bed without becoming winded was a major deal for me. I giggled out loud as I lifted my body for the first time from the bed without holding on to the nightstand; it was effortless and totally marvelous. The sound of Darryl's CPAP machine vibrating as he slept on the other side snapped me out of my mini wonderland. I tipped past him and headed toward our bathroom, which was my most favorite place to go in the morning. I loved to get naked in the mirror to see the new changes in my body. Not that my skin was especially smooth or aesthetically perfect now that I had lost weight, actually it was just the opposite.

My new frame had loose skin in every area, from my arms to my thighs, and everywhere in between. With the continual loss of weight I was experiencing, my formerly stretched skin that once contained pounds of fat was now flaccid and floppy. When I submerged my very different and unfamiliar body in the bathtub, my saggy skin would actually float to the top of the water I was in, like cream rising to the top of fresh milk. It was amazing to witness the way my body seemed to have morphed into a smaller version of itself. I ran my hand across my naked shoulders repeatedly just to feel my collarbone protruding. I rinsed the soap from my arms in anticipation of seeing the small but visible muscular structure that was beginning to take shape. Out of all the encounters though, the one that tickled me the most was when I was finally able to look down at my toes without having my stomach blocking my view.

My self-exploration was not without its woes however. My size 42DD breasts had deflated almost entirely, and left in their place were outstretched pockets of skin that looked like elongated, emptied balloons with nipples attached. My shoulders bore the evidence of my previously heavy chest in the form of darkened scars which had resulted from bras that dug mercilessly into my skin over the years. My waist and thighs, although much smaller now, displayed marks of abrasions as the result of my skin constantly rubbing against the rigid material of the tight and constricting girdles I wore every day since the age of twelve.

My developing arms clearly indicated how hard I'd been working on the bicep/triceps machines at Shapes. Serving as a reminder of how large my arms once were, I had king-sized "batwings" that appeared when I lifted them. Despite the imperfections, observing my body and all the changes it had gone through in the past several months was a joy for me every day. I felt stronger in body than I had ever been, and I was grateful to God that He kept me focused and never let me give up on my goal, even on the days when I begged Him to.

Since it was the morning of a brand new year and I was feeling pretty brand new about this time, it just seemed right to go ahead and weigh myself right where I was standing, naked and feeling good. Albeit a bit earlier than my usual monthly weigh-in at Shapes, I gingerly stepped on my bathroom scale, held my breath, closed my eyes, and crossed my fingers. I opened my eyes and clamped my hand over my mouth in shock when I read the numbers on the scale. In my usual skeptical style, I jumped off for a couple of seconds and got back on, doubting the number that had now appeared twice…231. I spent the next five minutes jumping on and off the scale just so I could see that magical number over and over again, like a complete lunatic.

From April 2007 to January 2008, I had lost a grand total 98 pounds, and felt more physically fit than I had ever been in my life. I dropped six dress sizes in that time span. I went from shopping at plus size stores to having the freedom to shop at any clothing store I wanted to. I had whittled myself down from a plus size 26-28 to a regular size 16-18.

I wanted to stay in my bathroom wonderland for the rest of the morning and simply bask in the afterglow of an accomplishment I thought I would never achieve. As much as I wanted to, I couldn't stay there forever. My existence on the other side of the bathroom door wasn't as sunny and bright. My victory on the scale would soon be overshadowed by the talk I knew I needed to have with Darryl. He had to pack his things and go.

What was supposed to be a temporary living arrangement until he found a steady job had turned into a year and a half long stint at my mother's house, and it was evident he couldn't care less. I fought so hard to defend Darryl to my family when we first got married, even going toe to toe in verbal shouting matches with my mother in his defense. I felt like such a fool. He knew that we had over-extended our stay, and he was okay with that. He also knew that my mother would never kick him out because he was my husband. I was an object simply to be used as a means to an end for Darryl. When I came home, I felt as if I was taking care of four kids instead of three. It all had to stop, and it would have to begin with me.

Hoping he would be still sleeping, I walked out of the bathroom to quickly grab my robe. When I turned the corner to the bedroom, there he stood, smiling as if he had been waiting on me to come out. "Good morning, you," Darryl said, eyes twinkling.

"Hi, Darryl, we need to talk," I said, rushing past him to get my robe on in a hurry.

"All right, but I need to go to my mom's house this morning. She needs me to do something." he said, eyeing me as I threw my robe on. That was so typical. He knew I wanted to discuss something important that he wanted no part of, so he evaded the conversation and pretended there was something more pressing he had to take care of right then. I had seen the whole song and dance before, and knew it front to back.

"Actually, we need to talk about this now. It's really important, Darryl," I said, tying up my robe and insisting that he listen.

"I already told you, Sue, I am still looking for a job, and if that is what you what you want to talk about—"

"Look, Darryl," I said. "Things are not getting any better, and it's been over a year now with your unemployment. I can't keep going to my mother and covering for you anymore. She is asking why you are not working yet and why you aren't helping out with the bills. She has every right to know, we are living in her house. You haven't been pulling your weight. I am tired of getting sick every time we argue; I am getting tired of feeling like you are using me for a warm place to lay your head. I love you, but I won't be used by you any longer. You aren't contributing, and you refuse to. You have to leave. I am giving you five days to find yourself someplace to stay."

I said it all so fast that I stuttered through half of my speech. I was nervous to hear his reaction; I knew it wouldn't be good.

"So, first of all, you are trying to blame your little attacks or whatever on ME? I'm making you sick now? Are you serious?" The smile he sported mere minutes before had turned into a contorted facial expression, his eyes wide and angry looking. "Look Sue, I don't have anywhere to go, all right? I am not going back to my mother's house with her husband who I don't get along with, and I don't have any money to go anywhere else. We are just gonna have to work it out," he said in a demanding tone.

"What is there to work out, Darryl? I have done everything I could as your wife. I have defended you, supported you, and made sure you were okay, even when your family didn't. The lies, the broken promises, not paying my brother and god-brother back like you promised you would, my car that you wrecked and promised to fix…the stress from this marriage is affecting my health, and I cannot let that happen. You don't care, and I know that now. I have to look out for my own best interest for once."

I hated that I started crying while talking to him. I hated that I nervously stuttered, sounding unsure of myself. Most of all, I hated that he saw me in a fragile state when I tried so desperately to appear strong. He smelled my weakness, and pounced on the opportunity to take advantage of it.

"Baby, I love you, and I love our kids. Please don't take their father away from them. I need ya'll." The emotional sucker punch—I should have seen it coming. I fell for it, too.

"You know that I love you too, but you aren't hearing me, so I have to take matters into my own hands. I would never take your daughters away from you. Just because you are not here, doesn't mean that you can't see them. I'll give you thirty days to find a place to live," I said as I walked out of the room quickly, attempting to gather my wits about me. He simply sat on the bed, saying nothing as I walked away. I desperately hoped that he would be packing up when I returned.

For the next day or two there was tension so thick you could cut it with a knife in the house. When I told my mother of my decision, her relief was unmistakable. I felt good about putting my foot down, something I could never do with Darryl before now. My feelings toward him were a strange mixture of love and intimidation. I often wondered if I made the right decision, in terms of telling him he had to go. Maybe he really WAS trying to get a job. My reasons for hesitancy were not unfounded. Up until that point, my life was a series of missteps and bad decisions. I wanted to do the right thing, but I wasn't sure if putting my husband out was it. I second-guessed myself for quite a while afterward.

My self-doubt was deeply rooted. I grew up the youngest child of three. My sister and brother were considerably older than me, my sister by sixteen years, and my brother by fourteen years. I was the little sister who somehow never got it right, and frequently ridiculed myself up for my indiscretions. Then there was the guilt factor that always loomed...Guilt from the sexual and psychological abuse I suffered as a child, guilt from not being accepted within some peer circles, and most recently, guilt about my lack of self-control when it came to food. My whole existence revolved around the notion that I thought of myself as inferior from childhood to adulthood. I never spoke up for myself, not even when it came to my own defense.

This was an important turning point for me. I made a decision to take charge; to do what I felt was necessary in terms of my relationship with Darryl. Yet, uncertainty abounded. If I kicked him out, the next step for me was divorcing him. Did I really want to do that?

What about what God said about divorce? How would I explain to our daughters that Daddy is not living with us anymore, because I told him to leave? What would my children think of me? The more the questions swirled around in my head, the more anxious I became. The more anxious I became, the more Xanax pills I took to calm my troubled and confused mind.

Some nights when the kids were sleeping, I would drive off to get some peace of mind. In the past, my nightly runs would consist of driving to several fast food places to gorge on hamburgers, fries, and ice cream in some darkened street or parking lot, but not this time. I'd discovered a new place where I could soothe my unsettled thoughts. A place that didn't make me feel ashamed when I left it, but tougher when I stepped out the doors. I discovered a place that was better than any McDonald's drive-through I ever visited: Shapes Gym. It was there that I received my "sweat therapy" many nights.

Permission to Shine (211)

It was February 15, and time to dodge the creditors again. I was so tired of not making ends meet, and my job at the bank lockbox just wasn't cutting it anymore. I was constantly robbing Peter to pay Paul in terms of the bills I had to pay. I was still paying for the car that Darryl totaled, plus the used van I had to buy to get to and from my job.

Unable to pay for both the old and new car notes, I stopped paying for the car, which was a strike against not only my credit, but my mother's credit, since she was my co-signer. I was way over my head with bills, and simply could not keep up on my little salary. My lunch hour consisted of returning calls about the various job inquiries I was making daily. I used my vacation and sick time going to interviews downtown. Nothing seemed to pan out until I received a phone call one Friday afternoon while sifting through dozens of checks on my desk. I ran to the break room and quickly answered the call. It was the human resources department for a downtown law firm who was interested in speaking to me about a receptionist position. I immediately set up the interview for the next day. I prayed that it would be worth me using my last sick day of the year.

The next day I woke up bright and early to find something to wear, which was a hassle at this point. All my clothes were way too big, even with a belt. I had no clue how much weight I'd lost since my last weigh-in; all I knew was my clothes were literally falling off me every day. With the emotional rollercoaster I had been on with the Darryl situation, my weigh-ins at the gym took a back seat. My mind was so preoccupied that I just went to the gym for my usual hour and left—-none of my usual small talk with other members. I just did what I had to do and left quickly afterwards.

After I took my shower that morning, I decided to get on the scale after being absent from it for over a month. When I looked down to see how I had done, to my complete astonishment, I found I had reached my initial goal and didn't even know it. I weighed 211 pounds—a total of 103 pounds…gone.

 I wished that I would have waited so that I could celebrate my victory with Shelly and the Shapes crew, but instead I ran like a madwoman up the stairs, still naked while yelling my fantastic news to my mother and sister, who were equally shocked by my nakedness as well as my finally reaching my goal. Now that I had attained my first goal, I wanted to keep going. So I made a new goal. My new fitness goal was to lose an additional 30 pounds, and to be medication free.

I frantically searched through my closet for something interview-worthy. Because money was so tight, I couldn't afford to replace all my clothes, but I did buy a pair of brown interview pants the week before, just in case I needed them. I was glad I made that call, because today I would need them. I paired my brown pants with a beige blouse and pulled my braids into a bun. As I adjusted my pants, I noticed how they flopped around my thighs a bit. Running up the stairs to the larger mirror, my mother said very matter-of-factly, "Sue, those pants are way too big. Here, try these on. I can't fit them anymore anyway." She handed me a pair of her size 14 pants.

"Those will be too small for me, Mama. I'm a size sixteen, remember?" I replied, wishing her advice on fashion wasn't so longwinded. I had a little under an hour to get to my interview.

"Baby, it will only take a second. Now please, put these on for me."

"Fine. Okay," I said, grabbing the pants and taking the other ones off at the same time. "After I show you that I can't put on these pants, then can I get out of here?" I sarcastically asked, putting one leg in the trousers. I was all set to prove her wrong as I slid the borrowed slacks on with ease and buttoned them. Mama just looked at me with a huge grin of approval.

"Perfect…see?" she said. "I told you!"

I grabbed her and hugged tight, as a nonverbal thank you for everything. Not just for the pants, but every single thing she had ever done for me and the girls. "Thank you, Mama," I said tear drops hanging off my mascaraed lashes.

"Get on out of here," she said. "Get. You already have that job. In Jesus' name, go on and show 'em what you got, baby!" Mama replied with tears in her own eyes. "I'm proud of you, baby. I really am. Now get!" Her approval meant the world to me; it always did. Mama had become increasingly smaller in frame due to her many health issues, but she was still as feisty as ever. When she said jump, you better believe I still jumped.

I walked out of the interview, excited. The law firm supervisor and manager seemed really impressed with my clerical background. I prayed that Mama's premonition was right about my being hired there. The pay rate was what I was looking for, and I really liked the office. Not too big and not too formal. I was told that I would receive an answer either way by the following Monday. I was on pins and needles the entire weekend, hoping to receive good news on Monday. Even better, maybe Darryl would have moved out already. He had two more weeks to find a place to stay, and I was counting the days. I still had to find a way to explain everything to our daughters, at least to Lanie and Johanna. At fourteen, Denai understood more than her younger sisters. She had unfortunately been a witness to the arguments and knew how much I was struggling to pay the bills. She'd understand the decision I had to make concerning her stepfather. It would take delicate diplomacy to explain why our living situation had to change to a much younger Lanie and Jo. I prayed that God would give me the wisdom to do it properly.

After the interview, I had some time before the kids got out of school to hit the gym. I kept an extra pair of workout clothes in the car for emergencies, and I would put them to use. I was on an adrenaline high from knocking my interview out of the park, and I was pumped and ready to sweat. When I swiped my key card, I was pleasantly surprised when instead of my name popping up, the most wonderful and thoughtful message appeared on the screen: "Sue is the QUEEN of the Shapes Circuit!" I am not sure which member of the staff composed the message to me, but I had never felt so special in all of my life. Someone took the time to deliberately make me smile. It was just a little gesture, but it meant so much to me. It was a moment I will never forget.

When I walked on the circuit to warm up, Shelly came dashing over to me with a huge smile and an invitation in her hand. "Hey, girlie, you are looking GREAT! All the gals here are so proud of you!" Shelly said in her loud, megaphone voice. Shelly was so encouraging, I wished that she could be on a recording in my pocket on the days when I felt less than encouraged about my situation at home with Darryl.

"What's that in your hand, Shel?" I asked, figuring that her absentmindedness had struck again, and more than likely she'd forgotten why she came over to me.

"Ohhhh, yeah…so, every year, all the Shapes locations in our region come together to do an annual fashion show for our members who have worked hard and lost weight. The managers and staff of each gym nominate seven members who have had success losing weight, with one particular member who is dubbed Shapes Woman of the Year. This member has lost the most weight since she started, and she comes out last at the finale. She is kinda like the Queen of the Ball, so to speak. She gets crowned, gets a ribbon, and she's presented with a dozen roses, just like at the Miss America Pageant. It's really a great time, and all our nominated gals love it. It gives us a chance to show them off for all their hard work. This year, all the regions voted on one particular member from our location to be Queen of the Ball, as a matter of fact." Shelly tossed the invitation back and forth in her hands.

I wondered who out of the Golden Girl crew was nominated. There were a lot of ladies who had lost quite a bit of weight. So many, in fact, that we had a chalkboard in the middle of the room that congratulated all the Shapes 'Biggest Losers' each month. I wanted her to hurry up and tell me because the suspense was killing me. "So who is it, Shelly? Renee, Barbara, Sue H.? Who?" My voice was shaking due to the relentless pouncing and bouncing I was doing on the cardio pads while we talked.

"Well here, take a look for yourself. All of us just decided this morning."

I stopped mid-bounce and reached for the red card. The invitation read:

Congratulations, Sue Lewis, you have been chosen as Shapes Woman of the Year! Please accept our invitation to our fashion show, where you will close out our ceremony with a walk down the catwalk. Your astounding weight loss has inspired many, and we want to celebrate your accomplishments. Of the entire Shapes members in this Chicago Region, you are the biggest loser, having lost 100 pounds. Congratulations Sue!

It was like I was in a movie, watching this happen to someone else. I was completely floored. My hands started to shake with excitement. *This must be what winning the lottery felt like*, I thought, as my open mouth grew into a huge nothing-but-teeth smile.

I always wondered what it felt like to win something. I had never won as much as a spelling bee. It was such an honor to have not only the owners of my gym nominate me, but owners from other Shapes gyms too. I had reached my goal that I set for myself the previous year of 100 pounds, which was something I thought I would never accomplish in my lifetime. But to actually be a part of their annual fashion show as the honoree was unfathomable.

There should have been tear stains all over that gym from all of the triumphant strides I had experienced each month, and with such a wonderful group of people cheering me on all the way. This time was no different. I looked around briefly to see my comrades, aka The Golden Girl Crew, applauding. I saw my buddy Sasha, who talked me off the ledge many times with her pep talks about the woes of plateaus. She smiled broadly as she gave me the thumbs-up sign, the rest of the staff rubbing my shoulders and giving me congratulatory hugs. It was like I was in some kind of dream state.

All the words Dr. Thomas told me came rushing back to mind. This wasn't supposed to me happening to me. I was the girl who got teased, the girl no one wanted to choose for games, the girl no one wanted to take to the prom. I was the woman who broke a salon chair with her massive weight. Now here I was, surrounded by so much moral and encouragement. For the first time in my life, I felt like a champion.

"You better get ready for your big reveal, Sue! The fashion show is in two weeks, girly! I have a couple of boutiques for you to go to and try some really beautiful gowns," Shelly said as she hugged me around my shoulders tightly. Not only was this a big deal for me, it was a big deal for Shapes Gym, period. Their annual fashion show would have all the glitz and glamour of an actual runway show, complete with wardrobe changes and everything. I would need to be fitted for an evening gown for the finale, and Shelly made certain all of the arrangements made and paid for, courtesy of Shapes. It was the most exciting time in my life. I couldn't wait. Me? The Belle of the Shapes Ball? Wow.

Overcast on Sunshine

I couldn't wait until I got home to tell my family the exciting news. On my way home, my cell phone rang. It was Stephanie from the

Human Resources department of the law firm that I just interviewed with a couple of hours before. My heart sank when she told me who she was. "Can you hold on a moment, Susan? Thanks."

Oh great, I thought. She put me on hold without even telling me what she called for. I wasn't supposed to hear from them until Monday…maybe I didn't do as well as I thought I did. With a call back so quickly, it had to be bad news. As I drove, my stomach churned until I felt sick. I had just been on top of the world mere minutes before; I went from elation to stomach constipation in no time flat. My nerves were so on edge; I prayed that I wouldn't throw up in my car while I waited for Stephanie to get back on the line with me. I needed that job so badly.

"Hello, Susan? Sorry I had to put you on hold, my boss came into my office for a moment. I wanted to hurry and call you to let you know that you have been offered the position that you interviewed for today. Mr. Moreno said that you were the candidate who met all of the qualifications, and he really didn't need to look any further. He said that you have the job, if you are still interested. Hello? Hello? Susan, are you still there?"

I was there…holding the phone, but nothing would come out of my mouth. I snapped myself out of my shocked stupor to yell out louder than I had intended to Stephanie, "Yes! Thank you, Stephanie. Thank you so much for calling me back so quickly.

When do I start?" My heart seemed to have leaped out of my excited chest.

"Can you start next Wednesday? Is that too early?" Stephanie inquired.

"No, Ma'am. I will be there and thank you again." I had to hang up the phone quickly before I started blubbering in Stephanie's ear. In an instant I became overwhelmed with gratitude for a gracious God who had heard my prayers for another job and answered it. He had given me the strength, and the presence of mind to reverse what I had done to my body all these years. After being held captive by my weight for so very long, I was now able to do things I never thought that I could. My body was stronger, so was my mind.

The one piece of the victorious puzzle left out was my relationship with my husband. My mind was still in constant turmoil with conflicting thoughts about whether to divorce Darryl, or try one more time. I didn't even know whether or not it was possible for me to gain back the respect that I once had for him. The truth was I loved him, but I didn't trust him anymore. That was a real problem.

My life seemed to be coming together all at one time, and not only was I excited, but my children were happy for me too. It felt so good to overhear Denai and Lanie talking about the accomplishments their Mommy had achieved. Johanna, who was much younger, took notice of the change in me as well. I was tickled when I noticed that Johanna's pictures of Mommy were stick figures now, instead of the circles that she once drew to depict how she saw me in her mind. I think that one gesture was the best part of my journey up until that point. My mother, who was falling ill more and more lately, was elated that I was finally getting my life in order.

My sister was also becoming more and more sickly around that same time. She suffered with terrible migraine headaches that left her incapacitated some days, while other days she simply refused to eat anything, saying that eating food "hurt" her stomach sometimes. Brenda lost a great deal of weight during that time, and just didn't look like herself. On top of that, she was suffering kidney failure, and was on intense dialysis three days a week, just like my mother.

Even though Brenda was going through more than her share of health issues, it never stopped her from living. She wanted to retire in a few years, and she worked every day to make sure she had a spotless record when she did. In her twenty-five years of working as an executive secretary for the Illinois Department of Employment Security, she rarely took off. I was so proud to call her my big sister. She was the most kind and thoughtful person that ever drew breath. Brenda was also my biggest supporter throughout my journey, cheering me on with every scale victory and making sure I had what I needed to eat on my revised diet. She rocked me to sleep during my frequent attacks, and held me in her arms as long as I needed her there. She was my rock. No one was happier for me than Brenda had been. I always wished that I could take her physical pain away from her. She never ever complained about the misery she was going through, but I could always look in her eyes and see her suffering silently. She would always say to me, "Baby, there is not a moment in the day when I am not in pain, but God is still good." Her strength was amazing.

I couldn't wait to tell my family about the fashion show and my new job, but I wanted my best friend to know first. As soon as I got home, I wasted no time calling my girl Nikki to tell her about all the great doors that were opening up for me. She knew how hard this journey was, and if anyone would be excited for me, it would be my best friend of over twenty years. Since I couldn't wait to call her, and I was in my car anyway, I figured I would do the next best thing and swing by for a visit.

When I got to her house, I was so excited I could barely get out what I wanted to tell her. "Hey Susie Bell, what's up?" she said, looking a bit surprised I was there.

"Hey, girl, you busy? I just had to stop by to tell you my good news!" I said as I walked into her door and threw my purse on the couch. "Before I get started…you look fantastic as always, Nikki. The weight is just falling off you! How much have you lost now?" I said, admiring her figure and wishing I had just a little more in my backside like she did. Nikki looked incredible, and I was so happy for her transformation. I was eager to know how her eating regime was going; maybe we could exchange some pointers or something.

"I dunno, girl, I told you, I really don't weigh myself. I couldn't tell you" She said while randomly thumbing through a magazine that I knew she wasn't really looking at. It hurt my feelings that she wasn't interested in sharing anything with me anymore. It was almost like we were strangers or something, like she didn't know me anymore. We didn't talk often, but when we did, it was very general, and she made sure that she didn't reveal too much to me. It seemed like we were so much closer when we were heavy together. Now things between us just felt…distant.

"Okay, well you look great anyway, no matter how much you have lost," I said, moving on past the awkwardness and getting to why I had come over. I was ready to celebrate with my best girlfriend, maybe go out for a drink or two or something. I was waiting on her to perhaps make mention of my weight loss, but there was nothing. "Guess what? I finally made it to my weight loss goal of 100 pounds, and I was nominated Shapes 'Biggest Loser' in the whole Chicago Region! Shelly wants me to close out their event on, get this…a red carpet! Of course you know I want my girl there, so I saved you two tickets. You think your fiancé might want to come too?" I rattled it off so fast that I had to catch my breath after the last sentence came out.

Nikki took turns looking at me, then looking at the magazine she pretended to be reading. Finally she spoke. "That's really good, Sue. That's good girl, but I don't think I will be able to make it. I think I have to work that night, but I will try to make it." Nikki looked up, finally giving me her full attention. Somehow I knew that she wouldn't try to make it.

"Well…okay…but I really hope you can make it," I said, feeling like a little kid that lost her favorite toy. It was becoming obvious that something had changed between us, and it bothered me that I didn't know what it was. I hadn't done anything to Nikki, yet I felt like I was getting the cold shoulder from my buddy every time the subject of our mutual weight loss came up. "I'm gonna head out, Nik. I was on my way home and just thought I'd stop by your way for a minute. Are you all right, Nik?" I asked, wondering why things felt so weird with her at that moment.

"I'm fine. I'm okay," she replied, nodding her head up and down.

"I'll call you tomorrow, okay?" I said, still feeling a bit hurt by her totally indifferent demeanor. I got in my car and drove half a block down the street to my house, wondering what had happed to our closeness. I didn't dare tell her about my new job while I was there; she might have fallen asleep in the middle of my telling her about it. I'll just keep it to myself, I thought as I put the key in the lock at home.

Shaking off the Nikki situation momentarily, I told Darryl about my news since he was the first one I saw as I walked into the kitchen. His reaction was lukewarm, but I wasn't surprised. He was down to just a couple days until his deadline to move out, and I didn't see one packed box or bag in sight.

My mother and sister were thrilled, and made plans to be at my "coming out" party with a few hundred other people from various Shapes communities. In between my gracious blessings from God, there were also thoughts that worried my mind and saddened my heart.

It seemed as if just about everyone I loved was suffering from some sort of health crisis. My mother's health became increasingly erratic. Some days were good, but when they were bad, they were awful. Her presence in the emergency room seemed constant. I also took notice of the odd way she held her left arm, as well as her slurred at times. When we insisted that she have an MRI to check things out, we were told that my mother had another transient stroke, or as it's commonly called a "mini stroke." This would be her fifth one in ten years.

My dad, who was going through his own health problems, was diagnosed with stage four prostate cancer at seventy-eight years old. He'd become quite weakened from his treatments, but rarely complained about it, so as not to worry me. I was his only child; and the only person he had to depend on, which kept me constantly worried about his welfare. I was nervous about him being alone in his apartment, and going to a nursing home was definitely out of the question for him. Aside from the cancer, my Dad was still very active when he felt well. He went on riverboat gambling trips and did whatever he wanted to do, whenever he wanted to do it. I didn't insist that he stay put. Any attempts to stifle his independence would have been met with much resistance to say the least. I let him do his thing, but kept close watch and made him promise to call me whenever he went out of town. My thoughts were often consumed with impending doom where my family's health was concerned. My horizon looked sunny, but I often wondered when the clouds would appear. I was petrified at the thought of losing any of them.

Strut! (185.5)

It was just a few hours before the fashion show was set to take place, and I was a bundle of nervous energy. The dress that was chosen for me couldn't have been more perfect. Shelly handpicked it herself. It amazed me that the boutique owner knew exactly what size to choose for me just by looking at me. When she presented me with an absolutely gorgeous size 12 fire-engine red bombshell dress, I smiled and politely returned it to her through the dressing room door. "It's stunning, but there is no way I can fit into this gown, Ma'am. I'm a size 14-16," I told her regretfully.

"Nooooo, honey, you think you are a size 14-16, but you are a 12 for sure. Try it on, you'll see," the gray-haired lady informed me in her thick Swedish accent. My mother taught me to always be polite to my elders, so I wasn't going to argue with her, but I knew she was wrong. All I could think about was putting one thigh in that delicate and very expensive borrowed gown and ripping it from one side to the other in my attempt to put it on.

"Fine, I will try it on, but I ain't paying for this dress when it rips," I said to myself, rolling my eyes and sucking my teeth defiantly.

Nervously and very carefully, I put the dress over my head. The satin-like material slid effortlessly down the rest of my body as the lacy hem hit the floor in perfect motion. I stared down at my feet as the beautiful train of the dress encircled my toes. I slowly looked up at the floor-length dressing room mirror like a deer stuck in the glare of a truck's headlights. The dress was a perfect fit. I rubbed my hands across the beautiful detailed beading along the sweetheart bodice as I cried silently, my teardrops getting lost within the shimmering beading details of the ultra-sexy dress. Immediately I reached for the hanging tag on the side of the gown to see if it was true...indeed it was a size 12. "Oh my God, it fits! It Fits!" I screamed out in hysterical happiness.

The little Swedish boutique owner flung the fitting-room door open before I could. She raised her hands in exaggeration and shouted, "I told you, honey! Look at you! You look beautiful, and what a figure you have! Va va voom!" She exclaimed, shaking her hands in a dramatic fashion, as if she had just touched something that burned her fingers. I felt my face get hot as I blushed through her complimentary commentary, grateful for her kind words. I was excited about my trip down the runway, but what would make the evening even more special was that my mother and sister, along with my daughters and Darryl, were all going to be there to witness it.

Denai, Lanie, and Johanna were so excited on the way to the event that they literally could not stop talking about it. "Mommy, you are a star now!" Lanie said to me from the backseat of our car. "Mommy has always been a star," Denai corrected her little sister.

"I'm proud of you, Mommy. You've always been pretty, but now you're *'pretty healthy!'* Denai said as she leaned forward in her seat and kissed me on the cheek. I could have floated straight to the ceiling of the car. Their accolades meant the world to me. If I never received another flattering phrase from anyone else, the fact that my children envisioned me as their "star" was all I needed. Even Darryl, who had been particularly quiet up until then, gave his own kudos to me for the honor of being chosen as Shapes' "Biggest Loser," which was surprising to hear considering his time had run its course at my mother's house. His move-out date was the following day, and I still hadn't seen so much as a duffle bag packed up yet. I made up my mind and refused to dwell on anything remotely negative that evening. All my diligence and determination had culminated to this moment. I wouldn't let anything spoil what I had worked so hard to accomplish.

The stage was set and the lights came on. Patti LaBelle's *"New Attitude"* was the chosen song I was to come out on. There would be many ladies that preceded me on the stage, and I enjoyed reveling in their accomplishments as much as my own.

I watched with pride as each one took the stage for their time to shine. We high-fived, shouted and applauded for one another in a display of great solidarity. Some of the ladies I knew from my gym, and others I had just met for the first time. But one thing was resoundingly clear, no matter the nationality. Black, white, or brown; we were all sisters that night. All of us connected with similar stories of hope and determination despite the odds. Virtual strangers ranging in age from early thirties to late seventies bonded instantly with hugs of support, compliments, and expressions of praise for one another. I relished in the thick atmosphere of optimism. It was truly an honor to be among such amazingly strong women.

I stood behind the velvet curtain as each Shapes honoree pranced to uplifting tunes like "*Celebration*," "*Pretty Woman*," and the Shapes gym anthem, "*Brand New You*." Before and after photos of the honorees flashed across a huge screen in the background, while each woman performed their best supermodel strut across the stage. I smiled as I peeked through the curtain every so often and reveled in the joyous moment these women were experiencing. I also wanted to make sure that my family had a bird's eye view of the stage once I came out.

I peered through just enough so I could see Johanna sitting on my mother's lap, bouncing happily and pointing to the sparkling designs on the stage. I scanned the audience to for Nikki, still hoping she would be somewhere in the crowd. I figured that she would be sitting with my family, but there was no sign of her anywhere. I held out hope that maybe I just missed her in the massive audience, or at the very least, she was just running late. I tried in earnest to shake off the disappointment of my best friend not showing up to support me, and vowed not to let it ruin the rest of my evening.

I heard Shelly's voice on stage. She was introducing herself as the owner of our gym, which meant it was almost time for my appearance. My stomach began doing flip flops as the rush of adrenaline pulsated through every part of my nervous body. I felt my knees shaking under my dress as I heard Shelly call out her seven honorees, with me being honored last as the Shapes Biggest Loser and award recipient.

I began to fumble nervously with my dress, trying make sure that all my loose skin was neatly tucked away in my girdle, and that the excess skin from around my sides wasn't spilling out of the top of my strapless gown. *Oh my God...what if my baggy skin comes flopping out as soon as I step out there?*

All I could imagine were my rolls of skin making their debut in front of all those people in the audience. My hands were dripping sweat, as every possible horrible scenario came popping up into my head. "*These heels are too tall, and the floor is probably slippery from the wax...what if I take a tumble as soon as I start walking or worse, what if I trip on that long, thick red carpet? Oh my God, I can't go out there!*"

As I fussed with my hair, tugged on my dress, and tried to talk myself out of my turn on the runway, I suddenly heard a deepened voice from behind me that almost scared the crap out of me...literally. "You look absolutely stunning, Sue...you are Sue, right?" the Barry White-esque voice said as I heard him walk closer behind me. I had been nearly startled half to death by a handsome gentleman who was dressed impeccably, clean cut and smelled magnificent.

"Yes...I'm Sue, yes." I said, stammering and trying not to swallow the gum I was nervously chomping on.

"It's a pleasure to meet you, Ms. Sue; the venue has been all abuzz about you and your absolutely amazing weight loss. You look, well, amazing!" He eyed me from my red high heeled feet to my loosely spiraled hair. "Well, thank you...and you are?" I replied, feeling a bit embarrassed by the shower of this sudden male attention.

His visual study of my figure was definitely not what I was used to. Up until then, I wasn't exactly showing off my body in what I wore, and I definitely didn't own anything as fitted as the dress I was wearing. I was so self-conscious about my body and my loose skin issue that I never wore so much as a sleeveless t-shirt after I initially lost weight. The dress, complimentary gazes, and interest I was receiving from this mystery guy was brand new territory for me, but it actually felt rather good to be noticed.

As his glance made its way back to my face, he apologized for his distraction. "I'm sorry; I didn't tell you my name, did I? My name is Eric. I was the emcee for the beginning of the program. Now I have the esteemed pleasure of escorting you as you take your walk down the aisle. Or should I say as you rip the runway with that dynamite dress you have on? I can tell that you are nervous. Don't be, you'll be fine. I'll be with you all the way." The gleam from his beautiful teeth and his melodious voice seemed to distract me as I fell silent for a moment. "Sue, are you all right?" Eric asked. I'm almost positive that he noticed how hard I was biting my bottom lip.

"Yes, I'm fine, Eric. Just nervous is all. Thank you for your pep talk. Just make sure you catch me if you notice I am a bit unsteady in these heels I'm wearing." He laughed, but I was deadly serious.

"You won't fall; you will be as graceful as you are beautiful. Here…take a moment to practice walking a few feet with me." Eric held out his arm. When I reached out to take hold of it, I noticed how tall he was standing right next to me. He looked like a giant as I looked up at him and he looked down at me with a mile-wide smile. I tried not to get distracted by whatever he was wearing that smelled like a slice of heaven. I focused on gracefully placing one foot in front of the other without looking like a newborn wiggly-legged calf. "You are doing great, Sue. See, I told you. You are a natural at this," he said, slowly building up my confidence.

Yeah, just don't let go of me...please, I said to myself, but out loud I declared, "Yeah, I think I'm doing pretty good, huh?"

"Indeed you are, Ms. Sue, or is it Mrs. Sue?" Eric's inquiry included a direct look into my eyes that seemed almost hypnotic.

"It's Mrs.," I replied, with just a hint of unintentional dismay.

"Your husband is very lucky, Sue. He has a true champion for a wife, and just as lovely, too."

"I really appreciate your kindness, Eric. I truly thank you," I very gratefully replied.

"No thanks necessary, Mrs. Sue, just stating the obvious."

I felt like a front-runner, and I hadn't even left from behind the curtain yet. Eric's encouraging words were really good to hear.

Thanks to my escort, my nerves disappeared and I was poised and ready to make my debut with my head held high. I noticed the applause became hushed from the audience as I heard Shelly's naturally amplified voice speak into the microphone (not that she needed one).

"I hate to use the term saving the best for last, because all of our gals are trailblazers in their own right. Please give another huge round of applause for our lovely and fitter than ever ladies of Shapes Gym!"

After Shelly prompted congratulatory applause for the ladies that preceded me, she took to the microphone again. "Ladies and gentleman, without further ado, it is my pleasure to introduce a young lady who not only garnered my respect, but the respect of my entire staff, as well as the members of my facility. I have watched her grow in resolve for nearly a year and set the circuit on fire with her determination not only to reach her personal weight loss goals, but to encourage other members to do the same. She is loved by us dearly, and we could not be more proud of her and the fact that she has lost over 100 pounds since April of last year…"

As Shelly spoke to the audience, I couldn't help but to peer out of the small opening of the curtain to see my before pictures flash across the huge screen of the venue. I was so glad I never threw them away like I thought about doing.

I couldn't help but to get teary-eyed seeing my former self on the screen. In an instant, I began to reflect on my journey as I watched picture after picture flash across the screen. I couldn't believe this was happening to me. Me. The child who hoarded food in her room, the teen who contemplated suicide because she believed she was unworthy of anyone's love, and the young woman who gorged on ridiculous amounts of food to drown her self-hatred. That was me up there on the screen. It seemed as if those photos were of someone else.

I felt renewed both in body and in spirit standing backstage. I was ready to take the walk that I never thought in my wildest dreams I would dare to take. There I stood, about to be honored for my diligence in losing over 100 pounds. Two months shy of a year's time.

Blaring through the speakers, I heard the opening lyrics to Patti LaBelle's *"New Attitude,"* which was my cue to get ready to take the stage with Eric. In all of the excitement, I realized that I was still holding on to Eric's arm from the little practice session we had a couple of minutes ago. I might have felt a bit of embarrassment, if he wasn't still gently clutching my hand with his strong forearm. I wondered for a brief second if his prolonged embrace was intentional, but either way, it felt good to be held on to. "Oh my God, I'm still holding on to your arm from earlier, I'm sorry!" I said, with a coy smile.

"What are you apologizing for? I'm holding on to you, too. Besides, with the death grip you have on my arm, I can't escape even if I wanted to!" We both laughed quietly. His lighthearted and good-natured demeanor was just what the doctor ordered as I waited for Shelly to say my name.

"Ladies and gentleman, it is my honor to present to you, having lost an astonishing one hundred and twenty-one pounds, and the recipient of the Shapes Chicago Regional Biggest Loser Award…Ms. Sue Lewis!"

The thunderous roar of applause was almost deafening. I never felt so humbled in all of my life. Unbeknownst to me, all the participants of the fashion show were behind me. Front and center was my trainer and buddy Sasha who had come to support me. All twenty-five ladies who I cheered for were now returning the incredible love to me in the form of hoots, hollers and cheers. The show of support was incredibly emotional for me.

"Well, that's our cue. Let's go, beautiful…show 'em what you got!" Eric said, with a flirtatious wink. As soon as I stepped out of the curtain, my eyes were immediately met by Shelly's. She was center stage, clapping louder than anyone. Her blue eyes glistened with tear drops as she mouthed to me, "You did it… you did it!"

Shelly returned to the microphone to tell the audience a little bit about my journey at Shapes while referencing my before pictures as they flashed across the screen. Eric and I took a leisurely stroll across the long stage, smiling and waving. Eric, who remained close by my side, turned toward me and whispered in my ear, "This is your time to shine, beautiful. It's all about you now, and the awesome job you've done. I am going to let you go, but I'll be waiting for you by the center of the stage. Right now, I want you to take your time, enjoy this moment, and soak it in. This is your catwalk, Sue. Now go own it, girl!"

Just like that, Eric released me to greet the crowd. The audience stood as I walked alone across the stage. Without Eric there, I felt a tinge of stage fright as I found myself self-consciously tugging on my dress, which was perfectly in place and not going anywhere. My fear slowly dissipated as I caught the eye of my mother. She was on her feet blowing me kisses as she cradled a vibrant bouquet of flowers in her hand for me.

My sister was a bit more vocal. Brenda shouted my name loudly and chanted, "That's my sister up there! That's my baby! GO GIRL!" I spotted my three daughters holding balloons for me, and Darryl showed his support with a thumbs-up signal to me. Feeling more comfortable and confident, I turned and twirled, displaying my gorgeous beaded gown. I looked for Nikki's waving hand, but I never saw it. My best friend for over twenty years never showed up at all.

As the music changed to the elegant tune of *"The Way You Look Tonight,"* Eric met me at the center of the stage as promised. He took my hand and led me in a mini dance in the center of the stage. It an impromptu addition that wasn't planned, and I adored the cutesy spontaneous gesture. There was not a hint of awkwardness or apprehension during our dance, just the feeling of being transported to Wonderland. I felt like a princess, complete with the handsome and gracious Prince Charming by my side as the audience "oooed" and "ahhhed."

No matter what happened after that night, no one could ever dampen the precious memories of my exciting time on the catwalk. Being honored for going above and beyond goals I thought I would never achieve in my lifetime was a magical experience I'll never forget. I will be forever reminded of how God led me through one of the most trying seasons of my life. I battled with self-doubt and fought an addiction to food that almost killed me.

When I began working out initially, I discovered quickly how much of a toll it can take physically. I wanted to quit, but God refused to let me. He gave me the physical strength and mental fortitude to keep my mind on what I needed to accomplish for my health's sake, no matter how difficult it became. Looking back, I know without a doubt that it was God who sustained me during that year. There was no way I could have achieved my 120-pound weight loss with my own human strength. I would have thrown in the towel if it were up to me. From a health standpoint, my blood pressure was more consistent, and I was looking forward to the day when I would be off all of my medications completely. There would be many other mountains to climb after my trip to the top of this one, but in that moment I took my time, just as Eric instructed—to relish the view from on high.

Coming Full Circle (174.0)

Nikki never mentioned why she didn't come out to my event, and she never bothered to call me to say congratulations. I suppose I might have felt better about it had she at least given me an explanation as to why she didn't come, but she never mentioned it, as if it had never happened. It became increasingly clear that the tides had turned with regard to our friendship; we weren't connected like we once were before we mutually underwent our physical changes. Something was different between us; I just couldn't put my finger on it.

Despite the fact that Nikki didn't show up at my event, I shook off the odd behavior like I was accustomed to doing with her lately. Our recent conversations were about her plans to marry her fiancé, Josh. Josh was a really nice guy, and no one was happier for Nikki than I was that she found a decent and hardworking man who loved her dearly. I was especially excited to hear that she wanted to celebrate her upcoming nuptials with a mini bachelorette getaway on the beautiful island of Nassau, located in the Bahamas. This would be my second time going with Nikki to Nassau; the first time had been an absolute blast, so I knew this time would be even better, especially now that we both were physically transformed. It was only April, and I wished that I could magically turn the calendar to July 12 so that we could get our tropical party started. I began counting down the days and putting money away for our all-girl trip.

Besides my best friend's upcoming nuptials, I had other reasons to smile for a change. My new job at the law firm was going better than I imagined. I was a front office co-receptionist with another lady named Dottie, and Dottie was a hoot too. She was an elderly Jewish lady with jet-black hair that stood out starkly against her very pale skin. She had a penchant for bright red lipstick that always seemed to be more on her teeth than on her lips. A very serious and devout unorthodox Jewish believer, and was quite opinionated about Christians, a quality that really rubbed me the wrong way. Nonetheless, she was harmless, and actually very nice to me.

One morning, to my surprise, the firm's manager, Raul, and my direct supervisor, April, called me into Raul's office as soon as I placed my purse down in my chair beside Dottie. Nervously I walked in; trying to figure out what I had done wrong in the past month I had been working there. To my surprise, Raul offered me another position within the law firm as a legal assistant.

I was floored, especially since I had absolutely no experience in the legal realm. The only experience I had was as a hair stylist and bank lockbox worker. For Raul and April to have that kind of faith in my abilities made me proud. I didn't have a background in anything remotely close to collection law, but I was eager to learn and ready for the challenge. I gladly accepted the job offer—which included a pay rate of five dollars more than what I was currently making the firm's receptionist. I was over the moon. I quickly packed up my Christian quotes from my side of the reception area, bid Dottie and her bright red lips adieu, and headed toward my new office space as the newest legal assistant at Wexler Walsh & Ryan.

There was also cause for celebration at Shapes as well. It was the month of April, which meant that I had reached the one-year anniversary of my membership at the gym that had become my home away from home, and its members my extended family. As I swiped in with my key card, the number of workouts since my first one appeared on the screen. In a year's time, I had worked out at the gym a grand total of 1,103 times. My eyes widened as I said the number out loud to Shelly, who was scribbling away at a Shapes clothing order for another member. "Yeah, you just haven't worked out enough in here, girly, you slacker!" Shelly chuckled.

On my anniversary, I thought it fitting to take yet another turn on the scale to see how far my progress had come since joining the year before. Shelly was prepared with the records of all of my weigh-ins dating back to my first work out.

I stepped on the scale as I saw Shelly, Sasha, and the rest of the Shapes staff gather around. Some even placed bets on how much I had lost since last year. I stepped on the scale to see how far I had come since I first walk through the doors of Shapes:

As usual, my eyes fixated on the rolling numbers on the digital scale. The numbers stopped rolling and remained at 174. In one year's time, I exceeded my initial goal of 100 pounds, with a loss of over 140 pounds.

There were congratulations and hugs that flowed from the members, the staff, and most of all, from the owner and my sergeant at arms, Shelly. She came over to me and grabbed me so tightly that the sweat from my gym shirt transferred to her own. "What did I tell you, girly? I told you that once you decided to place you determination in drive, there would be no stopping you, and you proved me right. I knew you had it in you all the time. I could not be more proud of you, Sue; you make us all so very proud," Shelly said, still holding me in her arms.

Shelly was more than the owner of a gym. She was a motivator, a cheerleader, and a drill sergeant all rolled into one loud, blond-haired, blue-eyed phenomenal health and fitness instructor. After the hubbub died down and the members went back to their step pads on the circuit, I sat down quietly in the corner of the stretching area—the same place that Shelly gave me her life-changing pep talk the previous year.

I marveled at the change in my prospective, not just from a physical health stand-point, but the psychological change as well. I still had a long way to go in terms of slaying the personal dragons in my life, but this one had been defeated by the Grace of God. I cried, pouted and complained my way through, but never gave up. Holding myself accountable, I adhered to a healthier regime that had now been set in stone. In April 2007, I challenged myself to want more than simply eating myself to death. On the heels of what could have easily been my untimely demise just one year prior, I made a decision to fight in order to live. Live. Not simply exist within an ailing, obese body, but to really pursue what it felt like to be released from that kind of toxicity. Sitting in the same place I started my journey a year ago, I closed my eyes and thanked God for never letting me go.

I had literally come full circle.

The Collapse

Decisions

After the fanfare died down that night, and all the feel-good congratulatory hugs from my crew at Shapes were generously given, I said my goodbyes for the evening and prepared to go home. As I drove out of the parking lot of the gym an ache of anxiety hit my belly. I had been in a warm and fuzzy state of mind, full of hopes for the future and the satisfaction of exceeding my weight loss goals. My body was in the best shape it had ever been in. My blood pressure was consistently stable, and I had tons energy to burn. I can't remember a time in my life when I ever felt as good.

From a physical standpoint I was stronger, but mentally I was still weakened. I had a different battle that needed my attention when I got home. Putting my foot down in terms of Darryl leaving the house was not going to be seamless. Darryl was supposed be gone a week ago, and he still hadn't mentioned a word about finding another place to live or so much as packed a bag yet. It was almost as if he was never a party to the conversation I had with him over a month ago. I knew the deadline had not slipped his mind. Not talking about it was a stall tactic, and at this point, I was very familiar with his strategies for delaying what he knew he had to do.

Nothing seemed out of the ordinary when I returned home. Denai was in her room yapping on the phone, and Johanna and Lanie were curled up around Darryl on the couch while they watched him play video games. After a round of my usual hugs and kisses for the girls and inquiring about school, I asked them to go to their rooms so that I could talk to their father. Darryl was no dummy. He knew where my strings were and how to pull them to get his desired result. "I made dinner, baby. The kids ate already, and Mama was glad she didn't have to cook. How was your day?" he purred.

"It was fine, thanks for cooking. What did you do today, Darryl?" I asked, to see if my suspicions would be on target. He let out a long, sigh before telling me that he had been trying to find work, and got a couple of leads that could be promising, which confirmed my suspicions about what his response would be. This wasn't the first time I had told Darryl that I wanted a separation and that he needed to leave. It was always the same scenario—I'd get hopeful, reconsider, and allow him to stay based on his promise to become more responsible and take his role of husband and father seriously. His promised proved to be hollow time after time. Hope turned into disappointment, followed by frustration.

Despite the false promises, I really loved Darryl and wanted us to work. The truth was he wanted this marriage to work too, but for reasons different than mine. I believe that perhaps some part of Darryl loved me, because I bore the only two children he ever had, but what he loved more was the fact that he could live without responsibilities. He didn't want to be an equal partner in our marriage; he was more comfortable being a spectator on the sidelines leaving all responsibility squarely on my shoulders.

Darryl continued with his spiel about his promising job prospects while I tried to figure out a way to tell him that his time was up, and that he'd have to leave. There was always a hint of hesitation that loomed whenever I was bold enough to speak up on my behalf with Darryl. He intimidated me. Although Darryl had never laid a hand on me in a violent manner, he still had a menacing demeanor nonetheless. He was about of 400 pounds, and had a bad temper when it came to him not getting his way. I saw how incensed he could get with others, and even with me, verbally. For those reasons I tried to choose my words carefully, although it really didn't matter at this point. Telling him he had to leave immediately would not go over well with him, period. I decided to go with the straight forward approach. No sense in mincing words.

"Darryl, your time here is expired, you need to leave today. I have been more than generous with extending my timeframe so that you could find someplace else to live. You can't live off my mother's good graces anymore. I won't allow you to use her that way." As if on cue, my voice began to shake as I spoke to him. I wanted so badly to say what I needed to say with strong conviction, but with Darryl, my articulations never came out that way. After I finished speaking, I took a few steps back and waited for the verbal backlash I knew I would receive from Darryl.

"Sue, I told you before, I don't have any place to go! Don't you understand that? But you don't care about that, huh? We have kids together, and you're just gonna kick their father out like that? I told you I got some jobs leads lined up, and when they call, I can start helping you out as soon as I can. I'm not gonna just live out in the street. You're just gonna have to wait until I find someplace to go before I leave here."

After loudly making his demands known, Darryl stormed into the bedroom and slammed the door. As I stood on the other side of the door, I was speechless. In the nine years that we had been married, there was one thing that Darryl knew about me above all else, and that was my inability to stand up for myself, especially when it came to him. He had become bold in his refusal to leave my mother's house, unlike the instances before where he'd pour on the "I love you" or "let's work this out" in order to get back into my good graces. His reply this time was full of defiant anger, as if he was had every right to stay there. His bold arrogance, although infuriating, was not surprising to me. It was amazing how he flipped in mere minutes from as sweet as a kitten, to an incensed lion, ready to pounce.

My mother, who was just upstairs listening to the confrontation, beckoned for me to come to where she was. "Sue, I heard everything," she said very calmly. True to form, my mother jumped into protective mode. Even in her illness, she kept a vigilant watch over me always. She kept herself just within reach upstairs, just in case I needed her intervention with Darryl. "I have the phone in my hand, and I am ready to call the police if he won't leave this house. I won't allow him to bully you into his staying here," she said with an icy tone while staring at my closed bedroom door where Darryl was.

Reluctant Departure

"I can take care of it, Mama," I said while walking back to my bedroom. I knew what I had to do, and I didn't want my mother taking care of the business I should be handling as if I were a child. I refused my mother's assistance and set out to complete what needed to be done with Darryl; however, that did not stop her from going with me to do it. When I went back downstairs to let Darryl know in no uncertain terms that he would have to leave immediately, my mother followed close behind me as if she was a hired bodyguard. "Mama, I'll be okay," I said, a bit annoyed at her insistence and over-protection.

"I KNOW you will be okay, because I am going to make sure you are." I understood her insistence but still bothered by it none the less. It was me who initiated this prolonged living arrangement in her house, and it should've been me who put the brakes on Darryl's free "stay-cation" there.

I didn't know what to expect when I walked nervously through my bedroom door. Darryl's angry response a few minutes before made me even more nervous in confronting him yet again. I walked into the room with my mother a few steps behind me, phone in hand.

Lying on his back and looking up at the ceiling, Darryl turned toward me and my mother as we entered the room.

"Sue, I've already told you, I don't have anywhere to go, what you want me to do?" he said as his eyes darted from my mother to me. Darryl's mannerisms and voice were noticeably more subdued than just a few minutes earlier as he made his case. My mother chomped at the bit to say what she wanted to say to him, and not mincing words in the process.

"Darryl, if Sue wants you to leave, you need to leave. This is my house, and ultimately the decision is mine as to who lives here. I am prepared to make sure that the police know that you are an unwelcome guest here. You have had ample time to make arrangements. You need to leave today." My mother always exuded an authoritative demeanor when necessary; I admired her greatly for that. In spite of prolonged illness, she still remained tough as nails. I appreciated her support, but I needed to step up to do I needed to do, even if I was uncertain of my ability to carry it out.

"Darryl, I can't do this anymore with you. You need to leave," I said as I carefully listened out for the girls, who were in the backyard playing. With the possibility of police intervention now becoming part of the equation, Darryl was persuaded to change his tune.

"I'll be at my mother's house. I'll get my things later." He brushed past my mother and me to reach for his cell phone to call his brother to pick him up. He didn't say another word, except to tell Lanie and Johanna that he would see them soon.

"Where are you going, Daddy?" Lanie said to Darryl as he grabbed some of his clothes and stuffed them into a duffle bag.

"Mommy will tell you why I'm leaving, sweetie," he said, briefly looking at me for one last shot of sympathetic drama before he left out of the door.

That evening, Darryl moved out of my mother's house, or at least he did physically. He left the majority of his clothes and shoes and a pile of laundry behind, but it didn't matter. That night I felt like a load of bricks had been lifted from my shoulders. There would be bad blood between us after that night. Darryl's behavior toward me became increasingly unpleasant to say the least. His tone was rough when he demanded to speak to "his kids" whenever he would call the house. The next few days I would attempt to explain to Lanie and Johanna why Darryl was no longer living with us, which was a difficult challenge. As for Denai, she appeared unaffected and perhaps a bit relieved herself. Her only reply was, "Oh."

My future was uncertain in terms of whether or not I would ask for a divorce from Darryl. We had been together for almost ten years, and although there were some bright spots, most of my memories were of broken promises, and a lack of regard for me. Be that as it may, I still hoped that somehow our separation would give him incentive to get his life together and realize that his family needed him to step up to the plate.

At every opportunity Darryl played the sympathy card by telling me how the girls were suffering because he wasn't there, while systematically preparing a pathway back to my mother's house. Guilt consumed me daily. Guilt from the church about my considering divorce, guilt from Darryl to sway my decision about our separation, and now serious concern about my sister, mother, and more recently, my father's declining health. It seemed as if I was either in the emergency room with my mother for her dangerously high blood pressure, or going with my father to the hospital after he was diagnosed with prostate cancer.

I continued to go to the gym as a way to ward off stress, but to my dismay, when I came home at night, the reemergence of my GAD began to make its rounds again. The terrifying episodes that I thought were in my past were back with a vengeance. I resumed taking doses of Xanax again to get me through the night, and occasionally through the day, too. Working at the law firm was challenging in and of itself, and the pressure to perform well in my new and unfamiliar position took its mental toll. I found myself in the break room of my office praying and crying that my GAD would subside, and sometimes it did. But when the episodes became too intense, I was forced to leave work in the middle of the day. Wearing a thin façade of normal on the outside, I felt like an absolute basket case on the inside.

I looked forward to "normal" days where everybody felt reasonably all right, and the girls were content. My mind was filled with so much emotional clutter, that it was a treat whenever I had a chance to get together with Nikki to talk about anything other than my chaos. Before I knew it, the time had come for us to prepare for her bachelorette trip to the Bahamas. It would be Darryl's weekend with the kids at his mother's house, and my family was well enough for me to leave without being too worried about them while I was away. A mini vacation could not have come at a better time. Excited would be a mild description of how I felt on the days and hours leading up to our bachelorette getaway to the beautiful islands of the Bahamas.

Brenda's Call

It had been a long time since I was this excited about anything. Nikki's all-girl getaway seemed like the perfect antidote to all the intensity that was going on in my life with my family. I was 140 pounds lighter and ready to meet the island natives with vigor and exuberance. This would be the trip of a lifetime and I couldn't wait to get started. Nikki's mother rented a limousine for us to travel to the airport to catch our flight, which was exciting in itself. The only limousine I had ever ridden in was the one that the funeral home provided when my uncle John died years ago. I was to meet Nikki at her Mom's house down the street at exactly 5:30 a.m. I barely slept the night before just so I wouldn't oversleep. Visions of palm trees, steel drums, and white sand beaches danced in my head like Mikhail Baryshnikov on Broadway. I might have slept an hour, maybe.

That morning I made a checklist of everything that I would take along with me. With all my meticulous inspections of my essential items like my passport, I.D.s, and clothes, I realized that I had only a few minutes to get to Nikki's house for our ride to the airport. My cell phone rang with Nikki on the other end inquiring why I hadn't gotten to her house yet. "You gotta be here in like, five minutes Sue," Nikki said not so calmly.

I grabbed my suitcase and purse as I dashed to the front door, but stopped short of opening it when I realized I'd forgotten something. In my frenzied rush, I forgot to tell my sister and Mama goodbye. For a split second, I had an internal conversation trying to decide whether to just call them on the way to the airport, or run back inside to tell them goodbye. Something within me urged me to go back inside, so I did, in a hurry.

I literally ran to my mother's room to find her sleeping soundly. I kissed her on the forehead and whispered in her ear, "I love you, Mama, I'm leaving now. I gotta run, but I just wanted to give you a kiss before I left." I am not sure if she even heard me, but I felt better that I said it. I figured I would call her when it was a little

Brenda's Call

later in the morning. The girls were with Darryl at his mom's, which meant that there was one more kiss I had to plant before I would be officially late for the limo to the airport. I ran downstairs to Brenda's darkened apartment and made a zig-zag dash to her bedroom, luckily unscathed by the obstacle course which was her living room, with all her knick-knacks and end tables situated throughout.

When I got to Brenda's door it was slightly cracked. I tiptoed into her room so as not to startle her out of sleep. I leaned over her bed and ever so gently hugged her as she lay there. "Hey Bren, sorry to wake you, but I just wanted to tell you I'm about to go. I wanted to tell you I love you before I left for my trip," I whispered as I kissed her forehead, which seemed unusually warm. She slowly opened her eyes and smiled at me.

"Okay, baby, have a good time. You deserve it. Have fun, but don't act a fool, you are too far away for me to come bail you out of Bahama jail." We both laughed for a moment, and then I noticed Brenda wincing as if something pained her. Brenda was sick more than she was well most of the time, and I knew it. She never wanted anyone to worry about her, but her facial expression always told the truth.

"How do you feel, Bren?" I asked, concerned and briefly forgetting that I had somewhere I had to go.

"I'm okay. Get on outta here before you get left behind now. I love you too, baby. Have a good time, and I will see you when you get back. Don't worry about anything, just go and have fun," she said softly.

"Okay. I will bring you back something really pretty…turquoise something, okay?" I said as I turned to leave. Before closing her door, I waved to Brenda and blew her a kiss. "See you when I get back."

"Okay, baby, see you soon," I heard Brenda say in the distance as I ran back upstairs and out the door to meet Nikki and our limo.

The next day, all settled in and taking in the beauty of Nassau, Nikki and I made plans to hit the beach and a couple of other tourist attractions. Nikki and I marveled at each other as we revealed our swimsuits to each other, our mutual weight loss and sculpted curves apparent. "We look gooooood!" I said as we both modeled in the full-length hotel mirror, admiring our new and improved smaller figures.

"Yeah, we do!" Nikki declared while twirling around to survey her smaller backside.

I hadn't been in a swimsuit since I was a little girl, and was a bit more hesitant to go out in public with one on, especially now that I had flaccid skin just about everywhere due to the weight loss. I tugged on the apron of skin around my midsection, stretching it out like chewed bubble gum in the mirror as my face curled into a frown. "This loose skin though, Nik, ugh."

"Girl, who cares…we are out of the United States, we don't know anybody here, and I ain't taking a camera…show those thighs off and shake what ya Mama gave ya!" Nikki retorted as we both giggled uncontrollably.

"Yeah, yeah…I think I will do just that," I said as I confidently put my hands on my hips and did a vigorous and very animated wiggle in front of Nikki, my loose skin flopping in one direction, and me in the other. We both laughed so hard that tears ran down our cheeks. With all things that weighed so heavily on my mind back home, it was an incredible release to laugh so hard until my stomach ached. It felt so good.

I happened to looked down to see my sister's gold hoop earrings that I borrowed sitting by my beach towel on the side of the bed. Just then I remembered that I hadn't called her yet to let her know we made it to the islands and that all was well. Between all the excitement of checking in at such a beautiful hotel and hamming it up in front of the mirror with our swimsuits on, I completely forgot to call.

"Before we leave for the beach, I need to call home to let Brenda and Mama know we made it okay," I said as I wrapped my beach towel around my waist and grabbed my cell phone. My eyes bulged a bit when the operator told me that I would be charged $5.50 a minute to call home from where we were, so needless to say, my intentions were to be on the line just long enough to let them know I was okay. As the static of the phone line popped in my ear, I hoped that Brenda would pick up the phone soon. It was a Saturday afternoon, which meant that Brenda should have been up and around, but it took an unusually long time for her to answer. After what seemed like a million rings, Brenda answered the phone sounding like she was underwater. Her voice was garbled, and she sounded as if she had been crying.

"Hey Bren, I just wanted to tell you and Mama that Nikki and I made it to the hotel, and that we are fine. But it sounds like you aren't doing so good, what's wrong?" I asked as Nikki stopped adjusting her swimsuit to look at me with concern.

"What's wrong?" she whispered to me, walking closer to the bed where I was standing.

"I don't know, we have a terrible connection and I can barely hear her" I said, shaking my head while holding my hand over the receiver. "Brenda...are you okay? What's wrong with you?" I asked again, hearing nothing but the popping static from the bad connection we had.

"Hey Sue, I don't know…my head hurts really, really bad. I've had headaches before, but not like this one." Brenda said, speaking slowly and sounding confused.

"This is a terrible connection we have, Bren, but it sounds like you are crying."

"No, I'm okay, I will be okay. Enjoy your trip. I'm glad you made it okay," she said, trying her best to hide the obvious pain she was in.

"I know Mama is at work today, but Jessica can take you to the E.R. It's probably your blood pressure that's elevated. They will give you something to bring down your pressure. Maybe your doctor needs to adjust your meds again."

Jessica, Brenda's best friend, worked close by and would've gladly taken Brenda anywhere she needed to go. I was concerned, but not overly so; Brenda suffered frequent migraines that were usually remedied with an adjustment to her blood pressure meds or lying off salt for a while. This wouldn't be the first time that she had to go for an emergency room visit for issues with elevated blood pressure or for problems related to her dialysis treatments; in fact, it was becoming more frequent. The E.R. doctors would give her the meds she needed, and she would be at home and feeling better in no time, I thought.

"As soon as we get off the phone, give Jess a call and she will take you to the emergency room. I will call you back in a couple of hours to check on you. You will be just fine, just take it easy when you get back home and lay off that salt ...okay?" I said as I picked up my sunglasses off of the dresser and signaled Nikki to grab hers so that we could leave out.

"Okay, I will. Talk to you soon, I love you, baby," Brenda said so softly that I could barely hear her.

"I love you too, Bren," I replied, hanging up the phone with a growing heaviness that filled my heart for my big sister. I hated that she suffered so much. She was always going through some sort of health crisis, but she always managed to bounce back, and this time would be no different, I thought as I grabbed my flip-flops to put them on.

"What's wrong with Brenda?" Nikki asked as she did one final check of her backside in the mirror.

"She will be okay, just a really bad headache, she gets them a lot. Jess is going to take her to the E.R. and they will give her something to lower her pressure. I bet she has been at the salt again. I am gonna call her as soon as we get back. By then she should be home." Nikki and I both walked out of our hotel room eager to dig our feet in the beautiful white sand at the nearby beach resort. Before locking the door, I looked at the phone to remind myself to call as soon as we returned from the beach and check on Brenda.

An hour and a half later, we burst back into our hotel room with sand between our toes and loud tipsy giggles, ready to hit some more spots on the island. Nikki and I threw our wet towels and sand-filled sarongs in the corner of the room while figuring out who would use the shower and change into dry clothes first. "Okay, Miss Bachelorette extraordinaire, you go first. I have to call to check on Brenda," I said as I riffled through my suitcase to locate my tightest fitting girdle and to pick out which outfit the island natives would see me in first. The sound of my ringing cell phone startled me to my feet. I wondered who in the world would be calling me all the way in Nassau unless there was some sort of emergency at home. I looked at the phone, hoping it wasn't about the girls being sick, or that there was something wrong with Mama.

"Hey Sue, its Wayne, where are you right now?" Wayne sounded completely unlike himself, his tone unusually serious.

"I'm in my hotel room, Wayne, why what's up? Oh, did Brenda make it home from the emergency room yet? I was just about to call her before you called," I said as I anticipated him telling me that all was well and that Brenda was resting.

"That's why I'm calling, Sue. It's Brenda. She is not good, you need to come home. She's—

Brenda went into a coma."

It boggles the mind how your body can go from relaxed to tight and tense in a matter of seconds. I felt my legs turn to jello as they began to shake where I was standing. I told myself I didn't hear him right. I told myself that even though the phone had a clear connection, that somehow I didn't hear him correctly.

"What? Coma? How?...Why?" I heard my voice becoming escalated as Nikki ran out of the bathroom with just her towel on, trying to assess the situation.

"Sue, listen to me carefully," Wayne instructed over the phone as I stood in the middle of the room, scared out of my mind as to what he was about to say. I had only heard my brother Wayne cry two times in my life; once when our uncle John died, and the other as he sang The Commodores classic *"Three Times a Lady"* to my mother, one Mother's Day several years prior. Wayne never displayed emotions to that degree, so when I heard his voice cracking into sobs over the phone; I honestly didn't want to hear anything he was going to tell me after that.

"Brenda never came home from the hospital, Sue…she suffered a brain aneurysm. She is on life support right now. Brenda went into a coma and never came out of it. She's…she's…gone. Brenda is gone, Sue."

Wayne burst into tears on the phone, completely inconsolable. Brenda and Wayne were close as twins growing up. They were each other's best friend. He was the younger of the two of them, but he fiercely watched over Brenda like big brother would. He adored her. She was everything to him, just as she was to me. In the background I heard the distraught voices of my nephew Wayne, Brenda's only son whom she named after our brother. I could only imagine what my mother was through. I knew she was completely devastated.

I still couldn't wrap my mind around what Wayne had just told me. Coma? Life Support?...Gone?

Everything seemed as if it was happening in slow motion, just like in a dramatic scene in a movie. Still on the line with Wayne, I felt my hand drop the phone as my body collapsed to the ground. It was as if someone punched me in the stomach. I faintly heard Nikki asking me what happened over and over again, but I couldn't speak. It was almost as if my vocal cords had become paralyzed. In complete denial, I hunkered in the middle of the room. All I could hear were my own screams. I saw Nikki's mouth moving, but I couldn't make out what she was saying. She immediately picked up the phone and resumed the conversation with an equally distraught Wayne. After a few minutes, she hung up the phone.

Despite the strange disconnect in our friendship as of late, that fateful day in a hotel room halfway across the world and away from everyone that I loved, Nikki lay on the floor with me and held me in her arms while my heart broke into tiny pieces. My only sister, whom I loved so very much, had died. To make matters worse, I was thousands of miles away from Chicago, and unable to be there to grieve with family. Even more heartbreaking, I couldn't physically be there with my Brenda, just to see her face. As I became submerged in a heap of inconsolable tears, Nikki displayed the kind of compassion and sympathy that only a close friend could provide. She rocked me in her arms and cried with me as if she personally connected with my pain. What started as a fulfilling weekend to celebrate her upcoming nuptials turned out to be a weekend steeped in great mourning and sadness for me.

After what seemed like hours, Nikki, still in her bath towel, helped me to my feet and we both sat on the bed. "Sue, we have to hurry back to Chicago. Wayne told me that although your sister is on life support now, the doctors will have to take her off in a few days in order to harvest her organs while they are still salvageable. It's the rules of the hospital." Brenda was incredibly generous with whatever she had to offer, until the very end of her life. It was typical "Brenda behavior" that she would make arrangements to donate any of her healthy organs to those in need in the event of her death. "Wayne told me that we should get back as soon as possible. The hospital agreed to wait twenty-four hours before they disconnect Brenda's machine," Nikki explained while still holding my hand.

"Brenda's Machine." It sounded so foreign, so wrong. I still couldn't wrap my mind around all that was happening. I just saw Brenda earlier in the day. I just kissed her and told her I loved her and that I was bringing her back something pretty. I was so glad that while touring the area, I had picked up a beautiful necklace for Brenda made of genuine turquoise stones from a local straw market. I started to wait to pick something up for her, now I know why I hadn't. I made up in my mind that I would still give Brenda that necklace, just as I promised. I looked over at the necklace I bought for her just a few hours earlier. It looked just like a piece of jewelry she would wear proudly; I could actually see her eyes sparkling and her beautiful smile as she put it on. As I imagined her beautiful face in my mind's eye, my eyes burned from trying to create tears where there were no more. Never in my life had I experienced a pain as great as that of the sudden death of my sister Brenda. The rest of the day, both Nikki and I packed up our things and tried to figure out how we would get back to Chicago quickly.

Nikki's mother, whose professional circle included some influence, managed to pull a few strings to secure a flight back to Chicago the next day. After our return flight, I didn't have long to make it to the hospital before they took Brenda off of life support. The hospital was about thirty minutes away from the airport, and that was with good traffic. All of my family kept watch and surrounded Brenda's bedside. Because each and every moment with her was precious for all of us, I didn't want to disturb the time that they had left with Brenda. I needed a ride to the hospital, and fast. I immediately called Darryl and hoped that he would at least have heart enough to take me to see my sister before it was too late.

Darryl and I weren't exactly on speaking terms ever since he was told that he had to pack up and leave my mother's house. I crossed my fingers in hopes that maybe he wanted to see his sister-in-law too, before she officially passed on. Darryl and Brenda had a pretty good relationship, and unlike my mother, Brenda tolerated Darryl a bit more than the rest of my family. Nikki offered to take me to the hospital, but I declined her offer. In my heart, I held out hope that my husband would want to take a moment to say goodbye too. I called him and he immediately answered the phone with his usual aggravated tone when he heard my voice. "Yes?"

I tried my best to pull my emotions together enough to talk without breaking down. The whole flight home, I couldn't even answer the stewardess when she asked me if I wanted something to drink without breaking down crying.

"Hey, Darryl, it's me. Um, I need a favor, please," I said, swallowing hard.

In true Darryl fashion, his answered was dripping with unnecessary sarcasm. "Favor? Oh, now you want a favor from ME? After you kicked me out of your house, NOW you want me to do a favor for you? Aren't you supposed to be out of town anyway?"

Brenda's Call

I started to hang up the phone, but instead I continued my train of thought and just blurted out what I was calling for. "Brenda is on life support. She is being kept alive by a machine. The hospital is waiting on me to get there. I need to get there, Darryl. Please help me get to my sister before she dies. I need to say goodbye to her before she dies." Before I finished, a rush of tears muddled the last part of what I said to him. I didn't even know if he heard it all, but by his reaction, I believed he did.

"Oh no, Sue. No, no, no Sue. Oh my God…what, how did this happen? I'm so sorry, I'm sorry," Darryl said as he began to cry too. "I am on my way. I will be in my mother's car…I am on my way. I will be there in less than fifteen minutes." His voice cracked.

"I don't have much time left to see her before they pull her plug. Please hurry," I said as I wiped my eyes with my hand. I heard Darryl hang up before I even finished.

In less than fifteen minutes, as promised, Darryl was sitting in his mother's car in front of the airport terminal waiting for me. I was surprised that he was there. It was one of the only times that he was truly there when I needed him to be. I was grateful to see him there. Darryl flew like lightening on the expressway. I have no idea how he turned a thirty minute drive into a ten minute one, but we arrived at the hospital sooner than anticipated with about seven minutes to spare.

We ran down the hallway and through the wards to get to the intensive care unit. I saw my mother first, then my brother as they came out of Brenda's room to greet me and Darryl. Denai was there with the rest of the family. She ran over to me and hugged me tightly, and whispered, "I'm so glad you made it, Mommy." Darryl and I both decided that Lanie and Johanna weren't prepared to see their aunt whom they loved so much in that state, so we opted to keep them with Darryl's mother. I ran into my mother's arms just as I did when I was little and needed her comfort. I hugged my nephew and looked into his blood-shot puffy eyes to kiss him on the forehead. I greeted my brother, who had wandered off by himself and was looking out of a window, with a tight embrace for several minutes as we both silently cried together.

"Brenda is in the room right there," Wayne pointed as he wiped his face with his other hand. All of us—Mama, Wayne, Wayne II, Denai, and Darryl—all went into the room together to see and talk to Brenda one last time.

When I walked in, I was immediately taken aback by Brenda's appearance. I barely recognized her. Her slender, beautiful face had blown up to three times its size from the swelling in her brain. Her lips and eyes were darkened and puffy, her head wrapped in a huge white bandage as a result of the emergency surgery performed to try to stop the hemorrhaging in her brain. There were several tubes that were sticking out of her thin body as she lay there, lifeless.

I never felt my body so numb, from my shoulders to my feet I was frozen in the spot where I stood. All I could think about was the last time I saw her, in her bedroom where I told her I would see her soon. It wouldn't be soon though; in fact, I would never see her again. I hated myself for going on that trip. My mind ran through all of the should'ves, would'ves, and could'ves. If I had only stayed in Chicago, maybe I could have done something. I could have gotten her to the hospital quicker. I blamed myself over and over again for not being there for my sister when she needed me, the same way she was always there for me when I needed her.

"She only has a few minutes left, Sue, you can go over to her you know," Mama said as the rest of the family gather around in a semi-circle around Brenda's bedside. Besides the buzz of the machines that kept Brenda breathing, the deafening sound of silence draped the room as great sorrow gripped each heart that surrounded her. I inched toward my sister as I looked at her unrecognizable face. If this would be my last moments with her, I would tell her all about my trip, just as I would if we were both back home and chatting over a cup of coffee.

I sat on the edge of her hospital bed as I pulled the turquoise necklace I bought for her in Nassau out of my pocket. I held her chilled hand and gently rubbed it back and forth. I needed to get closer to her. All of a sudden, it was as if it was just her and me in the room together, a little sister talking to her big sister. I moved my body closer to hers and positioned myself to be able to lay on her chest for a moment, just like I had when I was in the throes of an anxiety attack, and came to her for solace. I closed my eyes and told Brenda about the flight to the Bahamas and about the great time Nikki and I had preparing to go to the beach. I told Brenda all about the island men and how they love American women it seemed. I told her about the foods I tried and about the cute little boy that danced like Michael Jackson so that the tourists would give him money in the straw market. I laughed and talked to my big sister just like I planned to do when I got home.

"Oh, and I brought this necklace for you too, Bren! It's beautiful. Remember when I told you I would bring you something turquois back? Here it is!" I told her as I looked up at her with tears in my eyes, but with a smile on my face. I placed the necklace in her hand and placed my hand over hers. "This is yours; I want you to keep it, Bren…I love you, Bren, I love you, please don't leave me…please don't leave me. Please…"

I couldn't contain my emotions anymore. I lay there with my sister, holding her hand and crying for her until the doctors came in and told me us it was time for us to say our final goodbyes. I thanked God that he allowed me to get home in order to see her one last time, and to kiss her one last time. I couldn't come to grips with why God chose for me to be out of the country as my sister fought so hard for her life. It left me wondering why He would take someone that was so kind and who gave so much joy to everyone around her. It didn't seem fair that God didn't save her long enough to see her son continue to grow as a man. It didn't seem fair that He left me without the one person who never judged me, even if I was dead wrong. She was my advocate, and more than a sister. Brenda was my truest and most loyal friend. I never knew sorrow ran that deeply. I walked out of the room and blew Brenda one final kiss for the last time.

I thanked Darryl for taking me to the hospital and told him I would see him when he dropped the girls off in a few days. We embraced for the first time in a very long time. He hugged me tight and I hugged him tighter. "I'll talk to you soon," I said as I let go, reluctantly.

"Okay, talk soon. Sue, I am so very sorry, babe," he said, his eyes red from crying. I jumped in the car with Wayne, Denai, and Mama to head back to a different household. I would have the job of painstakingly sorting through Brenda's belongings and packing them up. Mama wasn't up to doing it, which I completely understood. After that day, I checked on Mama and made sure she was okay, but there was a silence in the house that spoke volumes as to how we all felt. Lanie and Johanna were devastated after learning that Auntie Brenda wasn't coming back to live with us anymore, and that she would now live in Heaven with God. I felt funny trying to explain something to my daughters that I could barely explain myself as to why Brenda didn't bounce back like she always did. I felt unequipped to explain why their auntie Brenda had to die.

That night I asked for Darryl to come back to the house, and he did. I needed comforting, and he gave it. Soon he was over all the time, and even started spending nights there. The nights turned into weeks, and before I knew it, he was back full-time at the house, unbeknownst to my mother, who never knew that he was spending so much time there. He'd come in late after she went to sleep and stay in the basement until she went to her dialysis treatments. He couldn't have been happier, and neither could I, until the same issues began to rear their ugly head once more. He would get a job, then within months, lose it. Then he'd take a long hiatus from looking for another one, blaming it on everything from the economy to his record, which he still hadn't gotten expunged, even when presented with the opportunity to have it done for free. It was business as usual, the same old song and dance of making excuses.

Here I was in the same boat with the same holes in it, and like before, I felt as if I were drowning. I hated the fact that I had let Darryl back into my heart and fell for his same tricks. I found myself eating more than I usually did. I was still going to the gym, but slacking off on my healthier diet. I found that the foods that used to give me so much solace came in handy whenever I would think about Brenda or stress about marriage. More and more, I ate instead of working out. Shapes began to see less and less of me as the months went on.

When it Rains...it Pours.

Darryl moving slowly moving back into the house wasn't the only thing that had changed since Brenda's death. My mother's health began to decline rapidly as well. I don't believe she really ever got over Brenda's death, if such a thing is even possible. As her health deteriorated, my mother was forced to quit her job, a position that she absolutely loved, but was no longer able to handle the physical demand of. The plucky, spirited temperament that we all loved so was gradually diminishing. Unlike the mother I knew, who loved to cook and go shopping for deals on the weekends, she barely left the house anymore and rarely got out of bed except to go to and from her doctor visits and dialysis treatments.

My mother's physical appearance changed as well. Once a healthy size 14-16, she dropped rather quickly in weight, and her appearance became increasingly gaunt and drawn. Her cigarette smoking escalated, and disturbingly so, which didn't do her rapidly declining health any favors.

Seven months after my sister died, my mother had another stroke. This time, the stroke left her weakened on the left side of her body and barely able to use her hand. She had great difficulty speaking as well. When my mother returned from the hospital after the stroke, she was barely able to walk and dress herself. My brother Wayne and his wife Tessa, who had their own house and family, split their time between their home and ours to help care for Mama. When her daytime care became an issue, a part-time nurse looked after Mama during the day while I worked. In the evenings I helplessly watched my mother, who had been the quintessential essence of Superwoman in every sense of the word, slowly morph into a weakened shell of her former self. With the passing of Brenda, the vigor within my moth Aware that we had less than twenty minutes to get to there, never fully returned. It was as if part of her soul died the day she had to bury her eldest and dearly beloved child.

With all that was revolving in my world, my stress levels were at their peak. Between worrying almost obsessively about my mother, the kids, and our household bills, I found myself eating a lot more and popping more Xanax to cope with my reality. Feelings of peace and contentment eluded my thoughts, and in their place were uncertainty, and the re-emergence of paralyzing fear.

In the meantime Darryl, who had practically moved back in, was still popping in and out of employment whenever it suited him. Yet something within me still desperately wanted to draw out what he had the possibility to be. I still loved him, and I wanted with all my heart to foster the competence I believed Darryl possessed. I wanted the abilities I saw in him to shine for his sake. I encouraged him to look into creating a business of his own, since working set hours and adhering to a schedule given by a supervisor obviously wasn't appealing to him. Of all the talents Darryl had, cooking was his area of expertise, and he was a natural at it. I suggested that he look into getting a small restaurant specializing in barbeque.

Whenever we had barbeques, dozens of people would ask if he ever considered opening a restaurant highlighting his superior grill skills. With Darryl's natural culinary talent combined with his gift of gab, operating his own food establishment had all the makings of a very worthwhile and profitable venture. I was ready and willing to make sacrifices and assist financially to make it a reality.

Ultimately, I was more excited about his future than he was. Every idea I gave him was either shot down or riddled with excuses. From home catering, to even purchasing a food cart just to get his name and brand out there, Darryl had reasons why it wouldn't work. He didn't so much as lift a finger to make a phone call to investigate any of the possibilities. His indifference left me feeling sour on the inside and ready to give up entirely. I didn't have the energy anymore, I just didn't. "I can't want more for you than you want for yourself, Darryl," I told him as I retreated, my words seemingly going in one ear and out the other. My disappointment in him began to transform into disgust.

Whoever made up the saying "When it rains it pours" wasn't lying. My family was coming apart at the seams. In the midst of caring for my mother and figuring out how to rob Peter to pay Paul with regard to the kids' needs and the household bills, my father's health took a sudden turn for the worst after suffering a massive heart attack. I received a call from my uncle, who told me that my dad was in a coma. I was devastated, to say the least. My dad had just received a cancer diagnosis a few months prior, and he was still dealing with the effects of it. Now here was yet another blow to his already fragile health.

My father and I had always been close; I had his mannerisms and his temperament as well. I loved him dearly, and I could not bear to think of him dying, especially after the emotional blow I just took from my sister passing not long before. In the midst of trial after trial, I leaned on my old habit of eating until I forgot what was troubling me. Soon I began gaining the weight I had lost. My scale seemed like it was going in reverse. My job performance began to slip; I began getting reprimands for inferior work due to my lack of concentration. Deadlines were missed, and I felt all control slipping away from me in every area of my life. The only peace I seemed to find was when I prayed for God's intervention in my circumstances. I couldn't connect the dots anymore; everything that was solid in my life had turned to quicksand.

My mother was a pistol even in her sickness; she wasn't exactly the kind of patient who did as she was instructed to do. With her left side just about immobile, she still managed to sneak cigarettes to smoke. How she hid them so well, I'll never know. She had also become very frail and weak because she had lost an interest in eating right after her stroke. To keep her strength up and to put some weight back on her, her doctor suggested that she drink nutritional shakes. Getting her to drink the shakes was nearly impossible. Realizing that her independence was slipping away from her, she began to refuse just about every thing we asked her

When it Rains...It Pours.

to do, from getting dressed to curbing her cigarette smoking. Every request was met with defiance, and as frustrating as it was, I totally understood why she was putting up such a fight with all of us.

My mother had been an independent woman all her life. Coming to grips with the fact that she needed to depend on others for the simplest of tasks, including personal ones like going to the bathroom and bathing, was very difficult for her, and left her feeling demoralized. Her frustration sometimes came out as anger for those of us caring for her. It broke my heart to see my mother so fragile in both body and mind. There were some nights when I heard her crying in her room because she couldn't reach for her remote control or get the glass of water by her bedside. As trying as it was for us, it was far worse for her. The state of her health after her stroke spiraled further and further downward, and across town in an intensive care ward, so did my father's.

In the days that followed, I spent my nights eating large amounts of leftovers, figuring out which bills I could pay, and listening for my mother call for me to help her go to the bathroom. Darryl, who had become increasingly difficult to spite me, went from dangling the promise of helping me get what the kids needed to "forgetting" to give me the money on a regular basis. After finding out that his unemployment was extended for the third time, I finally filed for child support. When he realized that a small portion of his check was being taken out for the support, he was livid, and the arguments between him and I ensued. He thought it unfair that I filed for child support.

"I need to live off that money, Sue!" He argued. The fact that he was also financially responsible for the care of our daughters was a non-issue with him. They were MY responsibility. Darryl created a world with the girls that included sporadic weekend visits at his mother's house with him, and then dropping them back off with a gallon of juice and a couple bags of potato chips. He would ignore my requests for essentials like school supplies and assistance with school uniforms. I knew how much Darryl made when he worked with Chris a few years prior. I knew that his unemployment checks were more than substantial to help out with the few items I asked him to purchase. I knew without question his motive behind insisting on making life as difficult as possible for me; he wanted payback for kicking him out of his cozy arrangement at my mother's house.

The proof was solidified when the girls started coming home behaving differently toward me after visiting with their father, almost as if there was subtle persuasion taking place during their visit. Johanna was the least affected because she was so much younger, but there was a marked difference in Lanie, and it troubled me greatly. Guilt began to take its toll again; I didn't want my children to suffer and be manipulated into thinking that I was the awful mother who kicked their father out with no place to go. I began to wonder if it would be better if I just surrendered. I was so

When it Rains…It Pours.

tired of fighting with Darryl. With all that was transpiring with my seriously ill father, whose prognosis was bleak, and my heart and mind weighed down heavily with my mother's situation, I simply didn't have the energy anymore. Fearing that drug addiction was looming, I found no other relief besides my bottle of Xanax. I recall getting on my knees in desperation when my last pill fell to the tiled floor of my bathroom and cracked into tiny pieces. All I could think of was getting as much of that pill as I could to take, because it was the last one. My bottle of Xanax was my escape from a world that felt like it was eating me up alive from the inside out.

I needed another release besides my resurrected desire for eating, and my growing fixation to Xanax to keep me rational. I began to feel incredibly guilty about my overeating and slacking off at the gym. To offset the damage, I stopped eating altogether which dropped my blood sugar to dangerously low levels. In exchange for overindulging in food, I turned to my frequent go-to, my Xanax as an alternative. When I feared becoming too dependent on the drug, I went back to overeating. This cycle became my everyday existence.

The concerned voicemails from Shelly and Sasha asking why they hadn't seen me at the gym lately went unanswered. I didn't want to talk to anyone. The muscular definition diminished significantly on my arms, my stomach began to protrude, and my thighs had trouble fitting into my pants. It became obvious that I was slowly gaining weight again. With all that I worked so hard for, and with all that I accomplished with my weight loss, in many ways I felt as if I was back to square one.

The Heartache

Social Media Medicine (200)

While trying to focus on my daily duties at work, I couldn't help but to overhear my co-workers loudly chattering in the cubicles next to me about some social website I had never heard of. They were rattling on about the happenings that took place in the various "rooms" on this site, and how entertaining it was. The name of the website was called Chat-Spot. Chat-Spot was a social website with a community of members who were interested in shooting the breeze about whatever. I decided I would check it out to see if it was all it was cracked up to be.

After visiting my father at the hospital, I came home to see a note on the kitchen refrigerator. Brenda's best friend and my self-appointed god-sister Jessica had come to pick up the girls for a sleepover at her house, to give me a bit of a break. Jessie was the best; Mama, Wayne, and I weren't the only ones still mourning the loss of our Brenda, Jessica was too. Brenda's death was a huge blow for her. For a long time, Jessica couldn't say Brenda's name without bursting into tears. She and Brenda had been best friends for over thirty years, and we all considered Jessica family.

Mama's caregiver had given her a bath and made sure she was fed before leaving for the evening. I tiptoed into my mother's room to find her sleeping soundly. I breathed a huge sigh of relief as I walked through the quiet stillness of the house. Dropping my purse on the bed, I looked at my bottle of Xanax, which was almost empty, and decided that I would try to hold off on them for as long as I could. My horrible anxiety attacks usually flared up as soon as I took my coat off in the evening. The best way to describe what happens during a GAD flare-up is to imagine yourself descending into a pit of torment for about fifteen minutes. The sweaty palms, dizziness, confusion, pounding headache, and uncontrollable shaking are just a few of the highlights. As soon as my foot hit the door of my bedroom, my next motion was to reach for my medicine bottle. I couldn't pop the pill in my mouth fast enough. Silence seemed to accelerate my panic episodes for some odd reason. My television served as my neutralizer, distracting me from the commotion inside my head.

With no intention of watching it, I turned my TV up loudly as I made my way over to my computer. I typed "Chat Spot" into the search engine to see what all the buzz was about. I immediately got to work creating a profile and searched for a decent picture of myself to put on my member page. I'd always been told that I had my mother's beautifully shaped eyes, so I chose the moniker "EYEZ" as my screen name. I snooped around the site a bit, going through the various chat rooms that were sectioned by age groups. I popped into each room until I saw a thread of conversation that interested me. In the 40s room, there were more mature people who chatted about everything from food to travel to sex, and everything in between. I wasn't interested in the sexual chatter, which there was plenty of. Because I was brand new at chatting online, I really didn't know what to talk about, or what to expect, so I just observed the various conversations between members.

In each room, there was a screen on the left side listing the members who were currently in that particular room. There were about 120 members in the 40s room, so I was quite surprised when I received a private message from a member named "TBTC".

TBTC: Hello Sue, are you new here? I haven't seen you in the 40s room before, I would have remembered you.

I really didn't know how to respond. I didn't know if he was flirting or simply being gracious by welcoming a new member. I kept my guard up and answered straightforwardly:

EYEZ: Hello and yes, I am new here.

I had heard about the jokers on Chat Spot from the girls at my office. I shook my head in disgust as I heard the tales they told about married men in the rooms trying to get some side action from the desperate women online. I kept myself guarded so as not to get too friendly with anyone initially, but as time went on, I really liked visiting the 40s room. In fact, I became a regular in the 40s room after a few weeks. Chat Spot kept my mind off the chaos with Darryl and the worries about my mother and father. When the kids were fed and Mama was tucked away in her bed, you could find me in the 40s room on Chat-Spot, joining in the conversations and even making friends with some of the ladies and a few of the guys online.

By this time, I was familiar with the regular "trollers" in the 40s room, the men who would flatter you with the intention of a possible sexual encounter. But not all the men were so brash and devious. TBTC was quite different. Eventually he introduced himself by his real name, Terrence. He was a fifty-six-year-old silver-haired gentleman who didn't partake in the sex conversations. Like me, he waited for more neutral topics to come up, or he simply initiated one on his own.

In our conversations, I found out that he enjoyed sports and cooking. He also enjoyed discussions about politics and current events. He was a board member of his beloved fraternity, Phi Beta Sigma. We talked about our personal lives, and I told him about my family and the difficulties I'd been dealing with. He told me about his wife and his three teenage children. I learned he was employed for many years at the university that was close to his home, and had plans for retirement from his position as the university's chief financial officer.

Our conversations became too lengthy for the chat room, so we began talking on the phone. Terrence lived about four hours from Chicago, he knew the city well, and a lot of our conversations were about historical information I never knew about my city. He was polished, kind, and extremely respectful. He never brought up anything remotely sexual during our conversations. He listened to me intently as I talked about the issues that my mother was having with her health. He related to it because his mother had recently passed away from a massive stroke. His description about what his mother went through before she passed was very similar to what my mother had been going through, almost identical, in fact.

I talked to Terrence for hours about my fears, my parents and the issues that were going on with my husband. He just let me talk and talk until I got everything out, never interrupting except to offer his sincere empathy to my situation. I felt so selfish hogging up all the airtime on the phone with my problems, almost never letting him get a word in edgewise. He never complained or behaved as if he was sick of hearing about my issues; he just intently listened and offered any advice that he thought could help. I felt like I was talking to my best friend when I was on the phone with Terrence. He made me laugh, sometimes to the point of tears. After Brenda's funeral, the calls and visits from Nikki stopped, and I was lonely for someone to talk to who wouldn't just hold the phone while I was on it, but would really and truly listen. My friend Terrence had become that person.

Besides being a great listener, Terrence was protective of me, something that I hadn't experienced since I was a little girl with my father. It was a wonderful feeling to have someone genuinely care about what happened to me on a day-to-day basis. I never even experienced that with my own husband. With Darryl, I was his breadwinner, accountant, and his personal bank when he needed something. Like clockwork, Terrence called me every day at noon to ask me if I had eaten yet. If the answer was no, he'd ask why. I didn't reveal to him my financial struggles, but he knew I was barely making ends meet. There were days that I didn't have any money for lunch because I had to pay a bill, or Lanie and Johanna needed lunch for a school trip. Although Terrence was four hours away from me, he would make sure I ate every day by having it delivered to me at work, and without even telling me he did it.

Researching what sandwich shops were in the vicinity of my job, he'd find one, and before I hung up the phone with him at my desk, the receptionist would come by my cubicle to tell me that Jimmy John's Sandwich Shop was in the lobby with my lunch that had been pre-paid for.

Not only was my lunch provided, but as the weather became cold, he made sure I was well insulated. In one instance, Terrence asked randomly what color my gloves were. I told him casually that I had to give my gloves to Denai because she lost hers. Two days later, gloves, a hat, and a scarf arrived in the mail for me. I was simply floored by his thoughtfulness, and a bit overwhelmed as well. Either this man thinks I'm some poor unfortunate charity case, or he is trying to get into my panties, I thought. Either way, I felt suspicious of his intentions and began pushing back from our contact. I had never had anyone be so kind without expecting something in return.

I told Terrence that while I was grateful, he need not pay for my lunches and winter gear for me. I asked him what he really wanted from me. I could tell that his feelings were hurt when I asked him that question; his tone became distant and softened. "I don't want, what you think I do. I like you a lot, I think you are one hell of a fighter, and you are as beautiful inside as you are outwardly. I admire you. You have been through so much, and I want to make things easier for you. I know lunch and gloves aren't much, but it's my small way of showing you that I care about you. I really care about you…if your husband won't see to it that you have lunch and that your hands aren't cold, then I will. If you don't want to talk to me anymore, I will be hurt because I consider you more than a friend, but I understand your reservations about me. I'm not Darryl though. I'm not after anything from you."

With that, Terrence said goodbye and hung up the phone, and I was left holding the other end of the receiver, confused by my feelings. I emailed Terrence and thanked him again for his awesome friendship and being a listening ear for so many months for me. I declined his request to visit me repeatedly. Deep down, I wanted to see him too, but conflicted because I knew in my heart it was an immoral reaction. We were both married. Nevertheless, as time went on, the marriage factor seemed less of a factor…for the both of us.

I decided that a break from Terrence was the best thing to do. Things between us were getting too close for comfort emotionally for me. Although I hadn't met him face to face yet, my affections for him were beginning to shift from a casual friendship to something deeper. These newfound feelings didn't sit well with me due to the fact that we were both married. My epiphany about us sat like a heavy rock in the pit of my stomach. Although not a fan of my decision to take a break from talking to each other, Terrence respected my choice. I needed time to re-evaluate things between him and I, and I suggested that he do the same as well. He complied with my request and stopped calling me, but every now and then I would still receive a delivery to my office with my favorite sandwich from Jimmy John's, complete with a note attached to the pre-paid bill that read: "Just in case....TBTC."

I tried earnestly to erase Terrence from my memory. I constantly found myself craving his presence in my life. Although I longed to hear his voice, I stood my ground. I deleted his number from my phone, and stopped logging in to Chat-Spot for fear that I would see his profile pop up. I had to make a clean break from him for both of our sakes.

Juggling Act

I was grateful for my position at the law firm, and it did pay better than where I was previously, but I still struggled financially due to playing catch-up with all the bills that were so far behind. As soon as I got one bill down to a reasonable size, there was another much larger one in its place. Because of the hundreds of dollars I owed the city for the parking tickets that Darryl had received, my van was now on the city boot list. Because I was afraid to park anywhere on the street for fear that my van would be booted, I left my car at home and took the bus to and from work, which was another expense. With Denai about to graduate from grade school, and Lanie and Johanna outgrowing everything seemingly at the same time, I felt as if I was walking on a tightrope, trying to balance twelve plates on my head without letting one fall to the ground.

Receiving absolutely no child support for my daughters from either my current or ex-husband, I grappled with which overdue bill to pay or purchasing larger shoes for one of the girls. I felt guilty about not being able to do as much for the girls as I would have liked, but they never saw a day without something to eat or clothes on their backs and a roof over their heads, thank God. I tried to make our home situation as "normal" as possible for them.

At fourteen, Denai understood and was usually sensitive to our financial situation. She understood more than I gave her credit for. Unlike most teenagers, she never whined about allowances or having extra money for the mall. She did all she could to help me care for her grandmother, which wasn't always an easy task. Denai helped prepare her meals and even bathed her grandmother, making herself available whenever she could. I couldn't have been more proud of her. In the evening, Denai finished her schoolwork and pitched in wherever she was needed, without a single complaint.

The Horrors at Hudson General

In summer of 2008, my father suffered a near-fatal heart attack at his apartment. The ambulance took him to the hospital nearest to his home, which was the infamous Hudson General. I flipped out when I got the call that he had been sent to one of the worst hospitals in Chicago. Hudson was notorious for their horrible bedside manner, uncleanliness, and doctors who behaved as if they couldn't care less about their patients. The running joke in Chicago had always been, "If you check into Hudson General, you ain't checking out." I hoped that the stories about Hudson's unprofessionalism and incompetence were just rumors. With no other alternative at the time, I gave the hospital the benefit of the doubt and ignored the negative buzz. Unfortunately, I soon found out first hand that everything I heard about Hudson General was true, and then some.

I really dreaded going to the hospital to see my father each day. When I turned the corner to the visitor's parking lot, my stomach tied in knots. The insensitive climate of the faculty seemed to permeate through its walls as I walked the long hallway to the intensive care unit. I spent the greater part of my evenings sitting by my father's bedside as he drifted in and out of various stages of consciousness.

My mind was numbed as I tried to stay positive about his prognosis, but my thoughts kept drifting to the worst possible scenarios. My father seemed fine in the days leading up to his heart attack. A little lethargic, but fine nonetheless. He went to all of his doctor's visits, and took his meds religiously. He even made the necessary dietary adjustments that were given to him by his doctor; I couldn't make sense of it.

I stared at his eyes as if I could will them to open up so that he would see me sitting there with him. The sporadic grip of his hand in mine made my heart burst with hope of a recovery. Softly, I'd urge him on with whispers of encouragement in his ear. "Come on, Daddy, you can do it, squeeze my hand again." I waited, anticipating the sensation of his weakened grip just once more. Some days were better than others with him. Some days he wouldn't move at all, which terrified me the most. I spent hours just looking for the rise and fall of his chest, relieved to know that he was still breathing. I often wondered why God would allow my father's senseless suffering, especially after my dad had grown so close to Him as of late.

My father received his salvation at the age of seventy-five, right after he found out he had cancer. I asked him to recite the sinner's prayer over the phone with me right after he received his diagnosis. I was overjoyed that he finally found Christ. Shortly after, most of our conversations were about the wonders of God, the Bible, and just being grateful no matter the circumstance. I recalled all of those wonderful conversations and revelations we shared as I sat beside his hospital bed. In the midst of all the buzzing machines and hospital clamor around us, I opened my small Bible to read verses from the book of Psalms to him as he lay there motionless. I struggled to get through each verse without breaking down in tears.

To say that Hudson General lacked professionalism would be an understatement. The intensive care unit where my father was taken was more like a huge break room than a unit where the hospital's most critically ill patients dwelled. There was always a lot of gossiping, laughing, and talking loudly over the patients with little regard to their circumstances. I was glad that I was there to oversee my father in the evenings, but shuddered to think what went on with his care when I wasn't there. Aside from the inconsideration of the doctors and nurses, the attention to care was noticeably absent as well. One evening when I came to visit, I immediately noticed tight restraints on my father's hands. The fabric cuffs were so restrictive on his wrists that it caused his arms to swell. The swelling was so bad; it appeared as if his arms would burst open. I wasn't a doctor, but I knew that there was no way that those cuffs should have been squeezing him in such a violent manner.

When I asked why my father was tied down so tightly, the nurse replied, "Oh, he has a trach. He needs to be restricted so he won't try to pull it out, and that's our policy here. He isn't in pain," the nurse said as she walked away, brushing off my concern. My dad had to have an emergency tracheotomy performed at the time of his heart attack to allow him to breathe, and while I understood why restraints had to be placed on his arms for his own safety, it was unacceptable for them to be placed so tightly that his limbs swelled. My insistence that the restraints be loosened was met with rolled eyes and whispers of disgruntlement from the less than concerned nurses, but proved effective. I wasn't the most popular visitor in the ward, but I didn't care. My father's treatment while trying to recover was my main priority.

I often wondered why people would go into a profession that requires care for the sick with little to no compassion whatsoever. I watched as the patients on either side my father would be overlooked as they called out in pain for assistance. I took note of the disinterested faces of the doctors who coldly checked the patient's vitals, without so much as a smile or a hello in most instances. How can people properly heal here? I often thought to myself.

Even though my father seemed to drift in and out of consciousness daily, I was thankful on the few occasions where he actually opened his eyes to look at me. Nothing made my heart more joyful than to see him awake, even if it was for the briefest of moments. He couldn't speak vocally, but his eyes always did. As the weeks went on, he even attempted to mouth my name, his lips forming a circle in his attempt to say "Sue." Some days his recovery seemed so promising that I left the hospital elated. Other days, it seemed as if my father had regressed back to the state he was in when he was first admitted into the hospital, and I believed it had everything to do with the poor care he was receiving at Hudson.

It was difficult to believe that the doctors and nurses there were trained professionals. A few weeks after his arrival, my father contracted MRSA, a highly contagious infection caused by a strain of staph that, if left untreated, could be life-threatening. I was not aware of my father's condition until his dialysis technician asked me why I never wore a mask and gown when I come to visit him. Totally taken off guard by the off question, the tech revealed to me that my father contracted the infection the week before, according to his records. As she spoke through her mask she said to me, "Oh, the nurse didn't tell you? Your dad has MRSA."

My blood ran cold as soon as the words came out of her mouth. I immediately thought of my sick mother and my daughters at home. I could have unknowingly contracted the infection from my father and given it to them. Absolutely livid, I immediately confronted the ICU nurse on duty about the new information I had just been given. This was the same nurse who saw me visit my father every day and told me nothing about his condition. No gown or gloves were provided for my protection, no mask to cover my mouth.

Thank God that even with the close interaction I had with my dad, I never contracted the infection, but I very well could have. I held my father's hand as I talked to him. I kissed his forehead and cheek when I left every evening. Yet I received no forewarning from the nurses that cared for him, ever.

To add insult to injury, the staff was very nonchalant after I informed them of their recklessness that could have had serious consequences for my family. The doctors shifted the blame to the nurses, and the nurses shifted the blame to other nurses. I ended up getting glossed-over apologies from the hospital administrators, and since I hadn't gotten sick, there wasn't much I could do in terms of punitive action against the hospital for their blatant negligence.

Code Red

The most unforgettable visit I had with my father was one Saturday afternoon. I arrived to see him as usual, and heard gurgling sounds coming from his room as I approached. When I opened the door I was shocked by what I witnessed. My father was literally about to choke from his own saliva buildup around his trach incision and mouth. The buildup had evidentially been there for some time, as it had begun to crust around his mouth and neck cavity. His panicked eyes were bulging as he looked to me for help. I quickly reached for a folded towel by his nightstand and cleared his mouth of the saliva that could have killed him had I not arrived when I did. His linen was soiled with blood from his IV, his bed sheets were heavily soiled with his own excrement as he lay there helplessly. Not wasting any more time, I went to work quickly bathing my father's body as tears fell from my eyes. To say I was angry wouldn't be an accurate description of how I felt after I cleaned up my father. I was utterly furious.

Completely out of character and enraged, I walked out of my father's room and screamed at the top of my lungs. I demanded to talk to the one of the hospital's administration representatives about the substandard care that almost caused my father to choke to death due to lack of supervision. I was incredibly insulted at the suggestion that I remain calm after numerous phone calls were made to the hospital administration with complaints about his substandard care, and all were either dodged or unanswered. Now they wanted me to calm down?

Throughout my life, I never opened my mouth to defend myself to anyone. I kept silent and admired those who were bold enough to speak out on their own behalf. That afternoon I allowed my voice to speak boldly in defense of my father. That afternoon, I learned something about myself in the midst of seeking to protect and care for the man that I loved with all my heart. I did have a voice, an authoritative voice that had the capacity to get things accomplished when the rubber hit the road. I knew in my heart that my daddy would have been proud.

It's funny what the threat of a gross negligence lawsuit can do to turn a situation around. Just like that, Hudson General quickly changed their lackadaisical tune with regard to my father's care. Reprimands went forth for the nurses and staff responsible for my father's neglect. I was met with apologetic promises of a turnaround where his treatment was concerned, and it made a difference immediately.

Not long after the incident, my father's MRSA tests came back negative; there was no sign of the infection at all in his bloodstream anymore. This was great news, because it made him a candidate for a hospital transfer. That evening after I walked out of his room, I prayed that God would intervene, and He did. That next day, my father was transferred to another hospital, one of the best in Chicago as a matter of fact. I imagined that Hudson General was overjoyed to get rid of me, and the feeling was more than mutual. I signed off on the necessary transfer documents on my father's behalf and confirmed that he would be transported by ambulance to his new dwelling by the next morning. I smiled broadly and bid Hudson General adieu.

August 17

My father was scheduled to leave Hudson in the early hours of August 16, 2008. There was a glitch in the schedule that caused him to arrive late that evening. I wasn't pleased about that, but grateful nonetheless that he was finally settled at Resurrection Hospital. I even liked the name of his new place. It signified revival and restoration. I felt positive about my dad being there. The hospital was a little distance away from me, which didn't matter to me. I was just grateful that he was in a faith-based facility known for their compassion and excellence in care.

When he was settled in, the hospital administrator called to inform me that my father had been successfully transported and was resting. She gave me an update on his vitals, which were stable, and also reported that he was semi-alert upon arrival, and was attempting to mouth words for a short period before drifting out of consciousness. For the very brief periods when he was awake, I don't believe my father fully understood what exactly was happening and why he was unable to speak; he wasn't cognizant enough to rationalize to that degree.

I was impressed that an administrator had taken the initiative to give me a call to update me on my father's arrival. Since visiting hours were over, I told her that I would see him in the morning. She told me that she would make certain that his nurse was made aware of my upcoming visit, as well assuring an opportunity to tour the hospital to become more familiar. The attention to detail was like night and day compared to what I had experienced at Hudson. For the first time since my father's heart attack, I felt a sense of ease with his care, and I hadn't even stepped foot in the hospital yet. My mother, who had been concerned when I told her of my father's condition, asked how he was doing on a regular basis. She smiled when I told her that he had been moved to a better facility, and within minutes asked what was wrong with him, as if it were new information about his being hospitalized.

My mother was becoming increasingly disoriented by the smallest of tasks, and was experiencing difficulty relaying her thoughts clearly. Her doctor confirmed that she was in the early stages of dementia. Neither Wayne nor I wanted to acknowledge it, but it had become evident that Mama's mental capacity was wavering. Her last stroke caused both physical and mental damage, which was a very hard truth for us to take. "Is your daddy in the hospital? What happened?" she'd ask me with a genuinely confused look on her face. It was so incredibly difficult not show my emotions when I witnessed the decline in her cognitive skills. One minute she was as sharp as a tack mentally, the next she was confused and unclear.

I tried to delicately balance my emotions around her. The last thing I wanted to do was to upset her by letting on that I was worried about her, really worried. "I will tell Daddy you said hello, Mama, I am going to see him tomorrow. Okay?" I said as I kissed her forehead before she drifted to sleep that night.

She looked up at me with her beautiful wide eyes and whispered as she closed them, "Okay, baby, yes…tell your daddy I said hello."

The following day was Denai's fifteenth birthday, and I had my hands full with an agenda that included finally coloring my greying hair, visiting my father at Resurrection, and taking Denai to the mall for her birthday. I woke up early to take care of the first order of business—dying my neglected hair. I was so busy with everything else that my hair looked like a grey bird's nest without my wig on. Just as I completed applying the black coloring to my roots, the house phone rang. As I made my way upstairs to grab the phone, my mother met me at the landing with the phone in her hand and a somber look on her face. "Ma, is it for me? Can you tell them to call me back? I have this color in my hair and—"

"Sue, it's your uncle Maurice," my mother said. "You need to take this call, baby. It's about your Daddy."

Uncle Maurice? I thought it rather odd he would call me. Uncle Maurice never called me. I reached for the phone and figured he was probably calling to get the address to the new hospital. I soon found out that he wasn't calling to get the address to the hospital, because he was already there. My father's doctor called Uncle Maurice when he could not get a hold of me via my uncharged cell phone, I soon found out.

The next voice I would hear would be that of my uncle on the other end of the phone with news that caused my knees to buckle. On August 17, 2008, my father passed away from congestive heart failure, the same day as his first born grandchild's birthday. In a strange way, looking back I thought it poetic that God decided to take my father to heaven on the day Denai was born. He was there with me through all of the aches and pains of my labor with her, he was one of the first people to hold her, and he adored her with all his heart. He affectionately called her "The Queen," and that's exactly how he esteemed her ever since she was born.

Denai was absolutely devastated, and the news of my father's death simply shattered my already fragile world. I felt like my heart was breaking beneath my chest as I stood there, the black hair dye running down my face mixing with the tears that were now uncontained. Gathering my wits about me, I managed to tell my uncle I would meet him at the hospital as soon as I possibly could.

I ran to the outstretched arms of my mother, who could clearly feel my pain. She didn't say a word to me, she just rocked me tightly in her arms as the stubborn hair dye continued to make its way down my face, and onto her face and shoulders—but she never let me go, not once. My voice rang shrill as I wailed until I had no voice left. The realization of my father's death slowly seeped in, while struggling to make sense of it. He seemed to be doing so well, I had just spoken the administrator the night before…he was even alert for brief periods after getting settled. All was supposed to be on the upswing. I just didn't understand.

Gathering my wits about me, I looked intensely into my mother's eyes. It suddenly occurred to me that she was going through her own brand of grief as well. Even though my parents had long since divorced, they still loved each other immensely, and it had become evident within the past couple of years. When Mama got sick, my father was often worried and checked on her often. When my mother found out my father had cancer, she was devastated at the news of his diagnosis. There was a deep friendship that had blossomed between my parents as they grew older. They laughed and talked more to each other than with anyone else when my father came to visit. I was thrilled that they mended their turbulent fences after many years of hard feelings between them. I felt my mother's sorrow as she released me from her embrace. Her pained expression mirrored the obvious heartache she tried to disguise, in her effort to stay strong for me. "Go see about your daddy, Sue. I'm so very sorry Baby, I'm so sorry" my mother said as she wiped the tears from my face with her trembling right hand.

Inhaling deeply, I kissed her on the cheek and whispered, "Okay, Mama, I'll be fine. You need to rest. I'll be back."

A Brother's Love

I composed myself for the sake of my girls, who hadn't found out yet. I broke the news about their grandfather's passing and attempted to soothe them, which was painstaking in itself, especially for Denai, who had plans to celebrate her fifteenth birthday within a few hours. She was heartbroken, but was even more concerned about me, true to her character. Her strength gave me the boost I needed to continue on with the business I needed to take care of. I didn't have time to wallow in sorrow; I needed to see my father face to face, immediately.

My next move was to call my brother Wayne. My father, who was Wayne's stepfather, wasn't exactly on Wayne's favorite person list; in fact, there was a disconnection with my father where Wayne was concerned for a very long time, and with understandable reason. My dad wasn't the best father that he could have been to my brother, and because of that, Wayne always had a bit of residual resentment toward my father. Wayne was always respectful when in my father's presence, but kept his interaction with him very brief. I understood why.

Nevertheless, Wayne was there for me every step of the way when my father died. Rushing to my side, Wayne drove me to the hospital while holding my hand the entire way there. When we arrived, I told myself that I would be able to handle seeing my father. My feet felt heavy and seemed to drag as Wayne and I walked the long hospital corridor to his room. I remained stoic until the nurse slowly pushed the door open to my father's room. Wayne held me tightly as I collapsed in his arms upon seeing my father lying there, lifeless. I felt as if I was re-living my sister's death all over again.

The white walls, the coldness of the air that filled the hospital room, the hushed manner of the nurses as they sympathetically touched my shoulder in condolence, the intense pain of my heart breaking, the denial of what my eyes were seeing—it all came rushing back in an instant. Inching closer to where my father lay, I ignored the stinging sensation of my hair dye, now hours old and practically sutured to my scalp at this point. I reached my hand out to stroke my father's soft gray hair, still in disbelief that he was gone. I am not certain of how long I remained in his room, but for as long as I was there talking, crying, and smiling at my daddy, Wayne was immovable. He remained by my side in silence, rubbing my trembling shoulders and softly patting my back in comfort.

I had no idea how I was going to make it through that night. My head felt like it was going to explode from grief and the details I had to iron out in terms of burying my father. I had no clue what to do or where to begin. I prayed for guidance and wisdom from God, and true to His character, He delivered. God made certain that everything was laid out clearly for me from the obituary to the funeral and burial details. Thankfully, I was able to locate my father's military records from when he served in the U.S. Navy. He was very proud to have served his county and spoke about it often. It meant everything to me that he be recognized for his service via the rendering of military honors at his burial site. My heart was overjoyed when I received confirmation that representatives from his beloved U.S. Navy would be present to pay homage to him. Without one single hitch, all the preparations for my daddy's funeral went seamlessly.

My father was to be buried within two days, and although the funeral arrangements were prepared, my heart was not. I found myself eating to sooth myself to sleep more and more in the days leading up to my father's service. My anxiety was out of control, even with the Xanax I had been taking. I yearned to feel numb. I wanted to talk to Terrence so badly, but I held off on calling him to tell him about my father. I knew he would want to come see me, and that was the last thing I needed, but the only thing I wanted. My nights were filled with hysterical crying into my pillow and eating until I felt sick.

Wayne's moral support got me through those difficult days leading up to my father's funeral. As siblings, Wayne and I were usually like water and oil when it came to getting along with each other. We bumped heads more than a few times in the past due to our difference in personality, but aside from our fallouts, his big-brother loyalty always shined though. I found a deeper reverence for Wayne during that very difficult period. He could have easily bowed out of helping me take care of the business associated with putting my dad to rest, but he put his own personal issues aside to come to my aid. He understood what my father meant to me and made himself available to me, all the way down to selecting the suit my father would be buried in. In the final days before the funeral, I discovered that my father didn't have a tie to match his suit; Wayne quickly supplied one of his own ties without hesitation. His loyalty and selflessness in the face of my personal tragedy was just one of many reasons why I loved Wayne so much.

I woke up the day of the funeral feeling dizzy and sick to my stomach. My blood pressure was becoming erratic again, just like it had back in my heavier days. My adverse coping mechanism was slowing emerging again, and its evidence becoming apparent in the form of weight gain and issues with hypertension again. After my massive weight loss, Dr. Thomas modified my blood pressure meds to a much milder prescription. In fact, I was well on my way to becoming medication free. Things had become much different now. The more strain I was under, the more I began reverting back to my old habits. Soon my waist size elevated, and so did my blood pressure, again.

My new blood pressure pills made me so sick that I could barely function most mornings. I felt as if I would pass out as soon as I stood up sometimes. I would need to get used to the meds all over again, but I didn't want to. The depression from my weight gain set off my anxiety, my anxiety caused me to eat, and thus went the vicious cycle that had now resumed in my life.

After much prayer that morning for a clear head and stable mind, I went about the task of making sure the girls were dressed, and that Mama had something to wear to the funeral. As I looked through my closet, I tried to find something that could fit properly. My weight had fluctuated so much that everything I put on was either too tight or…too tight. I decided on a flowing dress that hid the results of my overeating.

When the funeral home limousine arrived, all were present and accounted for at Mama's house: Wayne and his wife Tessa, my nephew Wayne and his wife Lorrie, as well as Darryl, who had arrived at my house just a few minutes prior to pay his respects to his father-in-law. I was glad to see him there, despite the fact that we rarely spoke outside of hello and goodbye without arguing. I was happy to see that he cared enough to show up.

He extended a hug to me that was more intense than a just a sympathy embrace. Pulling me closer he whispered in my ear, "You look beautiful, Sue, I miss you, and I am so sorry about Dad, I know how much you loved him." Between his overly intimate hug and the words he spoke, I was so taken by surprise I nearly teetered in the high heels I was wearing. I didn't know what to think about the display, so I didn't. I just accepted his condolences and compliment and focused on trying to get my mind together for the funeral service. Perhaps his words were sincere, maybe they weren't. I was so accustomed to his smooth talk and deception that I took whatever he said with a grain of salt. Besides, I didn't have the energy at that point to dissect his statements or why he said them.

The funeral was beautiful and it was befitting of the kind of man my father was. It was humbling to see all the people who came to pay their respects. My manager Raul and supervisor April took off work early to attend, and I was very grateful for that. A few associates of my father's came to give their condolences as well.

Although it was painful to say goodbye to my father, it helped to know that he would no longer be bound with cuffs around his arms anymore. He would no longer need to mouth the words he wanted to speak, and he was free from the painful agony that he had to endure toward the end of his life. It gave me a small sense of peace when I looked at his face one final time, and he seemed to be sporting a slight grin. That's the way I will always remember my daddy, because that is the way he lived. Smiling through everything, even in the midst of difficulty, he was always smiling. As I walked out to the procession of cars to prepare to go to his burial, Wayne stopped me as I walked to the car. He said he needed to speak to me, and that it was important.

We found a secluded area by a tree and he took my hand, "Sue, I need for you to understand what I am about to say. I know you are not going to like it, and you may get mad at me, but I need to say it anyway. I don't know if your father left you anything in terms of his savings or any type of insurance, but if he did, don't let your husband know about it. I don't trust him. If you tell Darryl, he will try to talk you out of it. He will try to get the money that your father left for you. I suspect he's gonna ask you, but don't tell him anything." Wayne looked into my eyes directly in a serious fashion. Every word he spoke was with conviction and emphasis. I became instantly offended by his words, just as he said that I would.

"How could you say that? Darryl would never try to swindle my father's insurance money out of me!" I said with an aggravated huff. Even while my mind knew that Wayne's advice held possible truth, my heart didn't want to believe it. My heart still wanted to believe the best about Darryl, even after what I already knew. Darryl had never stolen anything from me that I know of, but he certainly wasn't above manipulation to get what he wanted, and I knew it. That was Wayne through and through. It was in his nature to advise and protect, even though it came across as arrogant and bossy sometimes. I knew his intentions were pure; he was looking out for his trusting and naïve little sister. He was trying to shield me from yet another painful experience. Nevertheless, I shrugged off Wayne's warning, but took his advice on not revealing that my father had left me a small monetary amount from his insurance. I waited to see if Darryl would ask about it, just to prove Wayne wrong.

The Plummet

Dodging the Bullet

After a few weeks had gone past, Darryl was getting a bit chummier than he had been with me. He went with me to help me clean out and pack away my father's furniture and personal items from his apartment, which I really appreciated. He stayed nights with me and the girls for a while, and it did help with my anxiety episodes, which were out of control at this point whenever I was alone. With Darryl being there, I wasn't afraid, and he was well aware of it too. His nights turned to days, and the days turned into weeks of him being there.

He did come with transportation though. He was getting comfortable driving his mother and stepfather's brand new SUV truck they had just purchased. It was stylish and a real eye-catcher. His parents allowed him to drive it, taking them where they needed to go since Darryl wasn't working. Both his parents had medical issues that limited their driving. After his stepfather had been diagnosed as legally blind, their arrangement seemed like a good fit, until Darryl wouldn't adhere to the agreement they had made. His parents would take the truck away from him one week, and give it back the next.

I couldn't understand how a grown man could live like that, putting himself in a position to have his parents take his driving privileges away as if he were a child. It boggled my mind why he would choose to live that way. At forty years old, why wouldn't you make it a priority to have your own everything? My goals were set up differently. Besides working at the firm, I had my own mobile hairstyling business that was just getting off the ground. I had aspirations that spanned beyond where I was. I was grateful to be with my mother, especially since her stroke, but I wanted more for my life than where I was at the moment. Darryl and I were so completely different in that respect.

My dad's things had been packed away, and I said my final goodbye to his neighbors down the hallway from his apartment whom I had become acquainted with over the years. The move took a couple of days, and I was exhausted physically, but more emotionally than anything. On the final trip back home from my dad's place, Darryl recalled memories of my father, which felt nice. As he flipped from station to station on the radio, he nonchalantly made a few references to my father's belongings and how much he had acquired over the years. Out of the blue, he asked me, "So, did your father leave you anything? Did he have insurance? You never mentioned if he had any or not."

There it was. The question. Wayne's suspicions were right. Maybe it was all the stress I was under, maybe it was mental fatigue, maybe it was because I had finally flipped my lid, but I started laughing like crazy when he asked the question. "He was right," I heard myself say out loud. "He was right!" I said again.

"Who was right?" Darryl asked, looking perplexed.

"Nothing. Nothing, I'm sorry, what did you ask me again?" I said, just to be completely sure I heard him correctly.

"Did your father leave you any money?" he repeated.

"No, my father didn't leave me anything, he had nothing to leave," I said as I sat back in the passenger seat and stared out of the window in aggravation.

"Wow, nothing? Nothing at all?" Darryl continued prying for a different answer.

"Nope, nothing…can you turn into this McDonald's? I'm hungry," I said, quickly changing the subject. I just shook my head as the confirmation was made clear. Perhaps Darryl was just being nosey with his line of questions about a possible inheritance from my father, but I highly doubt it. His questions were always of a calculating nature, never random, and always for his benefit. I never told Wayne that he was right, but I did silently thank him in my head for helping me dodge that bullet.

Donuts and Setbacks

As Darryl sat comfortably at the computer desk in the early-morning hours, intensely engaged with his Farmville activities, I stepped around him to rush out of the door to catch the next train to work. Farmville was a computer simulated farming game, and

Darryl's new obsession. Each day, his mission was to grow as many fake vegetables as possible within a twenty-four-hour period to reap factitious rewards like fake money to "buy" more fake stuff for the "farm." I didn't have a problem with fun pastimes, but he took gaming to the extreme. It amazed me how he could be so dogmatic with "growing" these damn video vegetables and yet so nonchalant with looking for a job. In every instance, there were examples of how his priorities at forty years old were sadly out of touch with reality. He literally woke up in the middle of the night to check on the "growth" of fake watermelons and squash. While I worked and the kids were in school, he slept.

My marriage to Darryl felt so forced and strained. I began to think of my marriage to him as an arrangement of sorts, albeit a very unhealthy one. I wanted out, but was still wrestling with the guilt of a divorce. I'd heard over the years, again and again the sentiment of my pastor concerning divorce: "It's 'wrong' to walk away from your marriage." My divorce dilemma caused me to hold my head down in shame whenever the subject came up in a sermon at church.

I never thought of it in terms of Darryl willfully and happily making the choice to walk away from his responsibility to me as his wife and his children. I knew why he was with me, and it had nothing to do with loving me. Still I remained, because I "made my bed, and I had to lie in it." I thought many times about my situation as I lay down and stared at the ceiling fan, my fingers fumbling to find the box of donuts hidden under my blanket.

Our confrontations proved to be a fruitless cycle of repetitiveness. With the smallest of household tasks not done and walking into a house that was destroyed after I worked all day, I'd rip the computer socket out of the wall and hide the PlayStation, demanding that Darryl leave, only to have him return when my frustration died down. He played me just like a fiddle, offering to come back if I needed him. "Do you need me to come over? Can you sleep?"

In my muddled thoughts, I did feel like I needed him there, despite knowing what I knew about him. In the midst of my mental dysfunction, I had gained 60 pounds and eaten my way back up to 237 pounds. I was miles and miles away from that slimmed-down and confident woman I once was. My scrappiness had grown cold. My fight fizzled out. I was so ashamed about the weight I gained that I didn't go back to Shapes for nearly a year. After ignoring her calls and never returning her messages, Shelly finally stopped calling me. Sasha stopped texting me asking if I was okay or not.

Totally ashamed, I drove past the gym and never turned my head in that direction for fear of being recognized by a member. I'm sure everyone thought I dropped off the face of the earth, and that wouldn't have been too far from the truth either. My determination and my purpose plummeted so far into the abyss; I couldn't see my way out. It was like déjà vu all over again. I missed Brenda and my father so badly. I mourned their love and encouragement every day. I replayed my father's funeral in my mind like a broken record. I called my sister's phone at her work to listen to her voicemail over and over again until her employer deleted it permanently. My cheering section fell deafeningly silent, so I gave up, again. Between the turmoil in my marriage, my dependence on food and Xanax to disarm my anxiety attacks, and my mother who required constant care, I was frazzled and in a complete state of fear. Fear that I would lose my mother, fear of losing my job due to lack of concentration, and worst of all…fear of losing my mind completely.

I came home from work to find my mother's nurse looking a bit annoyed. My mother was having one of her episodes that including doing just the opposite of what her caregiver would ask her to do. Mama's demeanor was a doozy to deal with when she got that way. "Mrs. Currie has been a handful today. She was annoyed because the phone kept ringing and no one would say anything when I answered. Your husband is here; he must have taken care of it. There haven't been any hang-ups for a while. Your mom didn't want to get dressed, and she refused to eat her lunch. She said it didn't taste right." Mama's nurse took in a deep breath and she sighed in relief. I felt bad for her as she packed up her bag and quickly headed for the door. I knew how stubborn Mama could get when she was in one of her moods. In one fell swoop, her poor nurse said her goodbyes and was gone.

"Hey Mama, how are you?" I said, kissing Mama on the forehead as she lay in the bed watching an old Jeopardy re-run. "The phone rang constantly while you were gone; whoever it is keeps hanging up. It woke me up outta my sleep every time. Darryl must know who it is, because when he answered the last time he grabbed the phone and went to your room."

"Okay, Mama," I said. I was somewhat safe with the "Okay Mama" response. It was always wise just to agree with her unless you wanted a bit of her wrath. I warmed up some low-sodium, chicken noodle soup for her and served it with her favorite crackers, saltines.

"This soup is bland, where is the salt?" Mama said, frowning.

"Mama, its low sodium for your blood pressure. Do you want some pepper in it?"

"I guess so," she said, clearly not satisfied with my suggestion. Mama might have been forgetful with many things, but she never forgot how to hide the things she wanted and knew she couldn't have.

"Mama, give me your salt shaker," I said with my hand out.

"What? What salt shaker? I don't have a shaker in here."

"Mama, the one you keep hidden in your drawer, the same drawer you hide your cigarettes in? That drawer," I said with a chuckle as I shook my head. My mother rolled her eyes as hard as she could at me and relinquished the hidden shaker.

"Here, but you ain't taking my cigarettes," she said defiantly with a heavy slur in her speech.

Mama was a something else. It was times like that I was happy that she still had enough spunk to get sassy with me. Maybe it meant that she was getting better, perhaps that her mind was healing from the stroke she had the previous year. I didn't place much emphasis on the mystery hang-up calls that Mama said kept her up, but as the weeks went on, Mama would tell me about the calls that Darryl would answer before he'd leave the room in silence. She also told me about hearing him talking to a woman when she picked up the phone "by accident." Maybe it was his mother that called, but my mother wasn't buying that theory.

Terrence had been heavily on my mind ever since my father died. I wanted to call him so badly to tell him everything that had happened. I wanted to hear his voice and I missed our conversations. My birthday was in a couple days, and I wondered if he would remember, and he did. Darryl said nothing, and chances were the kids would let him know, and then I would get a "Happy Birthday" from him later on.

To my surprise, I received a voicemail at work from Terrence wishing me happy birthday the morning of my birthday. He asked if he could take me to lunch the next day, and that he really wanted to catch up on everything…no strings attached. I called back and immediately accepted his invitation to meet for lunch; the thought of meeting Terrence filled me with giddiness. I was so excited that I thought of nothing else that whole day but finally meeting my friend. When I gave the green light on our lunch meeting, he made arrangements for me to come to his side of town, four hours away in Bloomington, Illinois. He made the reservations for my travel via train, and the next day, I left work early and headed to Bloomington to see Terrence. On the way there, I thought of nothing but Terrence. In the back of my mind, I had some residual feelings of guilt regarding my meeting another man I had feelings for, but to be honest, I didn't give it much thought. The internal conversation that I had going on in my mind was as solid as concrete:

I'm not going to fall in love; I'm just going to have lunch. That's all. There is nothing wrong with having lunch on my birthday with a friend, right?...Right.

The train ride took forever as I held my ticket confirmation tightly in my hand. The ticket confirmation had Terrence's info on it. His name, address, and how much the ticket cost, along with his credit card information. He must really trust me to email me with all of his information, I thought.

I started thinking about how pitiful it was that I didn't trust my husband enough to disclose any of my bank account information to him in the nine years that we had been married. He had poor banking practices, with negative account balances and penalties which prevented him from opening accounts anywhere himself. Darryl asked several times through the years to be added to my account, but I never allowed it. He was incensed that I would not disclose my bank information or give him my debit card for any reason. I simply didn't trust him. Maybe it was intuition, but I didn't trust him to do the right thing by me.

An Affair of the Heart

The train pulled into the Bloomington station at exactly noon. As soon the doors of the train opened, my heart began racing within my chest. The butterflies in my stomach were going crazy with nervous excitement. I stood up to straighten my dress and proceeded to the exit, train ticket still clasped in my hand. Terrence said he would meet me as soon as I got off the train, and as promised, there he stood as soon as my foot hit the last stair. Terrence looked just like his profile picture on Chat Spot, but he was shorter than I thought he'd be. He was stocky, dark skinned, and grey haired, his salt- and-pepper goatee and beard neatly trimmed around the parameter of his oval face. He was not movie star handsome, but pleasing to the eye nonetheless. I couldn't help to return his bright smile when we locked eyes. "You look incredible, Sue, Wow," Terrence uttered as he scanned me from head to toe. "It is such a pleasure to finally meet you; may I give you a hug?" he said, taking a few steps back to allow me some personal space.

"Yes, of course you can!" I said, walking a bit closer on nervous, wobbly legs.

Terrence's embrace felt like a warm cup of hot chocolate on a very cold day. It was soothing and comforting, and he smelled like a slice of heaven. He held me tightly and I surrendered under his gentle but firm hold. "I have missed talking to you, Sue, I really have." Feeling a bit overly anxious, I let go of his embrace and stepped back a bit. The feelings within me were like a firestorm of emotion. I quickly began talking before he could notice how taken in I was by this first meeting of ours.

"So, are you hungry? I am starving! Where are we headed?" I said, attempting to dial back the energy from a ten to a comfortable three or four.

We ate at a cozy little restaurant with dimmed lighting and fabulous seafood. The atmosphere was casual, and the soft vintage jazz music soothed my nerves and helped me to relax. Terrence and I talked about almost everything before the first course even got to the table. He held my hand as I tearfully told him of my father's passing, to which he showed genuine sympathy and clasped my hand even tighter as I recalled my final moments with my father.

He wiped the tears from my face and showed such a tenderness that wasn't rehearsed or phony in any way.

By the time our meal was done, we were still rattling on as if we hadn't talked in ten years. As I inquired about his wife and family, he obliged me, holding nothing back. Terrence talked about his two daughters and one son that recently made the football squad at his high school. He talked about his daughters, who both attended the same university he worked for, and how nice it was that he was able to speak to their professors about their academic challenges. He was also thrilled about the opportunity to eat lunch with his daughters at school from time to time. He revealed in a despondent manner that his wife was a nurse who worked hard and didn't have the desire to do anything else but sleep when she got home. He did the cooking and tending to whatever the kids needed while she slept most nights. He revealed that he loved his wife of fifteen years, but felt deserted.

When asked how he happened upon Chat Spot, Terrence said something that hit home with me; he said that Chat Spot had become a source of sanity for him. Somewhere he could engage with others and not focus on the issues of his real life. I felt for him, mainly because I knew how it felt to be ignored and discarded. I gave him advice from a woman's perspective, and although he listened respectfully, it didn't seem to penetrate his obvious frustration with the lack of attention and affection he was receiving from his wife. Before I knew it, lunchtime was over and it was 3:00

p.m. We talked so much and sat there so long that the waiter sarcastically asked if we were planning to stay for the dinner items on the menu.

Time had certainly flown, and I hadn't laughed so much and felt so relaxed in a long time. I didn't want to leave, but I knew I had to get back home soon. "I can always change your ticket time going back home, Sue. Please don't leave right now. Stay and talk for a while longer with me," Terrence said, looking into my eyes and caressing my hands as we sat on the restaurant's bench outside. "Please don't go right now," he pleaded. The truth was, I didn't want to leave either. I wanted to stay with him and forget about what was at home, at least temporarily. My mind was at ease, and it felt good to be pampered. It felt good to be with someone who appreciated my company and wasn't afraid to show it. It felt good to hear that I was beautiful in every way. I was like a bee to honey at that point. I couldn't say no to such an invitation.

Throwing caution to the wind I answered, "Yes, I will make arrangements to stay a little while longer with you, Just let me make a couple of calls."

I called Denai to tell her I would be home late. She was to make sure my mother took her medicine and was fed properly. My next call was to Darryl. I told him something came up and that I needed him to make sure the girls had dinner and their homework was done. "Why will you be late?" he asked, sounding a bit annoyed at my request. Without hesitation, I told him there was a meeting that ran over and I shouldn't be long. Before he asked anything else, I hung up the phone. I didn't feel good about lying to my husband to stay with another man; however, I didn't allow the feelings of guilt to linger too long in my head. I was feeling too good to allow anything to spoil my cloud nine moment with Terrence.

As I walked back over to where Terrence was patiently waiting for me by his car, I told myself that this wasn't some sleazy booty call. This was a friendly date with a very dear friend, and sex wasn't on the agenda. "So, where are we going?" I said as Terrence held his car door open for me.

"Some place befitting a queen, some place where we can talk and relax a bit. I know just the place too…by the way, look in the back seat. I was so excited to see you; I forgot to give you these." In his backseat were two dozen perfectly shaped red and white roses with a fluffy white teddy bear that read *Happy Birthday* on it. "Happy birthday, Beautiful," he said with a mile wide smile on his face. I was simply floored and giddy as a schoolgirl. I gave Terrence a huge hug of thanks as we drove off.

As we pulled into a driveway, a huge sign that read Lexington Hotel met my eyes. The grounds were beautifully manicured, and there were men on either side of the doors in suits waiting to greet the visitors of the hotel. I turned and looked at Terrence with a curled lip. "Terrence, why are we here?"

"It's not what you think. I'm not trying to get anything, I just thought this would be a good place for us to talk and maybe get a light dinner. This IS your birthday outing, you know. I wanted to get a room, but if you feel uncomfortable then we can just chill out at the bar. Whatever you are comfortable with Sue, no pressure." Now I had a decision to make, do I go with what I feel, or not? I wanted to relax with Terrence a bit more, take my heels off and just relax. I would have plenty waiting on me when I got back.

Caught Up

We walked hand in hand to the room, laughing and talking like old friends getting acquainted all over again. We must have talked for hours between lunch and dinner, which Terrence ordered for us when we got to the hotel room. "Do you have any pictures of your kids?" I asked as I sat down and took off my heels.

"I think I have a couple of recent ones," Terrence said as he pulled out his cell phone and handed it to me.

"Wow, your sons look just like you," I said, shuffling through the photos on his phone. My roaming fingers paused momentarily at the surprise sensation of Terrence slowly and intently massaging my propped-up feet. "Um, what are you doing?" I said, putting the phone down and looking down at him as he knelt on one knee to get a better angle to rub my bare feet and legs. Terrence shook his head and continued massaging, ignoring my inquiry.

"Just keep looking at the pictures and relax. Are you gonna tell me your feet aren't hurting from walking all day in those heels, which look incredible on you, by the way."

I thought briefly about snatching my foot away, but the massage felt so good, I felt as if I had been shot with a tranquillizer gun. *Good grief,* I thought, *his hands are absolutely amazing.* I decided to loosen up and allow him to continue with his decadent skills in foot massage as I thumbed through more pictures of his kids. My eyes ran across a picture of Terrence and a middle-aged woman with chubby cheeks and a huge, pleasant smile. They were standing by a large Christmas tree surrounded by his three children and a cute dog. Suddenly the feeling of indulgence that I had been experiencing turned to shame which landed square in the pit of my stomach. I asked an obvious question that I already had the answer to. "Is this your wife Veronica?"

Terrence stopped his massage, looked up and answered without hesitation, "Yes, that's Veronica, the kids, and me with our Yorkie, Matilda; we took that picture last Christmas." I closed the pictures and put his phone down on the bed.

My shame turned into a deep reproach for us, both him and me. I did a quick review in my head of the current situation. I had been whisked away from my normal existence in exchange for the pleasant company of a man, who I felt genuinely cared about me. I was the grateful recipient of the kind of tenderness and affection that I forgot existed between a man and a woman. I was with a gentleman who had treated me like I was special, not a cash station. He wasn't asking for my money, only my time and company. He trusted me and I trusted him. It was an ease that I was so foreign to, and it felt so incredibly good. I was enjoying the ease of my mind, and most of all, I was enjoying the company I was with. The problem with this scenario? The man that I had fallen so hard for was married, and so was I. *"What am I doing here?"* I thought.

In an instant, I snatched my feet from Terrence's hands and jumped up so quickly that I nearly lost my balance as my body weight shifted toward the corner of an end table. As I leaned to the side to regain my footing, Terrence jumped up and reached out his arms to catch me. Because of the embarrassment of almost falling and the guilt of being in a hotel room with him, I cast my face downward, not wanting to look up…even as he rescued me from what could have been a huge knot on my head or worse.

"Sue, look at me…" Terrence said as he stared into my face, not a trace of a smile in sight. I looked at him regrettably.

"I should go; can you take me to the train station? I shouldn't be here with you."

Still holding my body in his arms, Terrence began explaining his position with regard to our relationship with certainty and firmness. "I am not going to tell how much I don't want my marriage and how I want to leave my wife. That would be a lie, and I won't lie to you. Like I have told you before, my marriage to Veronica has been problematic for years now, especially where our intimacy or lack thereof is concerned. To be honest, I just don't believe my wife loves me the way I love her anymore. The communication that we used to have is absent, and has been for a while. I try to interact with her and I am left feeling like a fool when I do. I finally just gave up. I go to work every day, provide for my family, and try to show affection to my wife, even though it's not reciprocated. When I encountered you, I didn't intend to feel about you the way I do. But you have a way about you that is different than most. I felt renewed when I found someone I could talk to, someone who actually wanted to talk to me too. I fell in love with that woman along the way. That woman is you."

"Susan, I love you. I know you are going to say that I don't, but I'm telling you I do. I don't just care about you…it's deeper than that. I didn't call you at your request, but the last few months have been horrible not hearing your voice. I should have been there for you when your father died. I know how much you adored him. To know that you had to deal with his death without me to comfort you…it's more than I can take. I had to tell you. You need to know that I love you, and I want nothing more than to take care of you, to make sure that your heart doesn't hurt anymore. I hate that Darryl takes you for granted. Any man that wouldn't cherish a beautiful, strong, and loving woman like you is a damn fool."

When he finished what he had to say, I was floored. I listened as Terrence told me how he felt about me. The emphasis he put on each word made me believe that he meant the words he said. I wanted to tell him I felt very deeply for him as well, perhaps even loved him too. My mind was a ball of confusion and pent-up emotion all at the same time. I tried to say something, but I was literally speechless.

Albeit wrong in every way possible, the only thing I could think of was kissing him right then and there. Terrence, apparently feeling the same whirlwind of passionate tension between us, leaned into me and kissed me. The kiss wasn't raunchy or lust filled, in fact, it was the exact opposite…soft, tender, affectionate, and gentle. Any apprehensions I felt melted away in those moments as I kissed him by the beautifully framed floor-to-ceiling window overlooking the posh hotel grounds. Everything felt right.

My mind and heart seemed to disconnect instantly. What I knew to be right and wrong suddenly became blurred, and the principles that I walked in with were overruled by my desperation to be loved. Not the synthetic type of love that seeks to gratify only on conditional terms. I had become accustomed to that kind of love in my marriage. I needed to be loved in the way that every human being wants to be loved, honestly and without reservations. That night I gave in to everything I wanted to feel and allowed myself to feel them with Terrence, another soul who also needed to feel wanted and cared for in that same way. That night, I willingly entered into a realm of fulfillment outside of my marriage...a realm that was not without bitter emotional consequences which haunted me every day and every night.

In our human frailty, we have the capacity to do things that we never thought we would. Within us, we all have the ability to go against what our convictions are for the sake of soothing our damaged spirit and bruised soul. In an instant, we are able to lend ourselves over to our longings in an attempt to suture our brokenness while giving ourselves permission to engage in actions that produce temporary relief, never taking into consideration the wreckage that could follow.

There were periods of silence in the car as Terrence drove me to the train station that evening. Although his hand embraced my shoulder, our thoughts were clearly preoccupied with all that had transpired. "Baby, are you okay?" Terrence softly asked as he gently tilted my chin toward him with his finger.

"I'm okay," I replied, which was a total lie.

As the train approached, Terrence escorted me to the platform. I felt his gaze, which seem to bore right into the side of my face as I stared straight ahead. "When can I see you again? This night has been more than I ever thought it would be. I miss you already...I love y—"

"I really need to board now," I said, cutting off the phrase I wasn't ready to hear right then. "Looks like the train is just about full, and I want to get a seat in the front."

"Okay, I'm sorry. I know I can rattle on sometimes. I enjoyed our time together, Sue, I hope you did too," Terrence said he brushed his hand against mine.

"Thank you for lunch and dinner," I said as I gathered my wits about me. We embraced quickly, and with a light kiss we said our goodbyes at the train station. As the train pulled slowly out of the station, Terrence remained on the platform, waving and mouthing "I love you" to me. He lingered on the platform until the train disappeared into the darkness of the night.

I settled into my seat and I lifted a nearby newspaper to my face. I had no intention of reading; I wanted to hide behind it. I wanted to hide my entire self within the folds of the pages if it was possible. Staring blankly at the newsprint on the pages, all I could see was the picture of Terrence's wife that he had in his phone. All I could visualize was Veronica's smiling face, seemingly taunting me as I tried to shake her image from my head. The four-hour ride from Bloomington to Chicago seemed like ten hours. My thoughts intermittently bounced from Terrence's confession of his love for me, to the guilt from our extramarital encounter. My mind knew without question that what transpired that night was wrong, yet my heart still felt deep adoration for Terrence, thus the perfect storm of conflict. The more I thought about what happened between Terrence and me, the more angst I felt.

"Are you all right, Miss?" The train conductor asked, taking my ticket and offering me a Kleenex from the small pack in his pocket.

"I'm fine, thank you...my allergies are getting the better of me," I lied while reaching for the tissue and wiping the stream of tears that flowed down my cheeks and onto the newspaper.

The train pulled into the Chicago station at about 8:45 p.m., an hour and a half later than I told Darryl I would arrive home. I knew I would have some explaining to do when I got there. I drove home in a rush, trying to piece together a legitimate account of where I was. I barreled through the driveway and turned off the car lights, grabbing my purse and shoving the receipt of my train ticket as far down in my purse as possible, reminding myself to throw it in the garbage when I got settled at home. The girls were sleeping, except for Denai, who was cleaning the kitchen when I arrived.

"Hi Mommy, where were you all this time? Darryl said that you would be home soon, but that was a long time ago." Denai said as a feeling of nausea in the pit of my stomach emerged.

"Hi sweetie, I had to work late, remember I told you?" I said as I took my coat off and headed toward my mother's room. I peeped my head around the corner to look into her room, and my mother caught my glance while sitting up eating a Popsicle.

"Hi, where were you? I was worried and I couldn't find you. I couldn't find you," my mother repeated, looking very upset, which made me feel worse than I already did for coming in so late and having to lie to my daughter on top of it.

"Mama, are you okay?" I said, feeling like the world's most negligent daughter on earth.

"Yes. But I tried to call you, and you weren't downstairs. Is Darryl here…again?" she said as the Popsicle she was eating seemed to soothe her nerves a bit.

"Yes, Mama, he is here." She said nothing to my response except to give me an irritated look, obviously not happy with the fact that Darryl was staying full-time at the house again. I didn't have the mental energy to go through the barrage of questions my Mother would surely ask with regard to Darryl living with us again. I kissed my mother goodnight and retreated to the basement apartment to find Darryl snoring on the couch. I took my heels off and tiptoed past him, showered, turned off the light, and slid into the bed with a huge sigh of relief. *"Maybe he won't mention anything about tonight in the morning,"* I thought while pulling my comforter over my head and falling asleep a few minutes later.

Broken Vows Revealed

I slept right through my alarm the next morning, which was a Saturday. I tossed and turned all night thinking about the deceit that I had been a party to; I began to hate myself for what I had done. I woke up every fifteen minutes, wet with sweat and my head pounding. My anxiety raged relentlessly without mercy, causing horrible bouts of nausea. My heart would beat out of my chest, it seemed. My conscious ate me alive with regret. "I need to tell Darryl, I have to tell Darryl what I've done," I kept telling myself as I looked over at him, sleeping like a baby. I made the decision to tell him once I had an opportunity to be alone with him. I needed to free myself from my mind's turmoil and ask his forgiveness for what I had done.

It was already 8:05 a.m. I was supposed to get up to make sure Mama had her breakfast before she took her 7 a.m. meds. I frantically ran upstairs to gather the oatmeal and eggs to prepare her meal for the morning. I looked into her room and was immediately panicked. My mother always got up at 7:00 a.m. to eat. She was still lying in her bed motionless and with her mouth open. This wasn't the first time she'd overslept, but the sight of her motionless body always petrified me. I thought the worst when I saw her like that. My mind always suggested that she'd passed away in her sleep. In a panic, I rushed to her side and watched for the rise and fall of her chest, the same way I did when my father was very sick. "Mama? Mama? Wake up. Mama?" I said several times, shaking her body a little harder than before. I closed my eyes tight and hoped that my mother wasn't dead. I shook her until she finally opened her eyes.

"Whaaaaa? Stop shaking me like that, gal!" she said groggily. I sucked in a deep breath of relief before exhaling a breath of gratitude that I had annoyed her enough to rouse her awake.

After preparing my mother's breakfast and making sure that cereal and milk were available for the girls when they woke up, I sat outside for a while on the porch in my pajamas. The park across the street from my house was as peaceful as could be. The only sounds were of the birds chirping in the distance. Now was a perfect opportunity to reflect, to gather my thoughts and words together as to how I would confess to my husband what I had done.

Terrence was still fresh on my mind as well. Guilt gnawed in my belly from still wanting to see him again. I didn't want to break ties with him; I didn't want to lose him. I never felt the way I did when I was with him. I craved to feel loved like that again; it wasn't about sex for me, it was about the affection and tenderness tied with it. My emotions were so frayed from the turmoil and stress of my marriage to Darryl that I was ready to sign divorce papers long before Terrence and I, but I gave in every time Darryl begged his way back with promise after promise, that he never really intended on keeping. Nonetheless, I still needed to tell him what happened. I wondered what his reaction would be as I tried to gather enough courage to reveal my affair to him that morning.

I decided to do the inevitable while my bravery was fresh. I was making my way down the stairs to the bedroom when I heard Darryl call my name. *Good, he's up*, I thought. His tone seemed agitated, which I wrote off as him being groggy from sleeping. I made my way toward our master bathroom. My computer desk was just a few feet from the bathroom, in a little space I always called my office. As I approached the office area, I noticed the glare from the computer screen reflecting off the wall. I turned the corner to the bathroom, and as I passed by the computer screen, I stopped dead in my tracks. I froze up when I saw the image of the Bloomington ticket confirmation that I had accidently left up the day before. Unbeknownst to me, he had printed a copy of the ticket confirmation and was standing by the printer holding it in his hand.

Darryl stared so intensely at me; it felt like his eyes seared my skin. "So, this was the meeting that you had to attend last night that made you several hours late coming home? You didn't tell me the meeting would be in Bloomington with Terrence Williamson. Who is Terrence, by the way? He sure was nice to pay one hundred and seventy-eight dollars for your round trip ticket."

I took a deep breath and asked Darryl to sit down as I prepared myself to tell him what he apparently already found out. "No, I don't want to sit down," he said. "So this is why you asked me to feed the kids? So you could go and screw another man? You going around screwing other dudes now? You are such a lowdown liar!"

My knees began to shake. I didn't know what his reaction would entail next. The tears began to fall from my eyes and my voice became shrill and cracked as I tried to speak. "I swear I was going to tell you, Darryl. I was going to tell you this morning. Yes, I did see another man last night; no, I am not going around whoring myself. I am sorry. I am so very sorry. Please forgive me. I feel terrible about what I have done. You deserve to be angry with me. I'm sorry," I said, my face covered with my tears.

"How can I believe anything you say to me now, Susan? How?" Darryl said as he raised his hands in the air very animatedly.

"Do you want to go to counseling, Darryl? I know we have gone in the past, but I am willing to go again. I feel empty in this marriage. I feel used in this marriage…we need to talk—"

"Don't put this off on me, Sue," Darryl yelled. "You are the one having the affair, remember?"

At that point, there was nothing I could say to make the situation any better. The gas was already poured and the match was lit. There was nothing left to do but to ask the question again. "Will you please forgive me, Darryl?"

"I don't know, Sue; I don't know what I wanna do," Darryl said as he put his coat on and stormed out the door. My heart was as sincere as it could have been when I begged for Darryl's forgiveness for the affair I had with Terrence. I hated what I had done and I felt disgraced by my actions. That night, Darryl didn't come home. He didn't come to my house for several days, nor did he call. I wondered what his next move would be. I still hoped that Darryl would go to marriage counseling with me. Maybe this time would be different. Maybe there was hope for us to stay together. From that point forward, my guilt dictated how I interacted with Darryl, which proved to work in his favor.

Darryl agreed to go to counseling with me. The counseling sessions were embarrassing as I disclosed details of my infidelity with Terrence to the counselor, who happened to be the associate pastor at our church. The counseling made things palatable for a short while, but every so often Darryl pulled out his "cheater" ace in the hole, to keep me in line.

Darryl used my guilt as the arsenal he needed to shut me down. His intention was never to leave the marriage, even after learning about my infidelity. Ours was the perfect mix of marital dysfunction; Darryl enjoyed the perks that came with being married and sharing no responsibilities. My feelings of shame and disgrace kept me from filing for divorce, no matter what he did. Every day I lost more and more pieces of my dignity until I didn't know who I was anymore.

As much as it pained me, I decided to cut permanent ties with Terrence. I told him that I confessed to Darryl what happened between us and that I couldn't see or talk to him anymore. He said that he understood, but was heartbroken about my decision not to talk to him anymore. Terrence still called to check on me, even if it was just leaving a message on my voicemail to say hello. The last point of contact I had with Terrence was via an email. He told me that he loved me and because he loved me, he wouldn't contact me anymore per my request. His final words in the email were:

"Sue, please understand the words that I am trying to convey to you. The only thing I want is for you to be happy finally. You deserve that and so much more. I wish that I could give you that happiness, but I can't. There is someone who will love you the way you deserve to be loved and won't take your love granted. I am jealous of this guy already, because he will have your whole heart and all the love you have to give. I'm so sorry I couldn't give you all of me. Love Always, Terrence."

I quickly deleted the email from my inbox, but not from my memory. I felt like I was letting go of the only source of happiness I had, the only person who truly cared for me. I felt as if I was mourning yet another person in my life that I loved, all over again.

My life existed in the way I was accustomed to in order to remain sane. I snacked constantly and popped Xanax to take me out of my misery at night. By this time, I refused to step on a scale. I wouldn't even go my doctor anymore unless I had to get refills for my Xanax and blood pressure meds. I didn't need a scale to tell me what had become very apparent. My weight loss was now my weight gain. I had to pull out some of my old clothes from back in my heavier days because everything in my closet was officially too small to fit in anymore.

I waited until everyone was away from the house and cried loudly in my closet as I packed away my size 10 jeans in the back of my closet and covered them with several old blankets. I didn't want to make the mistake of accidently looking at them when I passed by. I was so filled with anger at myself for how far I had fallen that I considered packing up all my smaller clothes and giving them away. I told myself that I would never look and feel the way I had when I wore that beautiful red dress at the Shapes ball two years prior...I found the pictures from the Shapes fashion show and in a tantrum, flung them in the back of the closet with my covered clothes. The pity party I organized while sitting on the floor of my closet was in full swing.

The Affliction

Peace, Be Still

My mother's health issues had leveled off a bit, and both Wayne and I were relieved. Aside from her emerging dementia issues, physically she carried on pretty well day to day with help from her meds. The medication she had to take for her various conditions numbered about thirty pills daily. Calculating the quantity of pills for her morning, mid-morning, afternoon, and evening doses was like a complex session of both arithmetic and chemistry. Mama's meds needed to be measured out perfectly, all the way down to the last tiny pill. We had to make certain that one pill didn't interact with the others in a way that would make her sick. I don't know how Wayne and Tessa did it. They sat down every Sunday for thirty to forty-five minutes with stacks of prescriptions, studying the bottles and what medicine corresponded to what aliment; from cardiac pills to hypertension, from diabetes to medication for blood clotting issues, and just about everything in between.

It was around 3 p.m. when I received a call from Wayne while I was at work. Mama suffered a massive stroke in the middle of her dialysis treatment. The ambulance took her immediately to the hospital from the dialysis center, and I was to meet Wayne at Christ Hospital. "I don't have all the details, but it was a massive stroke, and she's not conscious," Wayne said in a fatigued voice as he raced to the hospital from his job. In a panic, I left everything and told Raul and April that I would need to leave work immediately, and without hesitation I was out the door. As I ran to the train station, I began to prepare myself for the worst news. My heart sank as I thought about the possibility of losing Mama. Tears stung my eyes as I boarded the train home and prayed that it would take off quickly.

I kept thinking about not getting to the hospital in time to see Brenda and my father before they died. I couldn't take another scene like that. I prayed that God would intervene and heal my mother by the time I got to the hospital. Tears ran down my face at the thought of losing my Superwoman. My anxiety posed to attack me; I squeezed my sweat-drenched hands together to keep them from shaking so hard. My Xanax would have helped the symptoms subside, but I had none with me. Thinking about having a possible nervous breakdown sent me so far into a spiral of panic that I couldn't calm myself down. I shook my head back and forth like a crazed person as I sat on the half-empty train. "I can't get sick, I can't get sick, I can't…Mama needs me, God, please help me!" I found myself saying out loud. My head began to pound with a new and unfamiliar intensity as my prayers to God became more fervent with every breath I took. I was completely petrified that I would surely lose my mind within seconds.

I wished that I could will the train to go faster. It seemed as if it was going in slow motion. Suddenly I remembered the words my mother always told when there was a situation that appeared hopeless. As if she was sitting by me, I heard her voice quoting her favorite scripture in Psalm 91: "'He that dwelleth in the secret place of the most high, shall abide under the shadow of the Almighty. I will say of the Lord, He is my refuge and my fortress: my God; in him will I trust.' "You don't have to be afraid, baby. Trust God."

I closed my eyes and prayed so deeply that I blocked out everything else. All I could hear was the sound of my own voice calling out to God to save my mother and to rescue me from my panic attack. As I made my appeal to God, in an instant, a wave of calm engulfed my body. Starting at my feet and moving to the top of my head, the sensation circulated through my being as if I had put my finger in an electrical socket; only there was no pain associated with the feeling, just a sense of total peace that filled me. My mind was no longer frantic like it had been seconds before, instead it was subdued. The shakiness and pain in my head disappeared. My body felt heavy. I found it impossible to move, as if I was bound by something that held me.

I yielded to the Power that filled me. My encounter was familiar and welcome as my face curved into a smile and I basked in the protected realm I was in. I knew it was God who took over my fears and replaced them with assurance via the Holy Spirit. I had the same exhilarating experience several years before when I was contemplating suicide. I was visited by the same miraculous phenomenon when I cried out to God with my entire heart to help me back then.

On the Metra train that afternoon, I experienced a personal visitation from the Holy Spirit; God Himself, had reached down to soothe me just as He had done in my past. His comfort caused me to rest and I did just that. By the time I got into my car and drove to the hospital, it was not in a frenzied huff, but with a peace that surpassed my understanding. God had assured me everything would be all right, and I trusted Him at His Word.

Mama's Season

As I made the turn into the hospital visitor's parking lot, I received a call from Wayne letting me know he and my sister-in-law Tessa had just pulled into the parking lot of the hospital as well. We all met up and made haste toward the doors of the hospital. Grabbing name tags from the reception desk, we learned that Mama had been taken to the intensive care unit where she had been given meds in order to slow the clot that blocked blood flow to a her brain.

According to her doctor, we learned that Mama had an ischemic stroke. Ischemic stroke occurs when an artery to the brain is blocked. If the artery remains blocked for more than a few minutes, the brain cells may die, causing issues like slurred speech and problems articulating. Patients like my mother who suffer from other conditions such as high blood pressure and heart disease and diabetes are at higher risk for subsequent strokes. The fact that Mama was a heavy smoker didn't make for a favorable situation either.

We were relieved that the doctors were able to lower her blood pressure and get her stabilized after the stroke. As she lay there in her bed still in a sleeping state, she looked so weak and frail; her mouth was lowered on the left side as a result of the latest stroke, causing her beautiful face to be slightly distorted. Wayne, Tessa, and I waited for hours in her room, just to see her open her eyes. When she did, we were not prepared for what she said to us as she groggily came to. In a heavy slur she repeated: "I can't see...I can't see." To our deep dismay, our mother woke up to discover that she had been struck, eighty-five percent blind due to the stroke she suffered hours earlier.

Our worlds changed that day, but Mama's changed in a more defining way. She would have to accept the fact that she could no longer see as she once did. Although she had a very tiny percentage of her sight, less than twenty percent, it would not be enough to live as she once did. There were many challenges that emerged during that season in our lives.

There would be many decisions to make with regard to her care. She would need round-the-clock care to do everything from going to the bathroom, to eating, and every basic function in between. When one of the hospital staff made the suggestion of placing Mama in a permanent nursing home, it was a unanimous decision that we would never go that route. Both Wayne and I knew that Mama would never thrive outside the walls of the house, that she loved so much and lived in for over the last forty-five years. It would be an extremely challenging road ahead of us to take on the responsibility of caring for her while we both worked and had our own lives, but for us, the choice was clear. We loved Mama, and we would do what was necessary for her, in the same way she always did for us.

When Mama returned from the hospital, her cognitive skills had declined dramatically. Articulating what she needed and wanted, was a struggle for her to convey and for us to understand, leaving all parties frustrated as we tried to adjust to Mama's new way of life. When she wanted to eat, she said that she needed a "pot." When she wanted water, she called it the "sink." She became frustrated as the words she wanted to say didn't come out the way she wanted them to.

"Sue…don't you underrrstand? No…no, gimmie the box…the box!" she said while pointing at the remote on the nightstand. It took me a very long time not to tear up when she went on a tangent with misplaced words and indecipherable phrases. My heart broke for my mother. Her loss of sight and the extreme difficulty she had with speaking left her aggravated, impatient and irritable most of the time. The first few months of her transition weren't easy for her and as much as I wanted to make her comfortable, most of the time she just wasn't.

The real frustration came from the absence of her treasured independence. My mother was a woman who made her own money, bought her own car, paid for her own house and raised her kids on her own without the help of anyone else. She was a born leader if there ever was one. The stripping away of her self-sufficiency and her self-reliance took a huge toll on her. Now she had to depend on someone else for her every need, all the way down to having someone else wipe her bottom when she had to relieve herself. Along with her ability to see, a portion of her dignity was lost as well.

I prayed for nights that would go smoothly for Mama; many of them didn't. Although she was reminded to always let either Denai or me know when she needed to use the bathroom, she always tried to take the short trip across the hall to the bathroom on her own. In one instance, it proved to be a tragic situation. My mother's legs had become so frail that they weren't sturdy enough for her to stand on without assistance. Along with her declined cognitive ability, her reactions and reflexes became very poor as well—not a good combination.

The sound that will forever ring in my ears is the sound of my mother falling after trying to get out of her elevated bed on her own. The sound of her body hitting the hardwood floor in her bedroom was horrific and deafening. Numerous times, I'd awake to the loud thud and her screaming out in pain, "Lord help me, Lord help me." I'd run as fast as my legs would carry me upstairs to pick her up from the floor where she would by lying face down, and with her mouth bloodied from the fall.

In one instance, Mama fell so hard on her face that her front tooth was knocked out. Denai and I both would attempt to lift her body from the floor without causing any further injury. I'll never forget the pained looks on Mama's face as I tried with all my might to lift her body, her weakened voice crying to God, "Lord Have Mercy...Lord have mercy," as both Denai and I cleaned the blood from her bruised and swollen lips and face.

Mama also suffered with internal bleeding from time to time as a result of stomach ulcers. Her stool was so full of blood that it overflowed and covered her pajamas in blood. The psychological stress of seeing my mother suffer was more than I could bear many nights. It was nearly impossible to keep a tough exterior and not break down in sobs while sponging the blood from her body. I couldn't stand the look on her pained, yet beautiful face as she struggled to mouth "I'm sorry," as if she had done something wrong. I can't count the amount of kisses to her forehead I planted while consoling her and letting her know that she had nothing to be sorry for, the "I love you's" I offered, the smiles I tried so hard to conjure up while looking at her when everything in me wanted to weep with compassion for my Mama.

After tending to her and making sure she'd fallen asleep, my next move was to the medicine cabinet for my pills to stabilize my mind, and then to the food that would soothe me. It didn't matter what the food was, it didn't even have to taste good. I craved anything that would take me far from the visual of Mama crying out for me, while lying in a pool of her own blood on the bathroom floor.

When there was no more Xanax to take, when the binge eating left me nauseated instead of satisfied, I hit a brick wall of hopelessness. Day by day, I witnessed my mother's illness slowly consume her mind and wreak havoc on her body. She depended on me for so much and I felt completely inadequate as her caregiver.

Suspension of a Sound Mind

I kept up my "stiff upper lip" façade pretty well while working at the law firm. The last thing I wanted to happen was for my employers to see the kind of distress I was in. Life had to go on as normally as possible during the day, but at night was another story. My rational demeanor seemed to fall to pieces the moment my foot hit the stairs to my house. Like clockwork, my body began to shake and my heart palpitated. Not even my fast food binges could eliminate my anxiety at this point. My usage of Xanax was only effective when I took more than prescribed, leading me to an unhealthy dependence.

In 2010, my mother was hospitalized for her internal bleeding issues. In addition to the excessive bleeding, her blood pressure became erratic; with extremely high and low readings that not even her prescribed medicine could stabilize. When her hospital stay ran its course, her doctors arranged for her to remain at a local rehabilitation/nursing facility until it was determined that she was well enough to return home. During that time, both Wayne and I went to visit her every evening after work. When we could not make it there, Wayne's wife Tessa filled in. Most nights our mother would just lie in her bed motionless, staring at the small TV on the wall.

Mama hated being in that facility. She wanted to be in her own home, in her own bed, surrounded by things that were familiar to her. She didn't talk much at all, except to ask how her granddaughters were doing at home. "You know I am blind now, Sue," she would often remind me in her increasingly slurred style of speaking.

Having less than ten percent of her sight, my mother could see only shadowy figures. But she could still somehow make out our faces when we visited, which was of great comfort to all of us. Her blurred eyes could even see enough to recognize her favorite commentators like Wolf Blitzer on the CNN channel, the station she always enjoyed watching to keep abreast of politics.

Home is Where the Fear Is

Most people get a renewed surge of energy at the end of their work day; they looked forward to heading home to where there was a relaxed atmosphere. Not me. Home represented a place of mental torment for me, a place that sparked a kind of ridiculous fear that left me physically sickened by my anxiety disorder. Horrific visions of my demise robbed me of any kind of peace, no matter how hard I tried to shake it off. "You are going to die just like Brenda did tonight from a brain aneurysm; you won't survive what is happening to you." The relentless harassment continued on in my head like a broken record, not letting up for a second. "You are going crazy; you will end up just like Uncle Billy, in an institution, and Darryl will take your kids from you." The more insistent the malicious thoughts became, the more I panicked until I became sick to my stomach.

The torment of my mind continued relentlessly night after night. I isolated myself from my daughters as much as I could, spending just enough time with them to make certain they were fed, and that any homework concerns were addressed. My mind seemed to be stable enough to go through the motions of being a mother when I had to be, but there was something that happened at night to that sensibility and lucidness that went haywire. The mental confusion, the extreme headaches, and feeling as if I were detached somehow from my body terrified me in a way that words fail to accurately describe. My extreme fright caused my nervous system to shut down, and causing my blood pressure to skyrocket to stroke levels. The notion of dying seemed like a welcome relief to the suffering I endured many nights. The scariest part of it all was realizing that my anxiety was completely irrational. I was losing control and I had no idea why.

Many times I wanted to drive myself to the hospital, but opted not to for fear of passing out at the wheel. I isolated myself from my family during my fits of panic because I was ashamed to reach out. There was no way I could explain to them what was happening inside my head. "You're losing your mind. You'll be committed to an institution if you tell anyone, and your kids will be taken from you," I concluded. My paranoia reached illogical levels.

Without a refuge in which to hide from my irrational beliefs, I cowered in my bedroom and cried until my eyes became swollen and dry, until I had no more tears to shed. The sound of my own screams became murmurs of pleas to God as I sat in the middle of my bed, rocking myself back and forth. I reached for my mother's white Bible that was on my nightstand and clung to it, holding it against my chest so tightly that my fingernails jabbed into the cover from the pressure of my grip.

Everything that I had ever heard about, the Grace and Mercy of God when His children are desperate for His intervention would come into play during those horrific moments I spent alone in my bedroom. I needed God's intervention like I needed to breathe right then and there. Still holding Mama's Bible in my arms, it felt like the actual lifeline between me and the hellish abyss that was determined to pull me under and I didn't let go of it. My index finger held the place of the book of Psalms, verse 91. I closed my eyes and repeated the words of the verse over and over again…and over and over again, as much as my memory would allow me to remember.

As I rocked myself back and forth in the middle of my bed, I often waited on the moment when my mind would completely snap under the pressure. I began to repeat the verse until my heartbeat slowed and my negative thoughts were cast down and finally I was ushered into a deep sleep. That night, and well into the early hours of the next morning, I felt as close to God as I've ever been. When I began to pray back to him in confirmation, the words He sent to me calmed my restless mind and spirit.

"He that dwelleth in the secret place of the most high, shall abide under the shadow of the Almighty.

 I will say of the Lord, He is my refuge and my fortress: my God; in him will I trust…"

The Spirit of Fear

I felt as if I was just going through the motions from day to day. My routine had become a series of checks and balances, making sure the kids were up, bathed, and ready for school before I left the house for work in the mornings. Then I'd visit Mama in the evenings for an hour or so before rushing back to make sure dinner was prepared for Denai, Lanie and Johanna.

Darryl was sporadic with his visits with the girls. When he'd come over, there was always a plea from him to stay over. There were many times I wanted to give in to his requests, because I hated being alone in the house by myself. It was as if there was a demon waiting for me as the sun went down and my house became darkened and quiet. There was something about being alone that lit a fuse to my anxiety disorder; it exploded with terrifying episodes that are quite indescribable to anyone who has never experienced what it's like to be at the mercy of a severe anxiety/panic attack.

Any little thing roused my anxiety. My startle reflexes heightened to an abnormal level. If one of the girls tapped me or called my name as I slept, my first reaction was absolute fear combined with my entire body shaking. It was so bad that my daughters were afraid to wake me for fear I might freak out and begin trembling. Just like the average person physically reacts to a situation of imminent danger or even watching a scary scene in a slasher film, that was my reaction to a simple touch of an unannounced hand as I slept. I felt like the most incompetent mother in the world. At night my children walked on eggshells throughout the house, being careful not to startle me, because they didn't want to trigger their mommy's anxiety.

Although there was a sense of peace that was found when I prayed, sometimes I just couldn't pray. I couldn't get the words out. It was like I couldn't form my thoughts due to the intense attack. I kept my children close to me some nights, but most of the time I made sure they were in their own beds upstairs. I didn't want them to see me in the throes of an attack, which was a scary sight to see for an adult, let alone a child.

Denai witnessed my episodes many times, to my dismay. She encountered my fits of screaming and crying, balled up in the fetal position and rocking myself back and forth while shaking uncontrollably. I sat there, unable to control what was happening to me, asking her to please go back upstairs so she wouldn't have to see it. The first time Denai saw me going through an attack, she had to be about ten years old. She was scared to death, asking me over and over again, what was wrong with me. I couldn't answer her. I didn't even know myself at the time. At sixteen, she was more familiar with what was happening to me. I explained to her about my disorder and the necessary monitoring of my blood pressure when going through an attack to ensure my reading wasn't at stroke level, and many nights it was. I should have opted to call someone to take me to the hospital when my pressure had become critically high, but I was too afraid to. In my mind at that time, going to the hospital meant that I would die there, just like my sister and father had, or I'd remain there, as in my mother's case.

Denai kept a close eye on me during my season of illness with my disorder. She comforted her younger sisters when they heard me become sick from the anxiety. "Mommy is okay, she just needs to rest." I often heard Denai say as I struggled to gain control of myself. She listened intently for so much as a whimper from me; no matter how hard I tried to hide it from her. Many nights my daughter held me in her arms as if she was the parent and I was the suffering child in need of rescuing.

Some days were better than others. Even in the midst of everything that was happening with Mama and my bouts with anxiety, there were some bright spots. The children were adjusting better to my split with Darryl, and for a while, things weren't as turbulent in terms of Darryl and me. I spent a great deal of time thinking while Mama was in the hospital. I took long walks during my lunch hour watching the people hustle back and forth on the crowded sidewalks of downtown Chicago and wondered how my life had changed so drastically in the span of a few years.

The death of my sister, father, and the drastic decline of my mother's health struck several huge blows to my senses. Among those heartaches, I also count the decline of my life-long friendship with Nikki among them. Our bond since childhood seemed to have disappeared into thin air. I recalled the words she said to me at Brenda's funeral with regard to our companionship. "You may have lost a sister, but you will always have me, I will always be your sister." I wondered if she still remembered those words, and if they came from her heart, or simply out of pity for the loss I suffered.

The Awakening

When Did I Give Up on Me?

More than anything else that bothered me, even more than my split from Nikki or my dealings with Darryl, was going back on my promise to rid myself of the weight that almost killed me. In the spring of 2010, I had eaten my way back up to almost 250 pounds. In less than two years, I re-gained 85 of the 145 pounds I'd lost, and was still gaining. The commitment that I once had to weight loss and fitness had fallen completely flat. The circumstances of my life pulled me away from the liberation I fought so hard for. The determination I'd acquired and the sense of accomplishment that once made me so proud seemed like a distant memory, a beautiful dream. I didn't have the mental energy to think about it anymore as I sat on a bench looking out into the blue skyline of the city with a bag of McDonald's fries and a box of chicken nuggets sitting on my lap.

Suddenly, I didn't feel hungry anymore. I didn't feel like devouring the salted fries like I did when I bought them for my lunch. As if they knew my thoughts, the pigeons that marched back and forth in front of me clustered together, eyeing the box of fries I had taken out of the bag. "Lunch is on me guys," I said, tossing the warm fries to the ground along with the bun from my burger. I sat for a few moments longer, watching the grateful pigeons peck with delight and scramble for the remaining fries on the ground. I ate the meat from my burger and the sparse pieces of lettuce hanging off of it while thinking of the good old days when I worked out with the Golden Girl Crew from Shapes, and the feeling of euphoria every time I stepped off the scale victoriously.

Thinking about that time in my life made me do something I hadn't done in a very long time. Smile. I must've smiled for a long time, because an elderly gentleman sat down beside me and jokingly asked, "Who in the world are you thinking about that has got you smiling so hard like that? What's his name?"

I snapped out of my thoughts and replied with a grin, "Not him…me."

"You?" the old-timer asked, looking rather confused.

"Yeah, me," I said.

"I was thinking about the old me that I gotta find. I gotta find me again…I have to get her back," I said as I got up and brushed the crumbs off my lap and departed from the bench I was sitting on.

My response to the gentleman made total sense to me, but apparently not to him. I was already halfway down the sidewalk when I heard him loudly chuckle with a rather late sarcastic response. "Good luck! I hope you find her…you…or whoever you lost!"

"Thank you, sir! I think I know where I can find me again!" I shouted in the distance as I waved goodbye. The odd conversation between me and the old-timer on the bench was prolific for me. His words rang in my ears the rest of the day: "I hope you find the 'you', you are looking for." That comment sparked a fuse in my brain. I pondered it as I walked to the commuter train heading home: Where did I lose her?

Was it in between mourning Brenda?

When Daddy died?

Did I lose her while acting as Darryl's co-dependent?

When Mama took ill?

My fire...my passion to help others who struggle with obesity overcome it...my desire to reverse the damage I'd done to my own body...when did I lose that?

Where did it go? When did I give up on me—*again?*

"Getting It"

My thoughts were deep as I sat down on the evening train bound for home. Through my side vision, I noticed the woman who sat beside me was clearly looking at me for a few minutes at least, tilting her head to the side as if she was trying to figure out who I was. Annoyed by her relentless staring, I quickly turned to her, hoping she'd take the "stop staring" hint and look away, but she persisted.

Embarrassed and ready to move to another seat, she must have sensed my irritation and stopped me when I began to quickly gather my things. "Excuse me, excuse me," she said as she tapped me shoulder. "I know this is a weird question, but were you by chance featured in an article about extreme weight loss in *Heart and Soul Magazine* several issues ago? I have seen you on this train before, and I always try to catch your attention to ask, but I never had the opportunity. I tore out the article because it was so incredibly inspiring to me. Is your name Sue Lewis?"

My irritated expression turned into a huge and very humbled smile. Indeed it was me that the lady on the train read about in the magazine. I submitted my story when I lost the 140 pounds in the hopes of inspiring others through my story. Not only did I submit my story to one magazine, I sent it to several, hoping that the editors would take an interest in my journey. I was floored that someone would actually remember the article and even tear it out to keep it because they were so encouraged. I couldn't find the words to say to her, so I just hugged her. We ended up talking the entire way to her stop on the train. As she got up from her seat, she held my hand and thanked me for giving her the motivation she needed.

"I'm so glad I had the opportunity to finally meet you…by the way, I've lost forty pounds since reading your article. I took the advice you gave, and it worked. I've got a long way to go, but your story keeps me going. I won't give up either; I feel too good now to go back to where I was. Thank you, Sue." I could clearly feel the burn of her enthusiasm as she spoke about her new and improved body. I couldn't help but to smile at her excitement, recalling how good it felt to earn those scale victories. We embraced once more as I reached into my pocket to scribble my phone number on a piece of paper.

"If you ever need to talk, or just some extra incentive to reach your goals, call me," I said, feeling absolutely tingly with happiness for the young woman. "You can do it. Never give up, no matter what life throws your way, push through and keep your eyes fixed on your goal. You might stumble, but get back up because you are worth it…don't give up on yourself." She nodded her head in agreement and swiped at the tears that had accumulated in her eyes as she exited the train.

I stood in the vestibule of the train car, watching the train pull away, and thinking about the blessing that had just been given to me. I never asked her name, but I felt like I knew her. She was me two years ago. She had a lifelong struggle with obesity, just like me. She happened upon someone who gave her hope, just like Shelly did for me. She decided that she was tired of living a defeated existence and was ready to do something about it, just like I had done.

As I thought more and more about the lovely woman who just left the train, it occurred to me that there was a stark difference between us. She had a fire in her belly for transformation, one that couldn't be contained, I was positive of it. When she packed up her bags to leave the train, I couldn't help but notice the fitness magazines in her bag, her workout shoes, and a key tag that had one simple word on it: "Determined".

Where was MY "determined" keychain that once was affixed firmly to my consciousness? There were too many indications from God that pointed to what I needed to do. The lady on the train served as a reminder of what my purpose was. It wasn't to wallow in self-pity and revert back to my old way of handling difficulty. I couldn't eat my way happy anymore. I couldn't drug myself up as a buffer against reality anymore. God didn't take me from a life of self-hate to drop me back into it.

As I walked off the train, the sun shone so brightly I squinted for a moment. It was warm, and the blue sky was as beautiful as I ever remember seeing it. All of a sudden, I heard within my thoughts this message:

"I have for you…plans for good and not evil, to give you a future and a hope."

I am not a Bible scholar by any means, and memorizing a multitude of scriptures has never been my strong suit, but for some reason, God placed that verse from Jerimiah 29:11 into my memory as I journeyed to my car that sun-filled evening. I looked toward the sky in confirmation of what the Holy Spirit had just spoken to me. With renewed hope and an odd eagerness that came over me while walking toward the parking lot, I smiled. Not just any smile, but a full thirty-two teeth, Kool-Aid smile.

There is nothing like the peace-filled serenity of God. Nothing that can make you feel as exhilarated in a split second as He can. Without the means of any man-made synthetics like drugs, alcohol, or high calorie fast food to usher in feelings of contentment, I felt a surge of positive energy within me. A strong certainty that my circumstances were shifting poured all over me. When, where, or how they would I hadn't a clue, but in any case, what I knew for sure was that God had my back, because He just told me so.

The reassurance God gave me didn't mean that things were suddenly hunky dory in my world by any means. There would still be mountains to climb and rivers to cross, and lessons still to be learned. The funny thing about God is He sends us through tests of endurance to teach us the lessons we need to learn for our greater benefit. Many times we fail them, but He is gracious enough to lovingly send us back to the drawing board until we "get it." It's like the sixth-grade teacher who allows us to do a re-test, agreeing to toss out the failing grade we received on the first one. The teacher knows that student has the capacity to get it right the next go 'round, so she gives him a chance to score higher the next time.

During my "I get it" period, I discovered that God is so much more lenient than that sixth-grade teacher is. He will always grant us a more chances to get it right, no matter how many times we are determined to get it wrong. No matter how painful it is to re-take the test, He permits the unfavorable conditions in our lives to persist until we finally "get it."

For decades, I'd been either tardy or absent altogether for my lessons in the classroom of self-worth, self-love, and inner-strength, even after my first dramatic weight loss two years prior. Curiously enough, my 140 pound weight loss was just a partial cure for a much deeper issue. Through a shift in diet and consistent exercise, I learned HOW to lose weight, but the reasons behind my years of obesity and my propensity to "eat my emotions" were still very much present.

Facing the Truth

Flipping on the light switch in the bathroom, I walked right past the scale for the fiftieth time, avoiding its presence like the plague. I couldn't remember the last time I stepped foot on it. As I stepped into the shower, I looked down at my expanded belly as it angrily growled at me to feed it breakfast. Struggling to ignore the noisy protest, I sleepily made a mental checklist of everything I had to do that Saturday, the main order of business being to visit Mama at Manor Care. Mama had been at the rehab facility for a few months now, making very slight progress, but progress just the same. It would probably be at least a few more weeks before she was strong enough to return home again.

I made a mental note to take her favorite pink turban to the facility later on that morning; her thinning hair was getting longer, and was just about completely white now. My sister-in-law Tessa made sure Mama's scalp was oiled, and she French braided her hair on a regular basis to keep it neat, which was of great help to me. Mama didn't remember a whole lot, but she certainly remembered to fuss at me for forgetting her favorite pink turban. Sometimes I actually liked to hear Mama hassle me. It meant that she still had remnants of the feisty Mama that I knew and loved.

I felt the warm water cascade down my chest and began to think, really think deeply about where my life was going. There was hardly any evidence anymore of the smaller frame I worked my butt off to achieve, and the proof was in the pudding when I tried to wrap my favorite bath robe around me, only to discover that it wouldn't close anymore without a struggle. I sighed a breath of disappointment mixed with anger for going in reverse over the past two and a half years. I recalled a time when I couldn't wait to hop on a scale in anticipation; now it served as a symbol of disgust for me. Before leaving the bathroom, I glared at it as if it had wronged me in some way. All of a sudden, in a fit of rage, I pushed the metal scale fervently into the corner of my bathroom with my foot, almost slipping on the 9wet floor. I caught myself by grabbing hold of the sink, realizing how ridiculous I must've looked, almost falling on the floor because I had decided to have a fight with my scale. After regaining my footing, I laughed hysterically at myself while deciding to pick up the poor scale and return it back to its original home. "Get your mind right, Sue," I told myself as I exited, still cracking up at the mini-tantrum I'd just had.

After my eating my Special K cereal for breakfast, I waited for Darryl to pull up in his parents' truck he deemed his own to pick up the girls for their weekend with him. He was supposed to have gotten them up the day before, but never showed up, which was the norm. Bases on our mutual agreement, he'd pick the girls up for the weekend every other Friday, but rarely did, leaving me to try to soothe Lanie and Jo's hurt feelings without revealing how I really felt. He'd come up with excuses like having no gas money to get to my house, coupled with a bunch of empty promises to his daughters that held no weight. Typically, it was me who ended up taking them to him and picking them up because I couldn't stand to see them so disappointed.

While the girls were occupied upstairs, I decided to take my mind off the frustration I was feeling waiting on Darryl. I flipped on my computer, and my eyes were immediately accosted by the flashing indicator light informing me of new messages in my Chat Spot inbox, which were into the dozens. I hadn't thought about Chat

Spot since Terrence and I parted ways, which was several months ago. Since I had time on my hands, I began the task of sorting out and reading the messages that were clogging up my inbox.

I had been inundated with everything from Chat Spot spam, to random babbling from mostly male members with the usual off-color offerings of "mind-blowing intimacy," all-expense paid trips to meet them, and proposals of deep love and admiration for me simply because they read my profile and "immediately captured" by my "class and beauty". It's amazing how you can fall so deep "in love" with a stranger just by looking at them, I thought as I clicked the delete button and chuckled through barrage of messages.

Cleaning House

Darryl hadn't shown up. Hours later, he finally called to say he couldn't make it because he didn't have any gas money. He implied that I should bring the girls to him, adding that the kids really wanted to spend time with him, as if I didn't know that. Normally, I would've given in, which he banked on each time. The truth of the matter was he didn't want to expend the energy to pick them up, because it was MY responsibility to do that. "We wouldn't be going through this if I was still there with my kids!" he snapped. I refused to give in. I told him no, which never went over well with his ego. Let me speak to Lanie!" he demanded.

It was my usual stance to let him know that this was the umpteenth time he did not do what he said he would in terms of financial support, as well as picking up our daughters on his weekends. This line of conversation would immediately turn into an all-out verbal war which Lanie and Johanna would hear. The verbal venom that was spewed between us always left with our daughters in tears. I refused to take his bait, opting to stifle my aggravation as I called Lanie to the phone. My emotions were so inflamed, I began to shake as I handed my daughter the phone.

"Okay, Daddy…I understand. It's okay, see you next week." I never heard the conversation Darryl had with Lanie, but I knew from past discussions with Lanie that at every opportunity he made me the bad guy. The thought of him filling their thoughts with lies about me incensed me like nothing else ever did. I made it a point never to malign Darryl when making reference to him with the girls, no matter what he did or didn't do. The fact that he would go to such lengths made me wonder if I ever knew him at all.

In the days and weeks that followed, the pressure and strain of my marriage got worse. There was no love, only a barren wasteland of what used to be love and respect for Darryl. I felt as if he was a stranger, an unfamiliar being that I was shackled to. A calculating person who never had the capacity to love me in the first place. I had the sensation of being asphyxiated whenever I thought of spending the rest of my life being married to him. I kept thinking to myself, "This is not what love is supposed to feel like; marriage should not feel like a slow walk to death row."

Even though Mama was in the capable hands of doctors and nurses at Manor Care, my panic attacks arrived nightly without fail as I went through malicious exchanges with Darryl whenever I stood up to him. I prayed my way through, depending on God to relieve my mind of worry. Every night I cradled my mother's white bible in my arms as I tried to combat the thoughts that kept me in a state of distress. I meditated on Second Timothy 1:7, "God did not give us the spirit of fear, but of power, love, and a sound mind." I reminded myself that I DID have a sound mind, because God gave it to me. Any notion that is contrary to what God bestowed upon me is deception meant to destroy me. I allowed that affirmation to penetrate my thoughts as the Holy Spirit ushered a sensation of tremendous peace and stillness within me. The experience was too incredible for words. Into the wee hours of the morning, I used the Word of God to contest my mental affliction, disputing every thought that rose up in opposition.

Every night I sought prayer as my refuge against my raging mind. As my dependence on God increased, the need for artificial means to calm myself decreased. I didn't need them anymore. I tossed my Xanax and refused to refill the prescriptions. Even when I told myself I needed them, I resisted the urge to use the tiny white pills as my emotional crutch anymore. I declined the foods I normally binged on to soothe myself and I stopped buying them. Whenever

I wanted to go back, I reminded myself of the words of the man on the park bench. I made a commitment to "find myself," and if I were to make that declaration a reality, I needed to dig deeply for that change to occur.

I focused on the words of acknowledgment from the woman on the train who kept the magazine article as her own incentive for change. Out of all the incentives that cemented my mind shift, my daughters were at the forefront of them all. They were the reason why I decided to change my life in the very beginning. If I gave up on my goals, what would prevent them from following in my footsteps?

I had no more time to waste on self-pity. If I was planning to have a personal revival, I needed to purge myself. For the first time in more than a year, I stepped back into the doors of Shapes Gym. There were many new faces on the staff, and some of the members I became familiar with had come and gone, but there was one face that was still there, smiling and running to the door to greet me. Shelly. With open arms, she reinstated my membership without hesitation or judgment. She didn't even ask where I had been for so long, and I was so glad she didn't. Shelly's only statement as she bear-hugged me was simply, "Welcome back, girly, we missed you!" I never knew I could miss the sound of a high-pitched voice so much.

I got back into the gym and it was like day one all over again. I had been away for so long that the familiar aches and pains of getting my body acclimated to working out kicked my butt. But I didn't let that stop me from doing my full thirty-minute workout. Although slow to get started, I finished with a sense of accomplishment that felt amazing. I had my work cut out for me with getting back into the swing of things in terms of a consistent regime of exercising, drinking more water, and resuming my healthy eating patterns again. Being back at Shapes reminded me of the exhilarating feeling of the endorphins that pumped throughout my body as I worked out and the pump of adrenaline that made me feel alive. I was ready get back to work. The aches and pains were a small price to pay for what I was getting in return, my morale.

It was as if clarity had taken over my uncertainty. I knew the decision I had to make next and it was crystal clear. I met with Darryl the next day to let him know I was filing for divorce as soon as possible.

Strongholds Released

After years of uncertainty, I was ready to take the necessary steps to take control of my life. After ten years of the same garbage, my tolerance to Darryl' foolishness had run its course. My prayer life was becoming stronger and revelations were coming to the forefront. The assuredness I needed for my next move had been made laid before me.

Confirmation regarding my spiritual dilemma over divorce was given to me in the form of a stranger. I revealed my struggle as a Christian choosing divorce to a much older Godly woman who was a co-worker of mine, Mrs. Katherine. We were discussing issues within the life of a Christian. I told her about my decade of being married to Darryl, complete with a brief backdrop of the perpetual negligence, disparity and barrenness I felt being with him.

I told Mrs. Katherine how I was desperate to be released from him, but was conflicted due to my Christian beliefs. I told her I didn't want to make God mad at me; the thought of losing His love was petrifying to me. "God wouldn't love me anymore if I divorced Darryl. It's in the bible that God hates divorce, He will hate me too if I go through with it," I told her with a familiar anxiety that shook me when I even said the word.

Mrs. Katherine took a brief pause as she took in all that I revealed. "It sounds like your husband has abandoned you, Sweetie. God has something to say about husbands who abandon their wives as well, did you know that?" she said as she looked tenderly into my tearful eyes. Mrs. Katherine led me to a scripture that set my heart free from the guilt that held me hostage:

'But if any provide not for his own, and especially for those of his own house, he hath denied the faith, and is worse than an infidel" (Timothy 5:8).

As Mrs. Katherine held my hand, her words of wisdom flowed. "Sweetheart, release your heart from that torment it has been in. God loves you; nothing you do will ever change that. God never called for His beloved children to be unequally yoked to someone who is intent on the abandonment of his family. If your husband refuses to provide for his family, then he has most certainly deserted you and your children. Do what you must do with a free heart and mind, and God will continue guide you, love you, and keep you. Release yourself from the destructive stronghold of guilt. God never intended for you to be bound in self-reproach." I was grateful for the counsel of Mrs. Katherine. The wisdom she shared with me set my heart free, and provided the confirmation I needed. I knew what I had to do.

The Rise

FILED, STAMPED

I moved forward in the process of filing for divorce from Darryl. I was fortunate enough to work for a supervisor who was kind enough to help me with the particulars of filing the court papers. Raul advised me with what I needed to do and even downloaded the necessary documents for me. He would allow my lunch breaks to be extended for however long it took for me, to run back and forth to the courthouse, which was conveniently across the street from the law firm. He made what would have been a very expensive undertaking cost less than $50.00 total. All I paid for was the filing fees. I will be forever grateful to the management staff that assisted with the smooth transition. It was as if God was just waiting for me to move my feet, so that he could open the necessary doors for me to walk through. Within two weeks, my divorce papers were filed at the Cook County Courthouse. I felt like a world of heaviness was suddenly released from my heart. The liberation I experienced when I heard the clerk's stamp hit the paperwork with a thud was the best sound I had ever heard. In red ink, the circular stamp impressed the one word that made me giggle out loud and I didn't care who heard me: "Filed."

The clerk looked at me over her glasses and said with a chuckle, "I get that reaction all the time."

I wondered when I would receive a call from Darryl with some smart-aleck remark, or fuming about the filed divorce papers, he would soon receive in the mail. I waited for the confirmation, but had yet to hear from him about it. I knew that when he found out that I had actually gone through with filing, it wasn't going to go over well.

I knew him like a book. Darryl craved control and his ego drove him. For me to speak up on my own behalf and make a decision that would affect his comfort, had the makings of an all-out verbal brawl written all over it. I must admit that I was afraid to tell him initially. His demeanor was so intimidating to me that my usual response to his ranting was to quiet down and cower while allowing him to have his way. I threatened him with divorce so many times in the past that I had lost count. But this time there was a peace with my decision. My mind was steadfast and made up that this was the only way I could truly follow through with my commitment to love myself completely.

I'd been forced to be silent countless times in my life. Early on, people I trusted twisted and shattered my budding self-worth. From my stepfather to trusted neighbors, I was told to keep quiet as the sexual and verbal abuse continued. I too played a part in the systematic "hush-hushness" with my own insistence of self-silencing by means of stuffing ridiculous amounts of food into my body to muzzle the pain; I could not handle on my own. I was officially tired of it.

Sick and tired of the merry-go-round of trepidation, and now I was getting off and for good this time. I was done being afraid of what others might think of me, afraid of standing out in a crowd, afraid of standing up for myself. My self-esteem had been stolen long ago, by the misplaced guilt I carried around like a noose around my neck that got tighter and tighter into adulthood. It was plain to see that my asphyxiation was forthcoming if I didn't do something to save myself. If nothing changes…then nothing will be changed. It took me decades to get that, but finally, I got it.

I mentally prepared myself for the angry resistance, when Darryl found out about my filing for divorce. The perks from our marriage weren't big in magnitude, but he would fight with all he had to keep them. I carried him and the children on my job's health insurance, and he was the beneficiary on my life insurance too. A divorce would mean that he would legally lose that, as well as carte blanche to anything else I had as his wife.

Darryl was four hours late picking up Lanie and Johanna for the weekend. I figured it was as good a time as any to inform him of my courthouse activity as of late. My feet were steady, and my hands were tightly clasped together for support, when I heard him pull into my driveway. I purposely made sure that Lanie and Johanna were spending "sister time" with Denai at the local mall when Darryl finally did arrive. I knew if I told him that I needed to talk to him about something important, he "wouldn't have time for it," which was laughably ridiculous considering he didn't have a job or anything else constructive he was doing with his time. Hoping for the best, but prepared for the worst, I gave him the benefit of the doubt, and hoped for a diplomatic discussion while waiting on the girls to return. Regardless of what occurred from here on out, I refused to be intimidated by him anymore.

Darryl did his usual manic ringing of my doorbell several times as if something was on fire, something he childishly did just to aggravate me. "Why do you ring the bell like that, Darryl?" I asked as I felt my heartbeat accelerating and my palms becoming sweaty.

"Where are the girls? I got my car running." Apparently he had taken full pretend ownership of his parents' fancy SUV. I was still on speaking terms with my mother-in-law, so his façade wasn't fooling me. He had one foot on a banana peel, and one foot out the door of his parents' home because of his excessive driving of their truck and not helping out with the bills. The scenario was painfully familiar. Darryl loved to appear more together than he was, especially around me. For that reason, I totally ignored that part of his statement.

"The girls are gone with Denai, but they will be back soon. I need to talk to you. Sit down with me," I said as I ushered him from the porch into the living room.

"With Denai? Why? I told you that I was coming to get them an hour ago; they should have been ready to go. When are they supposed to come back?" He said with familiar hostility in his voice. "I don't have time to talk right now. I'll call you later about whatever it is that's so important."

I decided to strike while the iron was hot with what I had to say. "I'm just going to come right out with it. Two weeks ago I filed for divorce. The divorce papers are on their way to you, if you haven't already received them." There. I said it. I felt a feeling of slow release as I looked at him directly in his eyes, waiting for his response.

Darryl chuckled as if I told him a joke. A wide grin of sarcasm appeared across his face as he shook his head at me. "So, you're a big girl now, huh? You finally filed for divorce huh? It's cool, I haven't checked my mail yet, but I will be looking out for the papers." He turned away from me, still chuckling as he looked out of my living room window. "You're going back to your married dude? Is that it? You know, the one you were screwing last year? Whatever, Sue," he said with a condescending tone as he looked me up and down in disgust. "Tell the girls that I will be back for them next weekend. I can't wait in here for them to come back. Tell Lanie to call me when she gets back too." With that, he slammed my door and drove off, the wheels of the truck screeching down the street.

I was waiting for that same feeling of euphoria that I had at the courthouse, but it was absent. I was left feeling like a fool…a fool for thinking that Darryl had ever truly loved me…a fool to think that I could love him enough for him to change who he was. I'd been a fool for ushering him into my mother's house, my family and my life. "*I made this bed, I will have to lie in it*", I told myself as I sunk down into the couch.

After that, Darryl was angrier and more vindictive than ever. Ego driven, he didn't care about the casualties that resulted in his disdain for me. Unfortunately, our children were front and center for the nastiness that was spewed. For me, it seemed like déjà vu all over again. I witnessed the nasty dismantling of my parents' marriage and felt like it was my fault for somehow causing it. As difficult as it was, I sat the girls down and explained to them as delicately as I could about the divorce and why I had to make the decision. While my youngest Johanna was visibly saddened, I sensed indifference with Lanie after my gentle explanation.

Always her little sister's spokesperson, Lanie chimed in: "We understand, Mommy. We know you and Daddy don't get along too well anymore." The truth was that the girls were worn out from the heated exchanges too; perhaps they figured things might be better if we did divorce. The news hit Johanna the hardest. She was seven years old, the same age I was when my parents went through a bitter divorce. I knew exactly how Johanna felt. She didn't understand why Darryl and I couldn't be married anymore. No matter how I tried to explain, she was still much too young to understand the gravity of everything. It tore me to shreds to see her cry and ask why, over and over again.

I didn't hear from Darryl for a while after our little tête-à-tête in my living room about our divorce. He didn't call or do one of his drive-bys to see the girls for a while. I was hoping that he was taking time out to gather his thoughts so that we could reach a mature and mutual understanding. I still needed him to sign the divorce papers in order for everything to be final; otherwise he could show up in court to contest the divorce, which was the greater possibility. As hopeful as I was, I knew he would not be amicable about the divorce. He knew how much I wanted to move on with my life without him as my husband, and he knew the reasons why too. Yet, I kept hope alive that he would just sign the divorce decree, split the few items we had as a couple and work out child support. It had been almost a month since I filed, and I knew he had received the divorce papers by this time. I waited not so patiently for Darryl to return my calls to him.

The Lightbulb Moment

I tried not to obsess about Darryl and whether or not he would fight the divorce. I needed to take my mind off of him and focus on me for a change. Despite all the drama surrounding my forthcoming divorce proceedings, I felt good that I was finally taking control of my destiny. My commitment started with Shapes Gym, and that's exactly where I spent a good deal of my time when

I wasn't visiting Mama at Manor Care or tending to the girls. I split my evenings up so that I could at least get in a forty-five minute workout, while the girls were in their afterschool programs. At night, I felt rested, not the jittery fear that I was used to. My mind felt renewed, and despite the occasional anxiety spell, I felt so much better. My blood pressure was slowly becoming stabilized with the help of medication, and when my doctor asked if I needed more Xanax, I was proud to say, unequivocally, "No Thanks."

The only thing that would make my outlook even brighter was if Mama was to come home recuperated and feeling better. Things seemed to be headed in that direction too. Mama's doctors reported that although her recovery was slow, she'd made significant improvement, perhaps enough for her to come home soon. It was the best news I'd heard in a long time.

It's funny how frustration can either motivate you or discourage you. In my case, I learned quickly to use my fury as fuel for some kick-butt workouts at the gym. Every time I thought about the games that Darryl was playing, I moved a little faster, squatted a little deeper and jumped a little higher on the gym floor. I took every negative emotion I bottled up and converted them all into focused motivation, surprising even myself with the bursts of energy I experienced long after my workouts were over.

I felt it…I felt the fierceness beginning to re-emerge. The unstoppable feeling I experienced during my initial weight loss was back, but this time it included a prospective that was absent the first time around. The missing puzzle piece of my life wasn't wrapped in the massive weight loss that I achieved a few years prior. Although losing the excess pounds was indeed imperative for my health's sake, there was a hurdle much higher that needed to be tackled in order for me to be whole. The revelation that I uncovered was one heck of a bombshell that illuminated my consciousness like nothing had before.

My obesity was simply the by-product of the main issue, a lack of reverence for myself. The deep-seated guilt I internalized for everything from my parents' divorce, to the shame of sexual abuse, to the rejection from others because of my weight, stoked the flames of my self-loathing for decades. My lack of self-worth was the blueprint to all my relationships with men as well, most recently my ten-year marriage to Darryl. I settled for a marriage that was never based on love, but manipulation and self-seeking benefits for the other party. I conditioned myself to be grateful for the slightest hint of regard I received from Darryl… then called it "love" for ten years.

I thanked God for the wisdom that had been sparked. For the epiphanies that flowed from my thoughts in abundance as I examined my life. It was difficult to forgive myself for the past mistakes I made as I evaluated my choices. I went through a period of mourning, complete with a "shoulda, coulda, woulda" pity party afterwards.

After going over my regrets and missteps, I came to one solid conclusion. I wasn't the same voiceless person I was before. My idealisms, my perspective, my demeanor…they were all being slowly transformed. Changed. The realization hit me like a ton of bricks. The ugly lies I adopted as truth my entire life were being revealed. I shot them down, one by one in opposition while embracing my new truth: *I AM lovable… and indeed worthy of being loved.* It was the quintessential "light bulb" moment.

I didn't need a New Year's Day to proclaim my resolution. It was time to move on to what God had planned for me.

Get it Together

It wasn't easy getting back into the flow of my routine after being gone for so long, but I was like a dog with a bone with my weight loss ambitions. Even with the painful newness of working muscles that had been dormant, the "burn" felt a lot better than the regret of stuffing my mouth with food on a daily basis. On the gym floor, I was a bit slower because of the tenderness and pain in my knees. They had become fragile due to the extreme weight they were under for so many years. I was frustrated many times because I could not jump back into my old routine. My endurance took a while to get going, but I refused to stop. I had my eyes fixed on my comeback and this time it wasn't for me. God had given me a charge to help others like myself, like the woman I met on the train that used my story as her motivation. My new target goal was to lose the 85 pounds I re-gained and I was determined to follow through, no matter what.

Some days were victorious, some days not so much. The pain in my knees and back prevented me from going to the gym when it was severe, but I learned to rest a day or two then get back to work. I turned down the inclination to give up because of "I didn't feel like going to work out." To be truthful, there were many days I didn't feel like it. But what was the alternative? Giving up? Nope, I wasn't going down than road anymore. I'd hit the gym floor and tell myself I would do fifteen minutes, and then stop. After fifteen minutes, I discovered I had ten more minutes in me, then ten after that. It's all a matter of the mind. If my objective was to teach others how to be committed to their health, then I would have to set the example.

With the Grace of God surrounding me, He gave me the strength and fortitude to surpass even my own weight loss expectations. After retaining my focus, I lost 25 pounds within a month's time.

One thing had become distinctly different about me since my initial weight loss three years prior. In the midst of those three years, I discovered that it wasn't just physical weight that I was bound by…I'd also been lugging around years of psychological weight that was slowly ravaging my spirit. Although I still desired an equally fulfilling relationship, I was no longer desperate for someone to love me. True love would come when God sent it. In the meantime, I worked on loving me.

I finally heard from Darryl when he asked if I could get the girls ready so that he could take them to a carnival nearby. He asked if I wanted to go with them, which was such a shock I nearly dropped the glass of water I was drinking. I accepted the invitation, but reminded myself about Darryl's ulterior motive tendencies. I would stay cautious and vigilant.

Darryl's voice was surprisingly subdued as he explained the reason for my invitation to the carnival. "I figured we could discuss the divorce papers while the girls did their own thing at the carnival. I got the papers in the mail a few weeks ago. I had to let my friend look over the paperwork, ya know…to see if it everything was legit with them."

What struck me almost to the point of laughter was this friend who supposedly checked the court-filed documents for authenticity. Did he actually think that the papers were phony, or was this some kind of bull crap Darryl concocted for another purpose? My antenna went up immediately as I accepted his invite to the carnival. I gathered my copies of the divorce decree as well as the stamped original just in case there was still a question. "That sounds good, Darryl; I will get the girls ready to go. So, we are good to go with your signature?" I said.

"Yes, if that's what you want, sweetheart…I mean, Sue. You deserve to have my signature," Darryl said, sounding remorseful.

I knew him well enough to know something wasn't right about his newfound repentance. It had been way too easy and Darryl never operated on regret. Something about the whole thing smelled rotten to me.

"Oh, by the way, I don't have my mother's truck anymore. She took it back, which I am not happy about at all. Do you mind if we drive your van to the carnival? I'll give you a couple of dollars for your gas. You don't have to drive me home; I'll just take the bus," Darryl asked sweetly.

Drive my van? I shouldn't have been surprised by his nerve and yet I was. It was typical for Darryl to actually have the audacity to ask me to drive my van and burn my gas for his outing with the kids, especially after the nasty way he talked to me the last time we spoke. Turning off my anger for a moment, I gave him the benefit of the doubt, figuring he might actually be on the up and up and ready to sign his name to the divorce papers. He sounded like he was agreeable enough. He did mention that if a divorce is "what I wanted," he'd agree to sign. Hoping his friendliness toward me wasn't some kind of ploy, I agreed to drive us all to the carnival as he requested. To quote the English poet, Alexander Pope: "Hope springs eternal."

Delays and Deception

Lanie and Johanna were thrilled to see Darryl and me together, in any capacity. They sat in the back seat looking as happy as could be, smiling from ear to ear. "So, are you guys gonna ride roller coasters with us?" Lanie shouted from the back.

"Are we all gonna go out to dinner after this?" Johanna asked as she smiled so hard that her eyes closed shut.

"No and no," I answered as I smiled at them through the rearview mirror.

"Well, maybe we all can go out to dinner after this," Darryl interrupted as I cut him a look. This was another form of manipulation that I despised from him. Putting me in a position that made me look like the bad guy was his favorite mode of operation when it came to pitting me against him. He knew that I wouldn't agree to that, especially when I was trying to establish some sort of normalcy with the children with regard to our not being together anymore. Besides, he never even offered an apology for the bile he spewed when I initially told him about the divorce and now he was behaving as if all had been forgotten. He never apologized because he wasn't sorry. He meant every vicious word.

"No sweetie, you and Johanna are gonna have a blast at the carnival while Daddy and I talk for a little bit, then we are heading home, okay?" I interjected as I pulled into the tree-lined parking lot and grabbed my manila folder.

After I got the tickets and wrist bands for the girls, Darryl and I made sure that the girls were within eyeshot as we searched for a nearby spot. We sat down on a picnic bench a safe distance away from the ruckus of the carnival to talk. There was an awkward silence as I pulled out the divorce decree and turned it to the last page for him to sign. According to Darryl, he had already read it in its entirety with his "friend," so there was no need for a long, drawn-out discussion of the obvious, but I had a feeling that simply signing the divorce papers would be too easy for Darryl.

Darryl picked up the papers and scanned each line of the decree, then looked up at me with a slight smile. "So, you ARE serious huh?" he asked, as if this was the very first time he had heard anything about my seeking a divorce from him.

My eyes focused on his as I prepared to speak. Hesitation suddenly arose like it normally would whenever I was bold enough to speak up in my defense. The jitteriness of my nerves caused me to stutter as I began to speak to him. I shoved my hands in my pockets, as an attempt to stop them from shaking. I took a deep breath and readied myself to express my thoughts to him with conviction: "Darryl, our marriage was over long ago, but you know that. Saving us was my priority, it was never yours," I said as my voice shook. "There is nothing left for me to give and I am past the point of tired. I gave, you took, period. I don't wish you any ill will, I'm just moving on," I declared confidently, my voice becoming stronger with each word. "We can parent our daughters, but that is the extent of it. I can't do this anymore."

There. I had said it. And it felt good. For the first time, I stood up and didn't back down. I wasn't that voiceless little girl, who was shoved naked in a closet to be tormented and abused anymore. I wasn't the despondent young woman who felt compelled to eat herself into oblivion in order to cope with pain for over twenty years. And I definitely wasn't the naive, timid, and desperate young woman Darryl had married eleven years ago who bent over backwards and clung onto the wrong man just to say she had one at all. I wasn't that woman anymore.

My psychological makeover was officially in full bloom. The constant wear and tear on one's spirit can do that to a person. You get tired. After taking so much for so long, we simply become emotionally bankrupt. When our "light bulb" moment arrives and smacks us over the head with truth, we are prompted to run for the hills as quickly as we can, taking our hearts with us. I'd officially entered the courtship phase of learning what it meant to truly value myself. Divorcing Darryl was phase one of the plan to immerse myself in self-respect, as well as put a halt to any relationship that wasn't equally fulfilling across the board. I wasn't anyone's doormat to use whenever it was suitable anymore. I was headstrong and assured when I handed him the pen for which to sign the papers that would free me from him.

Ultimately, Darryl did exactly what I thought he would do, which was pull a fast one. After telling me that I deserved his signature so sweetly over the phone a few hours before, he turned right around and changed his tune by refusing to sign the divorce papers. "I thought about it on the way here, and I decided that I need time to think about this. I mean, I don't feel right about it all of a sudden. I don't think I am going to sign them just yet. Give me a few weeks to think about all of this."

I should have known that this would be the result of him purring over the phone all nice and friendly. What he really wanted, he got. In this case, he wanted my frustration and a ride to the carnival. I tried not to let him see how incensed I was at his shift in attitude. But I was sure he saw it, and I was sure it was the cherry on top of his cake. He didn't give a crap about our marriage, but he didn't want to let go of the benefits of it, which was to keep me bound in it. He craved control and seeing me flustered was the ego boost he desired. I gathered my thoughts and enjoyed the rest of the time I had at the carnival watching the girls enjoy themselves. After the dust settled that day, I decided not to let Darryl get the best of me. I might have to wait a little longer than I wanted, but all would work out for my good, just as God promised me it would. I went to bed that night with an odd sense of calm. I didn't question it; I just embraced it. I do believe that was the best night's sleep I'd had in a very long time.

The Revival

The Strength of a Woman

I arrived for my daily visit to see Mama at Manor Care and was delighted to find that she was in a peppy mood. She was quite chatty and alert, though still very weak in her body. Those extra sets on the weight bench I had put in at the gym came in handy when I went to see her. Lifting her to an upright position wasn't always easy. Although her delicate frame was slight, most of the time she could not bear her own weight when she got up to go to the bathroom. I did quite a bit of lifting to get her up and out of her bed at the facility. It was a struggle sometimes, but we eventually made it to her bathroom. I learned to stay very close to the door to help her up from the toilet. Mama had become so weak that she could no longer get up on her own from the toilet, resulting in frequent falls in the tiny bathroom, leaving her crumpled on the floor and wailing in pain. It took the assistance of two of us to get her into the upright position after falling on the floor. The pained frustration was clearly written on her face as we carefully guided her back to bed and tucked her in.

If you look up Super-woman in dictionary, there would rightfully be a picture of my mother beside its definition. Mama's determination was made of pure steel even after she was no longer able to care for herself. Stubborn through and through, both Wayne and I had to frequently remind her that she simply wasn't able to do things as she used to, and that she should ask for assistance, but that wasn't Mama. She was the caretaker; she was the one who was supposed to make sure we were all right, not the other way around.

Besides the bathroom challenges from time to time, it was good to see that my mother was slowly progressing. The time that I spent with her at Manor Care wasn't always full of chatter, but just being there with her was good enough. The best part of my visits was seeing her smile the biggest and sweetest toothless smile whenever I kissed her on her forehead. She was the epitome of amazing to me and still as beautiful as ever. Mama had always been my hero throughout my life, but at this difficult stage, enduring what would have caused others to give up qualified her for a much bigger and grander superhero cloak.

Finding a Good Thing

My evenings at home were a sight better than they used to be. I felt energetic and accomplished after coming home from a good workout. I felt my demeanor changing for the better and physically, I was feeling stronger than ever. The nasty skin breakouts I experienced as a result of extreme stress were a thing of the past. My skin was clearer and so was my mind. Every morning when I opened my eyes, I gratefully thanked God for my new presence of mind he blessed me with. Each day I felt differently than the day before, resuscitated and resurrected. Although difficult to put into words, I felt as if I had been raised from the dead.

I interacted with the girls a lot more, taking them out to dinner and the movies while taking advantage of the fact that Mama was safe and sound at Manor Care. Most nights when the kids were doing their own thing upstairs, I hopped on Chat Spot to chat with some of my buddies there; it took the edge off thinking about whether or not, Darryl would ever sign the divorce papers or maybe even try to drag out the process by contesting it altogether.

Spending time online had become my therapy and a getaway of sorts. I was considered a Chat Spot "veteran" at this point, a title that gave me a chuckle when I first hear of it. I became really close with many of the members I chatted with. Some of whom I considered to be like family. We exchanged numbers and skyped almost every night just as if we had known each other all of our lives. We were a close-knit bunch, which was ironic, because none of us lived in the same city nor had we ever met, up to that point. I thought it funny that people that I never laid eyes on were closer confidants than people I considered friends in my own city.

I felt fortunate to have found a network of both women and men that I connected with so closely that we called one another "sister" or "brother." The fellowship we all shared filled voids of genuine friendship for many of us. There was one particular member of our cyber huddle who intrigued me the most. His name was Cander.

Cander wasn't particularly chatty, but when he did say something, it was always something of substance he expounded on. He had the most endearing, yet driest sense of humor since David Letterman. Not everyone "got" cleverness, but I did. He possessed an intelligence and quick-wittedness that made me miss his presence in the room whenever he wasn't there. It was simply refreshing. Cander definitely stood out to me from the others in the room. He seemed to have taken a shine to me as well. His daily message to me made me smile, just by the simplistic nature of them. Two words and nothing more: "Hello beautiful." There were never any underlying sexual overtones or lewd requests like the usual messages I received, just that one simple compliment. After some weeks of smiling and returning his hello, I decided to say something more since he hadn't stepped up to the plate yet.

EYEZ: Hi, Cander, thank you for your daily compliment. I was wondering if you could expound on anything else, maybe?

I tried to match his dry humor, although the dry stuff wasn't tops on my list of workable jokes. I hoped that my response was corny enough for a comeback from the subtle Mr. Cander. I couldn't believe I was being as daring as I was, and for me, lightweight flirting was pretty darn daring.

Not more than a few seconds later I received a response:

CANDER_1: Hello beautiful. I could really go for some Hooter Wings right about now. I'm starving.

I immediately responded back with great vigor and excitement:

EYEZ: OMG! I LOVE HOOTER'S WINGS TOO!

Cander didn't realize it, but he was speaking my language. Anyone who shared my deep affection for chicken wings drowned in hot sauce was my kind of guy. Cander and I bonded over our mutual admiration of Hooter's Wings, and so much more. Out of curiosity, I asked him why he never bothered to strike up a conversation with me and why he only sent me the two-word message. Cander explained to me the reason why he never initiated real conversation with me was because he noticed on my profile that I was married and respected my status.

CANDER_1: I hope telling you that you were beautiful wasn't offensive. Your husband is blessed to have such a lovely wife.

EYEZ: I am actually in the midst of filing for divorce, Cander.

CANDER_1: Divorce? Yep, been there, done that 5 years ago. I'm just now getting my head together from my own. Has the process gone smoothly?

EYEZ: It's going about as smooth as a thorn patch full of needles on a cactus.

Our conversations gave birth to even more conversations as we discovered how much our lives were parallel to one another's. Even though I had grown quite fond of him, I approached our budding companionship with cautious eyes and ears, looking for the slightest mention of anything that would be considered risqué in his dialogue with me. I didn't want this to be another Terrence case where the attachment was based on sex in order to fill voided desires. Although he never came off that way, I still listened intently for anything that gave the impression that he might be in search of just a bed buddy. I had no intention of falling in love with someone on Chat Spot or anywhere else for that matter. I had my focus on ending the marriage that I was tied to.

It turned out that Cander had been through some pretty rough storms in his personal life as well. Cander was a Navy veteran who lived in a small town in Delaware. He had three adult children and a son in high school, and was a devout Christian with a strong devotion to Christ, which I greatly admired. He had been happily married, or so he thought, for sixteen years to his high school sweetheart, until one day she told him of her plans to leave him. His wife left him for their mutual friend from high school and a teammate of Cander's. Without explanation, she drew up divorce papers, seeking the greener grass on the other side. For sixteen years he provided, cared for, and sacrificed for his wife and children, and still that wasn't enough. She married the other guy soon after, leaving Cander heartbroken, withdrawn, and utterly devastated.

I could relate to a lot of the struggles he went through, especially practically bending over backwards for someone who only wants to take what you have to give. Besides his strong faith in God, I admired the sentiment he told me regarding his life with his ex-wife: "Things weren't always perfect, and there were many times we struggled financially, but I gave all that I had to give to my wife and children. That was my job as a husband and father. I provided, I went without so that they could have what they needed and wanted. I loved my wife, and although her demanding, self-centered nature made being married to her trying at times, I stuck in there. I would have never left her. Not in a million years."

We formed a united front of sympathy with regard to one another's personal battles. It was easy to talk to Cander, so easy in fact, that we spent hours on the phone, talking into the wee hours of the morning just about every day. I felt like I had known him my entire life. He had a kind-hearted nature that drew me to him, but the fact that he never brought up intimacy at all raised my eyebrows a bit. I mean, he talked about women he dated since his divorce, but never brought up…sex. We were both adults, and I hadn't slept with anyone since Darryl, and that had been at least a year. I admit I was being a bit forward when I asked him the question that had been burning in my mind for a while about his lack of pillow talk with me: "So, why don't we ever talk about the feelings we have for each other, you know…feelings? Like, uh…sex." Immediately, I felt silly that I even asked the question, and even worse, that I had allowed the longing in my loins to speak on my behalf. Bopping myself on the forehead, I wished that I could suck the words back into my mouth and shove them down my throat. *He is totally thinking that I am some brazen hussy now*, I thought to myself while in the midst of the very awkward silence that lit up the phone line.

After a rather long pause, Cander gave his response to my question: "If you asking me if I think about making love to you, then the answer is absolutely. I think about it all the time. But that is not all I think about…I think about you in general, more than I do anything else nowadays. I care for you very much, Sue, more than I ever thought I would care for another woman. Getting back to your question about the absence of sexual conversation, the fact of the matter is, we aren't there yet. We are not at the point where those kinds of conversations should take place. It's too soon, and frankly, I respect you too much to interject sexual discussions into the time we spend talking to each other. Bottom line, it's just inappropriate at this stage."

I am glad that he wasn't in the room with me at the time he said that, because he would have witnessed me with my mouth hanging wide open. If I wasn't embarrassed enough already, that certainly did it. Cander's intention was not to make me feel bad about my rather audacious question though. He simply wanted to let me know where he stood in terms of our budding courtship, and make it unequivocally clear the level of reverence he had for me. One thing I could say about Cander that was quite different from my personality—he was very forthright and direct, and I liked that about him. I took his answer in stride and tried not to let my embarrassment show as I thanked him and quickly moved on to a completely different subject.

After we got off the phone, I couldn't keep what he said to me off my mind. He said he really cared for me. I wondered if it was as much as I cared for him. I couldn't believe I felt those teenage-crush butterflies in my stomach at just the thought of him. Unlike any other feeling I had ever had before in terms of the opposite sex, it felt pleasant, it felt safe, and it felt really, really right. There was something about Cander that curved my mouth into a smile whenever I said his name.

A few days after, I received his "Good morning beautiful" text without fail, but this time, with a different message. His message put me in full "tummy butterfly" overload. Simply stated, and in true Cander fashion, it read: "Have a wonderful day, beautiful, and by the way…will you be my girlfriend?"

I sprang up from my bed, sat straight up, and immediately responded with a happy and resounding: "Yes!" We entered into an exclusive relationship with each other, Cander in Delaware, and me in Chicago, even though we had never physically met…yet.

Time flew by, and our courtship just blossomed into something even more precious than I could have ever imagined. I often wondered where he had been all my life, but then again, I didn't care as long as he was present now. At this point, we had already confessed our mutual love for one another. Nothing felt as genuine as when he told me that he loved me, and nothing felt as natural as when I told him how much I loved him too.

I definitely wasn't used to the flow and ease of a relationship like the one I had with Cander. Given the tension I experienced from the divorce drama with Darryl refusing to sign the papers, Cander was a great buffer for the aggravation, coaching me through and encouraging me to remain positive. Darryl was clearly enjoying this cat and mouse game that he was playing with me. I had been to his house on several occasions, on the premise that he was ready to sign the papers and each time he refused. When I caught on to the game he was playing, I stopped catering to it. I decided to simply wait until our court date with the judge.

My boss Raul did give me a glimmer of hope and great advice with regard to my upcoming court date with Darryl. "If your husband doesn't appear at the hearing, you can be granted the divorce by default. He must appear in order for the hearing to proceed. If he doesn't appear, then you are good to go." Time would tell, but in the meantime, I wasn't going to indulge Darryl's ego trips any longer.

Two weeks shy of our court date, I tore open the piece of mail that had "Domestic Relations Division" stamped on it. I knew it was either about the child support that I had recently filed for, or something having to do with my upcoming divorce proceedings. It turns out that the court pushed our divorce proceedings date back two additional months due to some sort of scheduling conflict. Patience was never my strong suit, so needless to say, I was beyond livid. I wanted to get this over with, and now it seemed like this divorce would never take place.

"Yes...Yes...Yes."

The only thing that took my mind off this ridiculous divorce delay was the buzzing of my Skype indicator on my computer. Cander was online and requested that I join him, which was odd seeing as we always had specific times when we Skyped each other. He had texted me first, with a message that said he had something very important to talk to me about, and that it couldn't wait until later. Before I logged on, I took a deep breath. My stomach was twisted in knots. I knew this was too good to be true, I thought as tears welled in my eyes. I began trying to prepare myself for the worst; Cander was the kind of man I had dreamed of my whole life. He made me happier than I had ever been. Now it was over. I tried to figure out what he would reveal to me as the annoying Skype signal kept buzzing. He's either married, gay, or both, I thought. I braced myself for the other shoe to drop as I began to log in.

"Hey, sweetie," Cander greeted with a softened tone.

"Hi babe, what's wrong? What do you need to talk to me about?" I asked in a hurry, hoping he wouldn't drag whatever it was out. If it was bad news, I didn't want to wait to hear it.

"Sue, after I got divorced, I swore I would never allow anyone else to hurt me the way my ex did. I became a recluse after she divorced me, only going to work and coming home to go to sleep. I finally came out of my shell when I met you. You changed my life and my perspective. You are kind, warm, and wonderful. When I think about you I am happy, when I am unable to talk to you, I get depressed. You are so beautiful on the outside, but more importantly, it cannot compare to the inter-workings of your soul. I can't imagine my life without you in it. I love you with all my heart."

With eyes full of tears, he adjusted his computer camera and lowered himself with his knee to the floor. In those seconds, I honestly didn't know what to think. My eyes widened as I thought perhaps he was going to pass out or something. Was he sick? Was he dying from some illness and this was his final goodbye to me? He appeared in view, clearly still on his knee as he stared into the camera. "Susan, will you marry me?"

I was stunned. For a minute, I had to process the question he asked. I never had a man ask for my hand in marriage before. The idea of marriage was suggested by me when I was married to both Aaron and Darryl. I was pregnant both times and figured I should

"Yes...Yes...Yes."

be married before the babies came, and they both just kinda said okay.

I asked Cander to say it again, just to make sure I heard him right, but mainly because I just wanted to relish in those sweet words again. "Susan, sweetie? Will you marry me?"

I cried rivers of tears the second time around and not "cute tears" either. They were the snotty, blubbering, ugly ones. Through my happily hysterical sobs, I heard my voice saying "Yes...yes...yes."

Cander smiled as he wiped the tears from his eyes with his hand. "Thank you, sweetie," he very sweetly responded. Who does that? I thought. Who proposes via Skype on bended knee and then thanks the woman for her saying yes to him? But, that was Cander—delightfully unique in all of his ways. I was simply stunned beyond belief at what had just happened to me. Cander explained to me that this was my unofficial, official proposal. "I will need to do something before I can make this an official engagement, that and, well, take care of the obvious—an engagement ring."

"Like actually meeting each other?" I said sarcastically. We both chuckled.

"Yep, I think we might have to fit that in too, sweetie," he said in agreement.

"You know people are going to think we are crazy, that this is crazy. You know that, don't you?" I said, snapping myself back to reality and imagining what Mama, Wayne, and the rest of my family were going to say. Explaining to my daughters would prove interesting as well.

Cander and I had plans to meet in Atlanta for the first time. The Atlanta locale was chosen for a meet and greet with our Chat-Spot group. I was excited to get away for a little while; I needed the change of scenery that sunny Atlanta, Georgia would provide.

My nerves were in bundles when I exited the plane to meet Cander for the first time. He would be waiting for me inside the airport. My legs felt like jelly as I walked inside the terminal and began to make my way to my new fiancé. I checked myself in every mirror in every bathroom on the way to meet him. I wanted to look as perfect as possible. As I checked myself out in the mirror, I was grateful that I'd started working on my weight again. I wasn't a size 10 yet, but I was a darn good-looking 14. "Not bad," I said to myself as I did a little supermodel spin and smiled in approval. I headed away from the fifth bathroom mirror I had visited with my little red carry-on bag in tow.

Approaching the terminal where Cander said he would be seated, I thought I might throw-up from the nervousness I felt. I knew what he looked like from a computer camera position, but what if he didn't look the same? I thought. Maybe he isn't as good looking as

"Yes...Yes...Yes."

he appeared to be on camera? I thought as I journeyed through the huge Atlanta airport. Suddenly, I had a case of serious cold feet thinking that he might not be what I thought. As I shook off the ridiculous notions that I was submerged in, I saw gate seven far off in the distance, the gate that Cander was supposed to be at. "He is your intended," I heard very confidently within my thoughts. That notion provided a sense of comfort that calmed my jitters and soothed my apprehensions.

My heartbeat sounded like a drum as I slowed my pace when I reached gate five. I called him to let him know I was mere steps away. "I think I see you," I said as I approached gate six and watched a man look in my direction and then suddenly duck behind a wall. I saw the man's shoe; it was a black loafer, just like the ones Cander loved to wear. At the same time I walked up, the man in the black loafers stood up. It was Cander. As if time stood still for a few moments, we both looked at each other and embraced. I remember thinking that I had never felt anything so satisfyingly decadent in my entire life. As he held me in his arms, he whispered in my ear, "Look at you...you are even more beautiful than I imagined you'd be." His voice sounded like the sweetest music ever composed.

Cander looked exactly like he did via my computer screen, except better. With smooth caramel skin, a neatly trimmed goatee, a shy smile, and boyish good looks, he was absolutely adorable. At forty-six, he looked great for his age. His attire was very casual and laid back. In simple beige slacks and a neatly pressed blue button-down shirt, he appeared polished and very attractive. When we finally released one another from our embrace, I didn't want to let him go. Everything that I hoped for was right before me. My future was staring at me with a huge, wide smile and tear-filled eyes.

Our weekend in Atlanta was absolutely wonderful. We met our online friends and had a fantastic time getting to know one another over cocktails, a lot of laughter, and dancing. Cander, clad in a very dapper tuxedo, threw me for a delightfully stunned loop when he gathered everyone together at the venue and asked for everyone's attention. With just few words of love and affection spoken, he dropped to one knee and proposed for the second time, only this time, his proposal was complete with a little velvet box containing a beautiful, sparkling engagement ring in his trembling hand.

For the first time in my life, I was acknowledged. Not only acknowledged, but proudly reverenced for the world to see by someone whose love for me was not contingent on what I could give him. My answer was the same, but this time, with more exhilaration than before. I could not believe how the puzzle pieces of my life were slowly finding their intended places. I was ten feet from the ground, levitating on raw bliss. Only God could have created such a surreal moment.

When all the proposal dust had settled, there were decisions that had to be made with Cander and me. We would discuss them in depth as we traveled back to Chicago where he would meet my family, and most importantly, Mama. I was nervous and excited at the same time; not knowing what their reaction would be was a bit unnerving to say the least. On the airplane, Cander leaned over to me and held my hand. We both admired the modest sparkling diamond on my left finger. "There is one last thing I have to do before our engagement is officially official," he whispered as he nuzzled my neck with his nose.

"Let's see, you proposed...twice, slipped a beautiful ring on my finger, and I said yes. That sounds pretty official to me," I said as I twisted my hand to observe my newly engaged finger from all angles.

"When we get to Chicago, there is one last thing I have to do before we are official," he said as he broke into a huge smile. I wondered what it could be, and since he kept it hush-hush, I would just have to find out when we touched down in the Windy City.

Mama's Gift

As the plane touched down in Chicago, I felt anxious to get back to my surroundings, especially Mama. Although I was grateful for the mini-vacation I'd had in Atlanta with Cander, I was ready to go check on her. When my sister died, I was far away from home and still harbored a bit of residual guilt because I wasn't there for her when she needed me. That memory was still fresh in my mind three years later. Although my devoted brother Wayne and his faithful wife Tess tended to Mama every day I was away, I still had to lay eyes on her myself. Plus, I was really excited to tell Mama about my being newly engaged to Cander.

Cander wouldn't be a total surprise to my family. As our friendship grew into a loving relationship, I did talk to Mama and Wayne about him often. Wayne, being the over-protective brother he was, cautioned me about all the things he had heard about online dating. "How well do you know him? Has he been in jail? Did you check?" Wayne rattled on as he opposed my decision to meet Cander in Atlanta. I really couldn't blame him. My track record wasn't exactly stellar with my choices in men.

I was three steps ahead of Wayne. I conducted my own security screening on Cander when things got serious with us. Contrary to my past relationships, I went in with eyes wide open when I decided to become exclusive with Cander. Part of my job function at the law firm was to do background checks, and I made sure that I did my homework when checking out Cander's history—complete with checking his residential, marital, and employment status, as well as any criminal or domestic issues he may have had. He was understanding and as transparent as possible, granting me with all the information I needed to see if he was on the up and up.

Without hesitation, Wayne asked for Cander's social security number, work location, home address, and all of his phone numbers. I wasn't surprised at his FBI-style debriefing of my fiancé. Cander, not offended in the slightest, gave Wayne the information willingly, telling Wayne that he would've done the same thing had it been his mother, sister, or daughter. His full disclosures made Wayne feel a bit more at ease with our relationship.

I didn't reveal that we were newly engaged however. Wayne and Cander's meeting would prove to be quite interesting.

While the girls were at school, Cander and I took a trip to Manor Care for him to meet Mama finally. We were both nervous, but Cander's nerves were evident as the beads of sweat formed on his forehead. "I hope your mother likes me, sweetie. I feel like I did when I went on my first date and met the girl's parents," Cander said as we walked down the long corridor to my mother's room. I slightly and maybe inappropriately chuckled at his adorable nervousness as I grabbed his hand.

"Sweetie, you will be just fine," I reassured as I lifted my hand to knock lightly on my mother's closed door.

Cander gently reached for my hand causing me to hesitate. "Wait, wait! Okay...now," he said exhaling deeply in an attempt to shake off his jitters. I shook my head and snickered harder.

Mama's nurse invited us to come in as she was giving Mama her evening medication. We walked hand in hand into the room where Mama appeared to be just waking up. "Mrs. Currie, you have guests. Your daughter and a friend are here to see you," the nurse said as she walked over to me. "Your Mom has been doing pretty well; sometimes she won't eat, but overall she is making some strides. She's a stubborn one." The nurse smiled sweetly and looked over at Mama. Mama hated the food at Manor Care. Wayne and I always bought her Burger King from across the street for dinner; she was a happy girl, when she got her hands around a Burger King strawberry milkshake.

"Hi Mama! How are you? I'm back from my trip," I said. Cander stood beside me while I kissed her on the forehead. Mama couldn't see, but she turned to make out Cander's shadowy figure beside me.

"Hi baby, how was your trip? I'm so glad you are back. I was worried about you," Mama said, her voice a bit weaker than remembered it. "Is Wayne with you?" Her cloudy eyes were trying hard to focus on the figure next to me.

"No Mama, Wayne is still at work. Mama, can you give me your hand? I want to show you something," I said as Mama reached toward me, her hand shaking slightly. Very gently, I laid my left hand on her lap and guided her hand toward it. I carefully ran her forefinger across my engagement ring as Cander looked over my shoulder at her, smiling with tears in his eyes.

"Wow, what's that, baby? A ring?" Mama looked down, trying in earnest to catch a glimpse of it while fingering the stone. She looked up, genuinely confused. "You know Mama is blind, I can't see it, but it feels really pretty."

"Thank you, Mama. It is beautiful. I wanted you to touch it first. Do you remember my telling you about the wonderful man that I talk to all the time, the one I fell in love with?" I said as tears rolled down my cheeks.

"Yes, baby, I remember…what's his name again?" Mama asked, still holding my hand and feeling the texture of the ring with her thumb.

"Cander is his name. He asked me to marry him, Mama. Cander asked me to marry him, and I said yes!" I declared as I looked back at Cander. Tears trailed from his eyes and down his cheeks.

"You did?" Mama said, her eyes wide and her mouth curved into the smile that I adored. "I am so happy for you, baby. I am so happy for you. Are you happy?"

"Yes, Mama, I am happier than I have ever been in my life," I replied, sobbing and sniffling.

"I wish I could meet him. Where is he?" she said, pulling herself up to a semi-sitting position. Before I could say a word, Cander jumped in, unable to hold his tongue any longer.

"Hi Ma'am, I'm Cander. It's a pleasure meeting you." Cander sweetly took Mama's hand and shook it very gently. Mama's eyes followed the direction of his voice.

"Hello, sweetheart, how are you doing? Are you going to marry my baby?" Mama said with her eyes fixed in his direction.

"It would be my honor to marry your daughter, Ma'am. I was taught that if you wanted to marry a woman, then a man should ask her parents for her hand. That's actually why I'm here in Chicago. I love Susan with my whole heart. She makes me happier than I have ever been. I want to spend the rest of my life making her happy as well. I would like to ask for your permission to marry your beautiful daughter. I promise to do everything in my power to protect and provide for her for as long as she'll have me. Ma'am… do I have your permission?"

Asking my mother for my hand in marriage was the final item on Cander's official engagement list.

My mother was very subjective when it came to men I became involved with. Rarely did she agree my choices. She always saw the writing on the wall, even when I refused to see it. Out of all her children, I was the one she worried about the most because she knew my vulnerability, and I how desperately wanted to be loved, and how that desperation drove my errant decisions. She wanted what any mother would, for her child to be happy with someone who truly loved them.

As if she was taking it all in, there was a silence that was almost deafening in the room. In the stillness of those seconds that it took Mama to respond to Cander's request, I wondered how she would react to what he said, and if she felt the same "rightness" that I felt when I was with him. Her intuition was always precise. I held my breath as I waited to see what her instinct told her about the man whom I had come to love with all my heart. I noticed her eyes filled with tears. These were the same eyes that cried with me while witnessing my distress over and over again. She watched me stumble though heartache after heartache at the hands of those whom I gave my trust to, and those who took advantage of my inability to love myself.

Her tears this time around weren't the same though. This time, her eyes smiled as she cried. "Yes…yes. You have my blessing, son. I believe that you really do love my baby, and I believe that you will take care of her," Mama said with more conviction than I had heard in a very long time from her. Her words, although a bit slurred, were understood.

Cander breathed a sigh of relief after Mama finished speaking. He gave her a hug, whispering to her his words of gratitude. "Thank you, Ma'am, thank you." We both embraced her, while covering her in affection and tenderness. Mama's gift to my husband-to-be was just the encouragement I needed to tell the rest of the family. There would be a new addition to our clan and his name was Cander.

The Journey

Ties that Bind

The news about our engagement raised some eyebrows, but no one had a heart attack when we broke the news. After several sessions of speaking privately to Cander, man to man, and having confidential conversations that I was not privy to, Wayne gave us the green light as well, which didn't surprise me. Wayne and Cander had similar character traits. They were both intellectual, hard-working, focused, and no-nonsense when it came to being dedicated to family. They definitely had a lot in common and bonded rather quickly over their similarities.

The girls, surprisingly enough, transitioned well too. It had been two years since Darryl and I separated, and they had pretty much realized that we were better apart than together. They met Cander, and Denai in particular, connected with him and he with her. After several visits with all of us together, I privately asked them what they thought about Cander. "We think he is really nice and we are glad that you are happy again. What do we call him, when you guys get married?" Lanie inquired.

"Whatever you feel comfortable calling him, sweetie. You just can't call him by his first name, he is still a grown up." I reminded them both.

"We call him Mr. Cander now; can we just keep that name?" Johanna asked.

"Works for me," I said, nodding my head in agreement. From then on, it was Mr. Cander for Lanie and Johanna.

At seventeen years old, Denai always looked to Wayne as a father figure because he was the closest thing to a father she'd ever known. After a time, Denai found out what is was like to have a father in her life consistently. One that didn't run out on her and make excuses. One that encouraged, nurtured and supported her in everything she decided to take on, the way any loving father would do. She settled on a name that described what Cander meant in her life and it suited him perfectly. "Do you think Mr. Cander would mind me calling him Dad? It would be kinda weird, because I never called anyone Dad before, but that is what he is to me. What do you think?"

"I think he'd be honored" I said, becoming emotional. Later on, she tried it out.

"Dad, will you see if you can fix the keyboard to my computer?" she said, looking for a reaction from him.

"Sure, let's take a look at it and see what's going on," Cander said with a gleam in his eye. "Did you hear what Denai called me? She called me Dad for the first time." He was as proud as could be at the title he was given by a young girl, who never knew she needed a dad so much until she found him.

It was December 20, 2010, and things were definitely in motion in terms of Cander and I constructing our new lives together. We set our wedding date for August 20 of the following year, with Cander making a permanent transition to Chicago in April. He left the computer analyst position he held for the past five years, he left his car and house with his son, opting to take the train to Chicago with just the clothes he had packed in two suitcases, and his beloved laptop. He left everything to begin a life with me, my mother and my three daughters. I often asked him if he was sure of his decision, giving him the opportunity to run while he had a chance. Not too many men I knew would give up their steady job, home and car, to come live in a strange city and marry a woman with a live-in disabled mother, three children, and a soon-to-be ex-husband, who was bitterly trying to cause as much disruption to her life as possible. That was enough to send anyone packing. When I'd ask Cander, "Are you sure you wanna do this?" His response was always the same.

"I love you Sue, and we can get through any difficulties together. I knew you had some issues going on in your life before I even asked you to marry me. Listen, if you have a sick mama, WE have a sick mama, if you have three kids to raise, then WE have three kids to raise. If you have an issue with your ex, then WE will handle him TOGETHER." The support Cander offered me was nothing short of amazing. Not only did he offer it, but he actually followed through, which was something that was so foreign to me.

While Cander was in Delaware tying up loose ends with regard to his move to Chicago, I was steadily doing the same here in preparation for our new life together, the main issue being finalizing my divorce from Darryl. If Darryl appeared in court and contested the divorce for the purpose of dragging it out, that would throw a wrench in all of the plans Cander and I had.

For the weeks leading up to the court hearing, I was a nervous wreck. My thoughts were constantly focused on the outcome of the proceedings. Darryl had me over a barrel and he loved it. My happiness didn't concern him, nor had it ever. He wanted his way and that was the theme of our entire eleven-year marriage. His sole purpose was to get back into my house and live there permanently, rent and responsibility free. The longer that he stalled the divorce, the more time he had to manipulate me into allowing him to move back in with me.

The pressure of everything caused a few flare-ups with my anxiety issue every now and then. I fought the onslaught of these attacks with fervent prayer. God never fails to deliver what He promises, and this time was no different. He granted me the peace I needed as I was reminded me that His plans were for my good, and not for evil" (Jerimiah 29:11). I clung onto that promise and gave myself no other choice than to believe that everything would work out the way it was supposed to.

There were many challenges ahead. One of which was that Mama was finally released to go home, but still remained under the watchful eye of her doctor and nurses, who came by every other day to check her vitals and such. I was happy that Mama was home again, in the place that she loved so much. Her blindness proved to be an ordeal for her sometimes, and her stubborn nature proved to be a test that I failed many times.

Under the weightiness of everything going on, I lost my cool at times, behaving very irritably with the girls and reprimanding Mama for her unyieldingness, sometimes with a harsh tone. During those times, she'd pout a lot and so would I, while trying to do things for her like put on her coat or get her dressed for her dialysis appointments. Mama could shoot you a glare and a scowl, like no one else could when she was upset with you. I felt terrible afterwards for losing my patience with her, reminding myself of her developing dementia and the fact that she was the one enduring constant suffering, not me. Each day going forward, I helplessly witnessed Mama regressing, becoming more and more fragile in her mind and body.

D Day Arrives

After what seemed like forever, the court date had finally come. It was a blistery cold and snow-filled December day, the day after Christmas. I arrived to work early and went over my divorce decree with a fine-tooth comb yet again. I jotted down notes, issues of

D Day Arrives

importance that I wanted to present to the judge, the most pressing being an order of child support and a concrete order of visitation that Darryl would be urged to abide by. My supervisors at the law firm coached and offered their moral support until it was time for me to leave for court. They allowed me to use my lunch and break combined to attend the hearing so that I wouldn't have to use my vacation leave in case I needed it for an emergency with Mama. I was so grateful to my bosses for all that they had done in preparation for my hearing. The time, effort and kindness they offered me was truly invaluable.

I walked into the courtroom fifteen minutes early. I took my coat off and pulled out my manila folder, intently studying all my documents and making certain everything was in proper order. I looked up anxiously from time to time to scan the room for Darryl as other litigants filed into the large courtroom and took their seats on the wooden benches. I was startled by the loud thud behind me as the guard closed the doors in preparation for the proceedings to begin. I twisted my neck around, eyeing each person in the courtroom in search of Darryl's face. He was nowhere to be found. After a bit of chatter and preliminary discussions between attorneys and their clients, the guard directed everyone to stand as the judge walked in and took her seat. The proceedings had officially begun, and still, no Darryl.

As the judge called each plaintiff and defendant by name to hear their cases, I anxiously awaited our names to be called; it was like waiting for paint to dry. Ironically, my name was called last. I sprang out of my seat and approached the bench. I did a final scan for Darryl. He never showed up. The judge called Darryl's name...once, twice, and then a third time. No response.

After explaining my petition to the judge, I couldn't help but to shed tears that were determined to fall from my eyes, no matter how hard I tried to keep them at bay. My words to the judge were an emotional appeal for my liberation to obtain the kind of life I so desperately wanted for myself. I believe that the judge sensed my desperation as she listened with a raised eyebrow. After informing her that we had no assets or property to split, making an appeal for child support and a set schedule for visitation, the judge rendered her decision.

"I hereby grant your divorce petition on the grounds of irreconcilable differences by reason of default. It is so ordered." I breathed a deep and cleansing sigh of relief as I stood there, waiting for my official stamped divorce decree. It was December 26, 2010, and ironically, Cander's birthday.

I can't remember how many times I thanked God after I floated out of the courtroom. My co-worker and friend was waiting right outside the courtroom. I ran to her arms and screamed..."YES!" as we both jumped up and down in the hallway outside of the courtroom. Since the birth of my three children, it had been the most joyous moment of my life. I was free. Free indeed.

Pieces that Fit

After Darryl got notification from the court that the divorce was granted due to his defaulting, he wasn't a happy camper. He'd banked on a different outcome. Because of his bitterness, he tried everything he could to be uncooperative and was just downright hostile towards me at every turn. I never asked why he didn't appear in court and I didn't care. I do have my theories as to why though.

Just like the theme of our marriage, his ego made him believe everyone was at his disposal. Darryl figured he could just blow off the hearing and there would be no recourse for his actions. His angry and sullen nature reached new lows as time went on, but I carried on. He did everything from inciting arguments with me to the despicable act of ripping the wig from my head and tossing it in the street, for the sole purpose of humiliating me in front of my children and neighbors. Still, I kept praying and believing that the tides would turn. Heck, I had been through storms before, and I wasn't about to let a few raindrops ruin the new happiness I'd found. Whenever Darryl's antics threatened to disturb my peace of mind, I focused on the future ahead. I kept my head held high and left the rest for God to handle on my behalf.

Time flies when you have your hands full, and boy was I up to my neck with multiple agendas. It was already the end March, and I was only partially done with my checklist for our wedding in

August. Cander was in full partnership mode, doing as much planning and booking as he could long distance. Our phone discussions concerning the wedding were like corporate boardroom meetings, all business. It was refreshing to be with someone who was a collaborator with me, and not simply sitting on the sidelines in a comfy seat. Cander was scheduled for his move to Chicago in mid-April, which would make things much easier with planning. I was so busy with wedding planning, tending to Mama, and making sure projects and homework were completed with the kids that I nearly forgot that my birthday was in a few days. The last time I had spoken with Cander, he said he had a surprise for me for my birthday. I wondered what it was.

Just as I finished making sure Mama was safe and sound from her bathroom trip, the doorbell rang. I hurried to the door, tying my headscarf securely on my head. My hair was a disaster and one of the things on my long to-do list for the day. I opened the door, and to my surprise, there stood my birthday gift. It was Cander with his two suitcases, and of course, his laptop. "Happy birthday, Sweetie," he said with a wide smile. I was overjoyed to see him standing there. I forgot what a mess I looked like and hugged him as tightly as I could. Cander surprised me with his move to Chicago a month early, just in time to celebrate my birthday with me.

Cander didn't waste any time with his job hunt once he touched down in Chicago. He was on a mission. He had initially looked for employment in Chicago before he left Delaware, setting up interviews with prospective employers for the week he was scheduled to arrive. His background was in information technology and we prayed that his field would be wide open in Chicago. Within three weeks of leaving everything in Delaware and stepping out on nothing but faith in a God who would provide for him and his new family, God did just that. Cander was hired for an IT position paying nearly three times as much as his salary from his former job in Delaware. God had been so incredibly gracious that it left us in a constant state of awe.

Mama kept me on my toes before the nurse got to the house each morning. I made sure her medication was administered; she was fed, and as comfortable as she could be before I left for work. Cander being there helped tremendously. He jumped right in and assisted where he was needed without a single pause. It was refreshing to see how Mama took to Cander's presence in the house. Her toleration for my now ex-husband was mildly cordial during the eleven years we were married, but nothing compared to how she interacted with Cander and so quickly too. She never saw his face, but she knew his voice when he came into the house. Every day like clockwork when he came home, he politely knocked and ducked his head into her bedroom with his greeting to her, "Hello Ma'am, it's Cander. How are you feeling today?"

Her eyes lit up like a firecracker as she replied, "Hi baby, Mama's doing fairly well, how are you, son?" My heart took wings every time she called him "son." My Mama didn't throw that term around haphazardly. She never referred to my ex that way in all the years we had been married. She only reserved it for a few. My brother Wayne and now Cander had received the prestigious title too.

Cander was proud to be the recipient of that title as well. Even after twenty years, the death of his own beloved mother still drove him to tears whenever he spoke of her. He felt some residual guilt that he hadn't been there when she passed away, a sore spot that we both had in common in terms of my sister's untimely death. He mentioned on several occasions how honored he was that Mama thought of him as her son.

Cander was indeed a son of hers, albeit late in their lives when they met one another. He displayed the kind of patience and care for Mama that amazed me sometimes. Never impatient in terms of her unique needs, and always willing to do what was necessary for her comfort. As Mama's health dwindled, she'd frequently fall out of her bed if she was too close to the edge of it, leaving her body awkwardly crumpled on the floor in intense pain. During the night when we slept, the sound of Mama's body hitting the floor shocked us and the kids wide awake as everyone scrambled to help. Although we were in the lower level of the house, Cander somehow made it up the stairs in seconds, beating me to rescue Mama as she cried and lay helplessly and sometimes bloodied. Swiftly, he'd carefully scoop her up in his arms and whisper in her ear softly, "I got you Ma'am, I got you," as he carried her to bed. I would be close behind with a warmed towel to clean her face before carefully tucking her into the middle of her king-sized bed. Those nights were very emotional ones for both Cander and me. Many times he held me through the night as I cried for Mama, feeling utterly helpless.

Everything seemed to be on schedule in terms of our upcoming wedding plans, thanks to Cander's tireless effort and assistance with getting everything paid off and the guest list locked down. It would be a mid-sized wedding, nothing really fancy, but I wanted it be fun and elegant. I had everything decided except for Mama's dress. I wanted her to help me pick it, and I was pretty giddy about it. Although Mama couldn't see the dresses I'd suggested, I described them for her as she thought about which one she'd like the best. "I can't decide, baby; just pick one for me that looks pretty and has a happy color, and don't forget about this scar on my arm, make sure you cover me up." She was referring to her stint site for dialysis, which I had already taken into account when picking out a dress for her. I was glad Mama mentioned that she wanted a happy color, and I knew just the dress for her—a beautiful long-sleeved sky-blue chiffon dress. It was definitely a dress fit for my queen. I made a note to myself to order it as soon as possible, so it would arrive in time for the wedding, which was a little more than a month away.

The Countdown

After hitting the gym a little harder since I became engaged, I was blown away when my size 14 wedding gown that had been a bit too tight when I tried it on a few months ago now needed to be cinched in the waist area and taken up in the hip area. I wanted to stick my tongue out at the saleslady in the dress shop who smugly insisted that I a find a different dress or get bigger size. For the first time in my life, the vision that I saw in the mirror wasn't one of unsightliness. I didn't pick myself apart like I'd been known to do all my life. I saw beauty; I saw the image of a glowing, beautiful woman. Even with the imperfection of my flaccid skin that hung loosely underneath my arms due to my extreme loss, it wasn't unsightly to me anymore. Instead it reminded me of a life-long battle with critical obesity that almost killed me and the hard-fought victory that was now mine. I always kept my hands tightly to my sides so as not to reveal my loosened skin, but not this time. I proudly placed my hands on my hips in defiance and smiled, content with the lovely lady looking back at me.

My healthier eating habits were now solid again. My workout routine had been incorporated into my life and I loved the result of the sweat that I put in. Along the way, I had discovered something that blew my mind. Consistent working out was very therapeutic. It proved effective, not only in alleviating my stress, but also made me feel more energetic and it was very instrumental in lowering and maintaining normal blood pressure readings too. Then of course, there were the "scale perks." During the course of that previous year, I re-gained 90 pounds and lost my focus. After recapturing my momentum, I managed whittled myself back into a toned and curvaceous size 12. I felt amazingly strong in both mind and body.

The cherry on top of my sugar-free cake? It was the first time in my adult life that I was totally medication free. After monitoring several consistently normal readings, Dr. Thomas confirmed that I didn't need blood pressure meds anymore. As long as I kept my fitness and dietary commitment, I could be free and clear of hypertension medication. The horrific anxiety episodes I experienced for the greater part of my life became a distant memory. I for the first time in my life, I didn't feel like I was insignificant. I felt strong, capable, and brave. Most importantly, I discovered someone who was worth defending and fighting for. Me.

It was down to the wedding wire. The date was three weeks away, and I could barely concentrate at work from the mental checklist that I obsessed over. My thoughts were interrupted by Wayne calling to let me know there was an issue at the dialysis clinic with Mama. Wayne asked Cander if he wouldn't mind taking Mama back to the clinic the next day because he couldn't take off from work. Her graft had become clogged, which prevented her from completing her dialysis treatment that morning. It wasn't a big deal; in fact, Mama had the procedure done before with no problem. The doctor would insert a vascular stent for the purpose of opening the clogged graft, and after a short recovery period, she would go home. Her appointment to repair the graft had been scheduled for the following morning.

The next day was an unusually hectic one at work and my mind seemed to be in three places at once. I attempted to tackle the surmounting pile of work on my desk while taking momentary breaks to get status updates with what was going on with Mama at the clinic. "Boy, she is not going to be a happy camper," I thought as I ruffled through legal filings that I was trying in vain to complete. My phone rang as just as I was preparing to dive headfirst into my surge of subpoenas. It was Cander calling from home. There was something in his hello that sounded different. Unsettled.

Transitioned in Love

"Babe, your voice sounds different, is everything all right?" I asked as I nestled the phone between my neck and shoulder and immediately took off my reading glasses. I heard the muffled commotion in the background, but I couldn't make out what it was. My heart began to pound within my chest as I sensed something wasn't right.

"Sweetie, it's your Mom. She got really sick when we got home, and she's unconscious…and…I called the ambulance, he's…here right now with Mama trying to revive her. Wayne is on his way from work right now...sweetie, are you still there, Sue?" I was frozen in my chair and my body felt limp. I heard Cander speaking and I tried to respond, but I couldn't. My supervisor April walked by and noticed my state immediately. She placed her hand on my shoulder and asked what was wrong. I heard my voice shout, "Mama...oh my God, Mama."

I realized that I was still holding the phone and Cander was still calling my name. "I'm on my way home right now," I said as I frantically grabbed my coat and purse.

"Sue, just meet us at the hospital. You don't have time to go home. The ambulance is taking Mama right now to Roseland Hospital," Cander instructed, trying very hard to keep his composure. I left everything at my desk and ran all the way to the train station, just in time for next train that was leaving in mere seconds. To this day, I still don't know how on earth I made to the train station in such record time.

As I sat anxiously on the train, I prayed that it would move quickly. It seemed as if the train was moving in slow motion. I spoke to Cander on the way to the hospital. Everyone else had made their way to the hospital's emergency waiting area, including Denai, Johanna, and Lanie.

Cander began to recount the events that took place after Mama's procedure at the clinic in detail over the phone as I listened and rocked myself in my seat for comfort. "Everything went seemingly smooth after her stent procedure at the clinic. She felt well enough to even make a few jokes about her not being able to drive herself anymore. Although she looked very tired, other than that, she said she felt fine. But she stressed that she was very tired over and over again. I helped her into the house, where Denai had just come home from school. Both Denai and I helped Mama out of her coat so that she could rest. As Denai and I eased her down to bed, she started convulsing. I called her name as she clung to me and looked at me with frightened eyes. I left Mama with Denai as I called nine-one-one. When I rushed back to her, Denai and I both held Mama, me on one side holding her hand, Denai on the other with Mama's head on her lap. With a few flutters of her eyelids, Mama's eyes closed, and they didn't open again."

My Superwoman made her earthly transition the afternoon of July 24, 2011. Just as God intended, she passed away in the loving arms of her devoted granddaughter Denai, and her Cander, the man she so lovingly called "son."

As I rushed through the emergency room doors of Roseland Hospital, I saw my family collectively in place: Cander, my girls, Wayne, Tess, and my nephew Wayne II along with his wife. I rushed to my brother's side and clung to him as I shed the tears I could no longer hold. The room fell silent as the emergency room doctor came in and asked us to gather in a room they called the "Family Room." We all knew what that meant. The doctor took a deep breath and announced in a softened tone, "It is with deep regret that I inform you that your loved one did not make it. We are very sorry."

There was a huge wave of collective sorrow that engulfed the tiny room which barely held the nine of us. We took turns embracing one another, the intense wails of deep sadness filling the room with ear-piercing resonance. After a long and hard-fought battle, our strong and graceful matriarch was suffering no more.

My heart was broken for the third time. I kept going over and over in my mind Mama's voice. I'd go into her room hoping to catch a scent of her essence on her scarf, her coat, anything. The only thing that gave me peace was that I knew that her physical and mental suffering was over. I saw the pained look on her face every day, and the frustration she endured when her words wouldn't come out right when she spoke. She was free from her sick body, never to suffer again. To wish that she was still in it, would be selfish of me. I loved her enough to cherish her memories; I loved her enough to understand why God loved her even more than I, and that He had decided that enough was enough. I cancelled the order for my mother's dress, but not the order I made for her corsage.

My mother's funeral was fit for a queen. She looked beautiful too. When my brother made the request for me to do my mother's hair and make-up for her funeral instead of the mortician, I looked at him like he was nuts. I told him I couldn't bring myself to do it, but after his words of encouragement combined with a bit of lightheartedness, I was persuaded. "You know how particular Mama was; you know that she wouldn't want just anyone doing her hair and make-up. She'd want you to do it." Indeed he was right; Mama had a real sense of style. I couldn't leave it to someone else who might jack her up; I had to personally make sure she looked like her fabulous self, so I did just that.

Choices, Chances, Changes

Memories of Mama saturated my thoughts more and more as the days leading up to the wedding closed in. Her eyes, her smile, and her vibrant personality that made me, and those around her, adore her. The decades of wisdom she expounded were tucked safely in my memory, along with her comical and often colorful commentary that made me laugh until my stomach ached. I felt Mama's spirit the morning I was to marry my Cander. I felt secure in knowing that although I missed her presence, she would be walking the aisle with me, in spirit. The only thing that dulled the ache in my heart for Mama was knowing that she didn't have to suffer anymore. Just like my sister and father, they had to leave me to be free. They needed to free, and I needed to sprout my own wings to fly on my own. In many ways I believe that God in turn, freed me too from my dependency on them.

As I continued to reflect, I began to think about how awesome God is. He collects the puzzle pieces of our lives and beautifully strings them together with such awesome intricacy. God brought together the lives of two emotionally shattered people to create a bond that mended each other's wounds and produced hope where there was none. Cander's presence in my life at just the right time filled the difficult gaps. He had come into Mama's life and they adored each other immediately. Before she left this earth, God made certain that she met the man, who would love and respect her daughter as a husband should. To think that God went all the way to Delaware to hand pick my husband for me and deliver him to Chicago still makes me smile in amazement at what God can do.

As I looked in the mirror at my reflection in my wedding gown, I cried tears of happiness, but mostly gratitude. I couldn't believe I been so abundantly blessed. As I arranged the curls in my hair to accommodate my veil, I began to reflect on the last few hours before I became Mrs. Anderson. I was not the Susan I once was. She had become a facet of my past and a distant memory. Through God, I had been resurrected and transformed from the inside out. Through life-threatening obesity, depression, addiction, mental disorder, setbacks and self-hate, He never took His hand off my life. Even when my anguish dulled my sensitivity to feel His presence, He was always there.

The fragrant smell of fresh gladiolas filled my living room as the photographer snapped photos of my gorgeous flower girls Lanie and Johanna, who were hamming it up for the camera. My flawlessly beautiful junior bridesmaid Denai, made sure I was properly cinched into the built-in corset of my gown. My bouquet held an exquisite vintage pendant that belonged to Mama so that I would have a piece of her that walked the aisle with me. I had my handwritten vows to Cander safely tucked away in my bra and the limo was on the way; everything was set.

I heard the doorbell ring as I put the finishing touches on my make-up. It was my supervisor, awesome friend, and bridesmaid, April. She had traveled all the way from Wisconsin to take part in my wedding, and she'd arrived complete with coffee in hand for me. I couldn't believe I was about to marry the man of my dreams in a little less than an hour. "So, are you ready, Sue? You ready to take the plunge?" April asked as she helped me adjust my veil and tiara while the photographer captured each moment.

"Girl...I am beyond ready!"

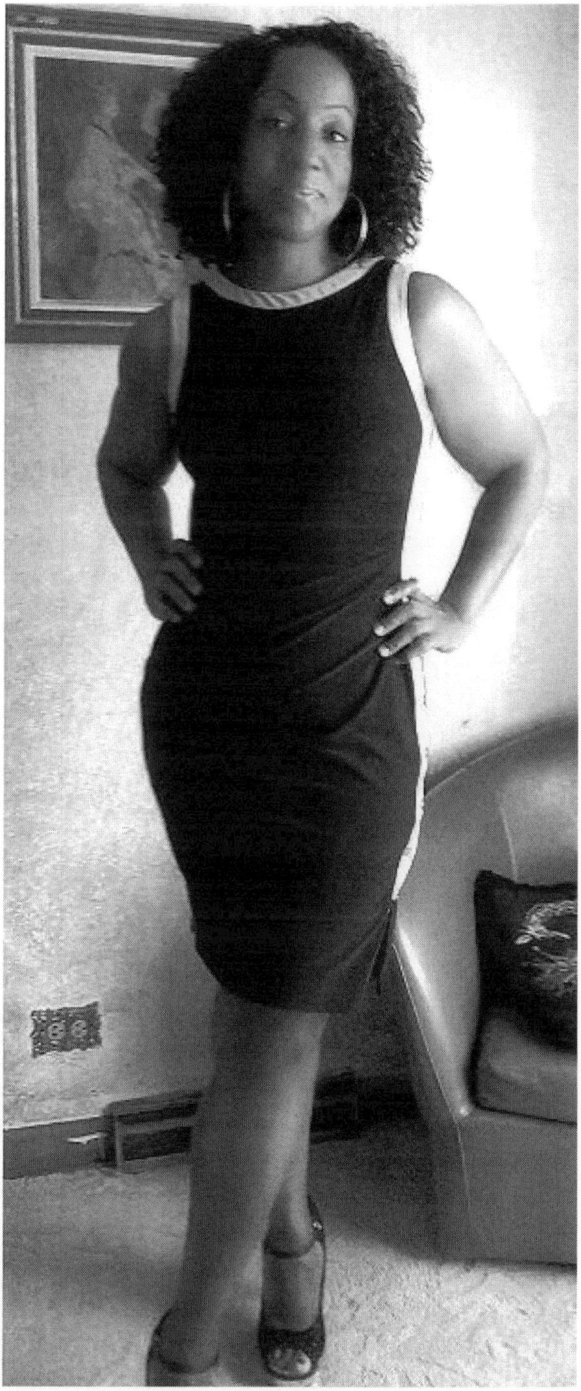

How I did It!

The Mechanics of Weight Loss

"In the long run, we shape our lives and we shape ourselves. The process never ends until we die. The choices we make are ultimately our own responsibility."

- Eleanor Roosevelt

The Girlfriends & Coffee Segment

Pull up a chair and let's chat!

Think of this section of the book as a bit of girlfriend to girlfriend chit-chat over a cup of your favorite coffee or tea. A laid-back conversation between you and I about the ups and downs of weight loss, along with a bit of practical advice about health and wellness; not only physical wellness, but the kind of emotional wellness that will align everything else in our lives.

The information given within these next few chapters has proven extremely effective during my journey to a 140 pound weight loss. Knowledge is a powerful tool, I've discovered. It is the key to unlock the power that is within you to change your life. In the wise words of my beloved mother: "When you know better, you can do better."

Get comfy; pour your cup of coffee or tea. You bring your notepad and pencil to take notes. I will bring the encouragement as you embark on the most gratifying and life-altering journey of your life!

What keeps our mind in Bondage?

Obesity is without a doubt one of the most harmful forms of mental bondage. Its oppression has a snowball effect on just about every area of one's life.

Being overweight is one of the most stigmatizing characteristic in America. One cannot live through a single day without encountering numerous forms of fat prejudice in magazines, media, even when applying for a job.

Obesity not only weighs us down with heaviness physically, but emotionally and psychologically as well. It hinders us from living the quality of life we deserve, and robs us from living a substantially longer life without the dependency of prescription medicine to control ailments that are directly associated with obesity.

 In our day-to-day, we often find ourselves struggling to maintain a delicate balance of work, finances, home, and raising children, just as an acrobat attempts to balance plates while walking on a thin wire. Sometimes everything comes crashing down emotionally. Stress creeps in, and for those who struggle with a healthy relationship with food, our favorite fast food restaurant or break room vending machine becomes a convenient go-to. The thing is, this brand of soothing is short lived. We often find ourselves searching for the next quick fix a few hours later, which usually accompanies the guilt of overindulging. The struggle between balancing daily stressors and binge eating is one that is very familiar to me.

When we are in the midst of a personal struggle like obesity, sometimes it is difficult to see past our current condition. The mind is a very powerful instrument. The power of suggestion is a strong influence in what we believe to be true. Once we anticipate that a specific outcome will occur (I will never be able to lose this weight), our subsequent thoughts and behaviors will actually help to bring that outcome to fruition. Negative thought patterns are the breeding ground for failure and hopelessness. Negative self-speech is toxic to any effort we put forth in our lives.

True liberation from the chains of obesity lies within the power of your own mind. Ultimately, you are in the driver's seat. It starts with putting the brakes on the negative speech. For us to start to consciously create the life of our dreams, we must take total responsibility for our lives. As we take full responsibility for what happens to us, we discover that we create our lives by our thoughts. Everything on the outside is a reflection of what is happening on the inside.

From the Bible to Buddha and beyond, our greatest teachers have told us via their writings that the words we speak contain tremendous power. Our thoughts become tangible, whether positive or negative. Essentially, our thoughts construct our reality.

There are many things in life that we do not have control over, but taking command of our health is within full reach.

Automotive and assembly line industrialist Henry Ford said: "Whether you think you can or think you can't, you are right." His sentiment is the true catalyst for change in any area of our lives, not just weight management. If you think you can't, it will stop you from succeeding. If you think you can, it will drive you to success.

It's YOUR Time!

Webster's dictionary defines the word *"CHANGE"* as:

To make radically different; to transform. To give a different position, course, or direction to   replace with another. To make a shift from one to another.

Are you ready for some good news? You have already been equipped for change in your life, no assembly required. The ability to change is inherently within you; however, you must ignite it with action.

God has designed you in His image-strong, capable, and resilient. You have already been prepared with everything you need to alter the course of your life with regard to your health and wellness, but ultimately the decision is up to you. We cannot change God's timing, but we can be prepared for when it comes. Now is your time to make that shift. Now is the time to do something that your future self will thank you for. Haven't you waited long enough?

Now let me caution you, if you are looking for a quick fix for weight loss, or the "skinny" on where to buy the latest diet shake (pun intended), that will magically make the pounds disappear, then you have picked up the wrong book. Permanent changes equal permanent results. Nothing worth achieving has ever come easily, including reversing a lifetime of bad eating patterns with little or no physical activity.

You want to talk about excuses? I wrote the book on them. I had a million and one reasons why I could not lose weight. So instead I ate more to combat my feelings of failure. I've tried the pills, the shakes, and endured the painful B12 shots, hoping to achieve what could only be done with consistent commitment and a willingness to put away my excuses. The gratification that is received when you hit the marks along your weight loss journey is the by-product of the hard work and dedication you put in, and no pill can give you that.

If you are still reading this, I'm guessing that you are a part of the "Let's do this" crowd. Great! I won't promise a road that isn't a bit bumpy or downright frustrating at times. The temptation to give up WILL creep into your thoughts. Just know that it's temporary. Here is the promise I can offer you: The payoff you will receive is worth every second of the journey.

Here's the real deal. Every day our lives are filled with choices to make, the end result being a decision. If you are truly ready to challenge yourself, defy the odds, and completely transform your body and mind from the inside out, it starts with a decision.

Are you REALLY ready to change YOUR story?

Eat ANYTHING You Want, and STILL lose weight!

Did your eyes perk up when you read the above statement? Bingo! That is the tactic of every "quick fix" infomercial that is out there. Advertisement pros that work within the multi-billion dollar diet industry use the "rapid results" approach to lure you into thinking that weight loss can be magically achieved by popping a few pills, wearing a specially designed weight loss girdle, or shaking some foreign ingredient on your food. These weight loss infomercials are quite convincing and designed to target the large population of people who are obese and desperate for something that will work for them overnight. By preying on emotional distress and vulnerability, weight loss companies suck large sectors of weight loss seekers into false promises, convincing them to pay big bucks in anticipation of a miracle.

You've seen those commercials before. The svelte and toned perky woman beckons you to purchase products that promise quick weight loss in just a few weeks, just like it did for her. Then the overly excited paid spokesperson giddily announces to you, "Eat what you want and STILL lose weight without dieting or exercise!" or "Take this pill, sprinkle this on your food, and watch the pounds just melt off!"

Here is what is these commercials don't mention. The models flaunting their toned bodies on the infomercials usually don't achieve their results by using the product that they are selling. In fact, if you look at the fine print at the bottom of your screen during the commercial, you will most likely see the phrase "Results not typical." This is the company's way of legally protecting themselves since most of the people who purchase their weight loss products will not experience those same results. This is an age-old deceptive marketing ploy to pull viewers into the fantasy of "as easy as one, two, three" weight loss.

Then there is the wave of fad diets that have swept the internet. Do a quick Google search of diets and you will be flooded with every variety under the sun. The Hollywood juice diets (lose weight and get a body just like your favorite celebrity…by next week!), the lemonade diet, the cabbage soup diet, and the popular master cleanse diet craze—just to name to few. I have tried them all. We run out and buy all the necessary ingredients, then follow the recipes precisely with dreams of losing a significant amount of weight within a week or two. These diets make claims of life-changing results that are not realistic, and in some cases, physically unhealthy. Marketing execs know their targeted audience well. People who are driven to lose weight fast, because of social issues and emotional meltdowns, are looking for the quickest means to get out of that state.

The truth of the matter is there is no quick-fix weight loss that will last any substantial amount of time. The latest fad diet makes bold promises of weight loss, and while you may drop some pounds temporarily, it soon returns, and sometimes with a few more friendly pounds added to your waistline to boot. It's not realistic to eat cabbage soup every day for the rest of our lives. By the same token, strictly consuming only meat as some diets suggest is just as impractical. Our bodies need a healthy balance of the right foods to operate efficiently. Adhering to restrictive diets is just another version of the "rapid rewards" program. You may lose weight initially, but as soon as you begin eating regular food again, you gain the weight back. There is no way around it. If there was, trust me, I would have found it, sold the rights to it, and be living on my private island by now. Until there is a change in the way we think about food, healthier eating habits established, and regular body movement, permanent weight loss is beyond our reach.

The decision to change a lifestyle that has been a part of us for so long is difficult. Why? Because it requires personal discipline.

The truth is very simple when it comes to weight loss: its mind over matter. A conscious choice must be made. As my own journey can attest to, the battle isn't won overnight. Sometimes you will fall behind, and setbacks will occur. It's a normal part of the process.

Get back into the ring and don't allow defeat to fester. You're worth the fight.

Simply put, your success has one determining factor: you. Before any kind of positive change can take place in your life you must have a firm conviction about what you want your life to look like. Then begin to draw the blueprint on your own terms. This is your destiny, no one else's. Regulate your control; remember, you're in the driver's seat.

It really comes down to one question: How sick and tired are you of going backwards? How fed up are you with being on the hamster's wheel, going around and around, yet getting nowhere? How badly do want your circumstances to change and what are you willing to sacrifice to make it happen? What people and things are you willing to release for the sake of your own welfare and happiness? Your physical and mental health is too precious to forsake. Life is short, start creating your reality now. Don't wait.

Decisions, Decisions, Decisions…

There are always three major factors that come into play when embarking on any journey: Decision, Destination, and Preparation. Think about it for a minute. In order for us to arrive at a particular destination, we must first decide where we are going in the first place. Once a decision has been made on where we are headed, we have to then prepare for the trip. This preparation includes carefully organizing all that is required (food, clothes, supplies, etc.) and gathering those things together beforehand. There is nothing more frustrating than being ill-prepared for a long trip. The same steps are required for your success on the journey to weight loss and healthier living. The decision you make when you put action behind your words, will be the ground zero of your journey.

So, now that you have the mindset that you are ready to make some serious changes to your health, now what? You act.

Sounds simple enough, right? But why is it so difficult to stick to something like deciding to lose weight? Why do the factors in our lives always seem to pull us away from what we really want to accomplish? The answer is not an easy one. It is a matter of properly placing priority in our lives.

Let's face it; there are plenty of things we make time for without even realizing it. When I am talking to someone who is looking for guidance on how to lose weight, the conversation always goes something like this. I ask:

"How many times a week do you do some sort of physical exercise?"

The response is usually:

"Oh, I would, but I just don't have the time. My life is just so busy!"

Then there is this question I throw out there:

"Well, what is your favorite TV show? How long is it?"

Gotcha. Chances are, the person faithfully tunes into their favorite TV programs for at least thirty minutes to an hour at least three days a week. When asked if they could spend a portion of their TV time working out, the response is usually:

"Oh, I didn't think of it that way," or sometimes just silence, indicating that time might be better spent in front of the TV instead of working on accomplishing their fitness goals.

Even the busiest of us can carve out some area of our day working toward improving our health, even if it's just thirty minutes. It all comes down to prioritizing what we deem as important. Write down your daily schedule, look at it on paper. Decide what time of day you can commit to some form of exercise, even if it's a rigorous walk around your local park.

Cutting out some of the extras like our favorite TV shows and replacing them with exercise makes a huge difference in the long run. Before you know it, doing something good for your body will not feel like a sacrifice anymore. It will turn into sheer liberation. The feeling of accomplishment coupled with the increased energy and stamina you receive will far outweigh any of those TV shows you thought you could not live without. Again, it comes down to the one thing: choices.

Finding your "Motivational Mojo"

There is no shortage of "how to" books, seminars and videos that detail the mechanics of weight loss. There are plenty of fitness gurus who can walk you through the process for a nominal fee if you so choose. I'm convinced that the problem isn't that we don't know the method to weight loss; it's that we haven't figured out the method of adhering to the principles of it. To get that, we must put into practice self-control, which is not easy, but necessary in terms of achieving our goals.

Begin a crusade of knowledge in your quest to restore and improve your health. Do your research about proper nutrition and exercise. Take the time and effort to put the things you've learned into practice. These are essential components to your preparation phase.

During your journey, you will learn more about yourself than you ever have before, and you will begin recognizing an emotional connection between you and food. That's why this is called a "journey"– it takes time to learn about who you are, where you want to be, and how you're going to get there.

Then there is motivation, a reoccurring theme in the weight loss arena. In order to stick to any goal long term and see it through, something has to drive us. Stimulate us. As a motor is an essential segment of a car, maintaining motivation is just as important to every segment of your healthy mind/healthy body journey. Your determination to adjust the necessary elements of your day-to-day life to accommodate your physical/mental renovation must stick, otherwise we just hop on and off of that perpetual "hamster's wheel" I referred to earlier. Bottom line, if we are going to do this, let's not half-ass it. We aren't talking about losing a couple of vanity pounds for the sake of a new outfit for vacation; we are talking about REAL transformation here, inside and out.

"Eh, Maybe Tomorrow…."

Trust me; there will always be something in the way of what you need to do for yourself if you allow it. You deserve to have the best life possible, with your health at its optimal level, but it is you who is in charge of that mission. There will be times that you simply don't feel like it. Your cheering section will sometimes consist of just yourself. Good! Don't allow others to dictate where you are going. If no one motivates you, you must be a team of one. If you wait on others to jump on your personal success bandwagon, you may be sadly disappointed with the lack of participation you receive. This journey will require a joint effort consisting of God and you…His Strength, and your effort.

So how do we get started? How do we get our "mojo working" in terms of readjusting our eating habits and our approach to a healthier lifestyle? Here are a few key points to note:

One goal at a time. One of the reasons why we have difficulty staying motivated long term is because of the numerous things going on in our lives. You name it—work, kids, relationships, etc. — all these factors pull us in several directions. We are left feeling mentally drained and with not much energy to stay focused on one thing for too long.

As women, we are the masters at wearing several hats and juggling our dishes on a thin wire, trying not to drop one plate on the ground. When there is so much going on in our lives, it can zap our energy and focus. It's probably the most common mistake people make when trying to accomplish too many goals at once. Making your health a priority is a decision you must make for you. Make it your primary goal. Be intentional. Your health is too important to allow it to be pushed into the back burner of your life. Make the necessary room in your life to work toward that goal, otherwise you will be spinning your wheels and never getting to where you want to be.

Be Inspired. Another way to find your "mojo" is to become encouraged by those who have taken the journey before you and succeeded. When I first began my weight loss journey, I promised God that if He would stick in there with me, guide me and grant me with the strength and determination to successfully lose the weight, I would spend the rest of my life motivating and sharing my testimony with others who struggled just as I have. What I didn't anticipate was the bonus blessing of not only transforming my physical body, but my mind as well. The same can happen for you. Look to those who have been in the trenches and have overcome their battles.

Get excited! If you want to break out of a slump, get yourself excited about a goal. Visualizing what your goal looks like, keeps you engaged and excited about your purpose. Once you have done that, it's just a matter of carrying that energy forward and keeping it going. Cut out pictures from magazines, stick a motivational quote on your mirror or set a family photo as your phone background, so there's always a visual cue to remind you of your goals.

Here is a motivational tool I used on a regular basis to keep my weight loss focus: hang "the outfit" on your bedroom door. You know that pair of pants you bought a few weeks back that are a size too small? Instead of shoving them in a drawer, hang them on your bedroom door. See yourself sliding them on effortlessly. When you reach your goal, how good is it going to feel when you can take them off your door and fit into them? The answer: so ridiculously good!

If you don't have that special outfit that makes you feel like a fox, go out and buy one! The same concept can be implemented with your "big girl" jeans. Hanging your "before" jeans in plain view is a constant reminder of your goals. This also serves as a reminder of where you never intend on going back to.

Prepare for "The Pushers." These folks will come in the form of well-intentioned parents, friends, and work associates. These are the people who encourage you to go off your diet "just this once."

That's not really a problem, until "this once" becomes time and time again. If every time you see someone and you go off the rails at their suggestion, it may mean you need to distance yourself or have a serious talk about your weight loss efforts with your family member. Remember, not everyone will understand your weight loss journey and why this is serious to you. Do not be deterred by the "just once" crowd. You know what you are looking to get accomplished, so stay focused. Peer pressure doesn't end after high school. Keep your eyes on the big picture. Don't fall victim to the dieting "yo-yo" syndrome. It's ok to say no. Keep your mind fixed on where you want to be in six months, or next year. Make a serious effort to resist temptation when you're in an environment where food is part of the festivities. Stay focused. You will be so happy you did.

Do it for you. Have you ever heard yourself say something like: "I don't have time," or "I don't get a break from the kids," or how about the oldie but goodie, "I will start Monday?" As you probably already know, Monday always becomes next Monday, which then becomes next year. (What's wrong with starting in the middle of the week anyway?) The truth is, there will never be the "perfect" time to focus your energy on getting your health in order; "something" will always be there.

The fact is—you are worth the time and effort it will take to do something for yourself that will reap tremendous health benefits for a lifetime. The benefits that far outweigh sliding into that foxy outfit we spoke about earlier.

Your body is your temple. The only one you will ever have. Taking care of it properly could mean the difference between living a full life as it was intended or simply existing while going through it. Your body, with all its imperfections, is special. Your body houses all the organs that keep you alive. It gets you from place to place. Your body pumps oxygen to the brain that enables you to think, feel and function. Loving and respecting your body requires you to fuel it properly, not fill it with things that will cause it to decay.

Remember, this is your unique journey. There will be challenges that come in the form of people and circumstances. Situations can cause you to stumble and lose momentum, which is why ultimately; your motivation must come from within. Don't count on other people to be your only source of inspiration. Encourage yourself. Celebrate your weight loss milestones. Even when you fall off the proverbial wagon (and you will, it's a part of the process), don't lose focus. You will get there. Every day, people set their sights on personal goals, work hard at them, and achieve beyond what they thought they ever could. You are no different.

Pay it Forward. Your change could very well set the precedence for your family and friends to change their lives too in terms of health and fitness. There is a chain reaction effect that comes with making positive changes. Those around you may not be on board at first, but when they begin to notice the change in you, physically and emotionally, they will want to know how you did it. They will want to follow suit on the heels of your success. It's very possible your weight loss could even save the lives of your loved ones.

Bottom line is—this starts with you making up your mind and sticking to the plan of healthier eating and regular exercise. It may not seem like it now, but you could set the tone for your children and their children to develop healthier habits that break generational patterns of heart disease, diabetes, certain cancers, and a host of other obesity-related ailments. Knowledge is power. When you have access to it, you have the power to transform your life and to help those you love in transforming their lives as well. Now that is the true definition of "paying it forward."

Are You REALLY Ready?

I have had the pleasure of meeting many women of different backgrounds, who ask the same question when they hear of my weight loss journey. "Sue, I need your help. I am ready to lose weight and become healthier." My initial response is very simple, and causes a slight pause for most.

I ask that because along with wanting to change your life, you have to be willing to put the effort it takes behind it. That is where "the disconnect" happens. Between the wanting and the doing, the direction of your life changes the instant you actively and aggressively pursue a new goal. At the precise moment you start down that new path…you are headed towards a new destination and a different future than if you had you remained on the old path.

Being intentional about achieving your weight loss goals is just as important as motivating yourself to accomplish them. In order to achieve your objective, you have to be just as steadfast about getting your physical condition in order as you are with everything else in your life you care about. Yes, it will be challenging to do, especially if you are a nurturer by nature. We as women are hardwired to take care of others, but rarely do we focus on our own well-being while doing so.

We sometimes allow our health and well-being to take a back seat to our sense of duty, not realizing that we may have to pay for our decision to do so in the long run. It's a cost that can carry a hefty price tag. Medications to control obesity-related illnesses and hospitalizations take a toll not only on one's health, but wallet as well.

The Stats

According to the CDC (Centers for Disease Control), obesity-related conditions including heart disease, stroke, type 2 diabetes and certain types of cancer are the leading causes of preventable death. The estimated annual medical cost of obesity was a staggering $245 billion in 2014. Even more distressing is the medical costs for people who are obese were actually $1,429 higher per person than those of normal weight; that alone is a huge motivation factor.

Putting an undue burden on our loved ones to take care of you because of what could have been prevented through a healthier lifestyle is a sobering realization. For me, that was a wakeup call. I watched my mother's health slowly decline with each passing year she was here. From high blood pressure, to diabetes, to heart disease, to multiple strokes—because she did not take her health seriously. Trust me; you do not want your loved ones having to care for you because you're are no longer able to care of yourself.

Make no mistake about it. Losing weight is difficult; until all of a sudden it's not anymore. It stops becoming difficult once we realize how good becoming healthier feels. The transition of switching from one lifestyle to another, however, can be a constant struggle between your mind and body. There's a reason why formerly obese people who work hard to transform their bodies get all the glory, while the "in shape" individual who has always been fit does not receive as much praise.

You might think that the fit individuals should get some credit for never allowing themselves to become out of shape in the first place. While that is very impressive and they should be commended for their endurance, the individual who underwent the huge weight loss transformation receives all the accolades because they overcame an internal struggle which consumed their lives. For that very reason, millions of people read transformation stories and become inspired because they relate to that person, on a personal level. This is what drives me to teach others what I learned in my own battle. I know what that liberation feels like. It's the key that releases you from your own prison of self-doubt and discouragement. To get to that place, your mind has to be renewed. A new way of thinking has to be realized about what you can accomplish.

The Lifestyle Shift

Like small children learning their ABCs for the first time, learning to re-train your mind on how and what to eat will be a big challenge initially. Unhealthy eating habits don't just sprout up out of nowhere; they are usually formed early on. For those of us who have battled serious weight issues all of our lives, we have most likely been inclined to follow bad eating patterns that we have adopted while growing up. Some of us grew up eating what was most affordable, not necessarily the healthiest of food choices.

Don't get me wrong, the food my granny prepared was delicious, but the downside was that those southern dishes were full of saturated fat, salt and loaded with unhealthy carbohydrates. For those of us who have had a lifelong battle of the bulge, the inclination to become overweight typically begins at a very early age. In other words, there is a learned behavior of unhealthy eating patterns present well before we have reached adulthood.

These patterns continue on because we simply don't know any other way. Meanwhile, the body is being set up for numerous health challenges due to years and years of unhealthy foods. Even though you may understand the relationship between eating specific foods and your risk for the above preventable ailments, it can be difficult to undo years of unhealthy eating habits. However, the benefit is the prevention of arthritis, osteoporosis, stroke, diabetes and other illnesses that are affected by the dietary and lifestyle choices, we make every day.

This journey isn't a sprint to see how quickly you can get the weight off only to go back to your unhealthy ways. For many of us, we have been there and done that.

The re-occurring theme here is a lifestyle change. The willingness to change the way you think about food, as well as a closer look into the reasons why we turn to food as our comfort source. This journey is complex because it involves not only transformation of the body, but of the mind as well.

The Pitfall of Success: Self Sabotage

Have you ever talked yourself out of starting something due to your fear of failure? I think we all have. Especially when it comes to a huge undertaking. Most of us limit ourselves. Especially when it comes to losing weight. We do not achieve a fraction of what we are capable of achieving because of fear. Here is a moment of honesty from me to you. On this journey, there will be twists and turns. Situations that will tempt you to give up. Setbacks and naysayers will play a huge role, but believe it or not, our biggest adversary is usually ourselves. Often times, we subconsciously sabotage our quest to lose weight via our negative thoughts.

Negative patterns of thinking about your capabilities can keep you from reaching your goals, and in essence, these patterns become a type of crutch or safety mechanism that protects you against disappointment. In other words, what you tell yourself becomes truth. It's a cycle of defeat I am very familiar with. This is the major reason why preparing yourself mentally to take on this challenge is crucial to your long-term success in weight management.

When it comes to our self-defeating thoughts or negative self-talk about weight loss or any goal for that matter, we must pay close attention to the patterns that begin to surface. We must become familiar with the excuses we make that prevent us from moving forward toward success. Here are some examples:

- This won't work, I can't do this…

- I will have to give up too much.

- I just don't have the time now…

- I'm too stressed right now. My kids/job/schoolwork is preventing me from really focusing on myself right now.

Sound familiar? Each of the patterns listed above has its own set of consequences that manifest in a variety of ways in our lives. Some are very obvious, while others might be a little difficult to identify. The key for us is recognizing negative self-talk and nip it in the bud. Create a new speech pattern for your thoughts. This will take some intentional practice on your end. After years of negative thoughts regarding my weight, it was very difficult to recognize the pattern of negative self-talk. It can be so gradual that we become comfortable with it. It's like an old friend that won't let us down. "If I never try, I will never be disappointed."

Another way we sabotage our efforts is the company we keep. You know the old adage, "misery loves company"? This statement could not be truer when it comes to getting your health in order. Negative people are always looking for ways to dishearten your efforts, especially if a serious effort to lose weight is not in their game plan. Check your circle. Step away from associates who are intent on distracting you from your goals. Refrain from hanging out with people who claim to be on board with you, yet aren't very positive. We become like the people we spend the most time around, so make it a point to affiliate with positive, goal-oriented people. People on the same page as you are.

In short, continual self-sabotage drastically alters your life. The scariest aspect of self-sabotage is that if you make it a habit sooner or later, you may find yourself not living the life you truly desire. In fact, you'll likely experience great difficulty accomplishing the goals that you've set for yourself.

In order to experience long-term results, we have to break out of that mold of negative self-talk, this means getting out of a very familiar comfort zone for many of us. So, how do you go about breaking the self-sabotage cycle? First, recognize your abilities and embrace them. Practice makes perfect! For many of us, negative self-talk is so familiar; it has become our immediate go-to emotion when there is a challenge before us. Because old habits die hard, it will take some practice to reverse it.

Surround yourself with positive people moving in the same direction you are. Look for motivators, not detractors. Remember to remind yourself that weight loss is not a race; it will take time to get to where you want to be. Be patient with yourself, and don't expect perfection from yourself. When you fall off the wagon, just jump back on. Recognize when you are embracing negative thoughts and replace them with positive words of affirmation about yourself. Reshaping negative self-talk helps you change your self-definition from someone who can't lose weight or achieve this or that, to someone who can. Ultimately, you must choose to embrace thoughts of confidence in your ability to make positive changes in your life.

Ready…Set…GOALS!

Weight loss goals can mean the difference between success and failure. Realistic, well-planned weight loss goals keep you focused and motivated. They provide a plan for change as you transition to a healthier lifestyle. Goal setting is talked about often when making the decision to lose weight, but how often do we actually do it? It's usually an afterthought. Our goal is usually very general, like "I want to lose weight." There is a problem with that; this non-specific goal does nothing for us. How are you supposed to plan out your weight loss if you have no idea what you're planning for? So where do you begin?

Be realistic. Now that we have decided to lose the weight once and for all, we want it gone like yesterday, right? Be careful that you don't set your expectations too high from the start. That is a sure set up for failure. Remember, you want permanent results, not the temporary kind, and for that reason, your journey will take time. Don't try to rush the process. Losing weight too fast can lead to swift weight re-gain. Setting realistic goals now will help you to keep the weight off later. To put it in perspective, look at it like this way—it took a lifetime of unhealthy habits that resulted in the weight gain, it will take some time to reverse years of those unhealthy habits and develop a different way of eating, a different way of thinking.

Set a big goal initially. Once it has been established, break your ultimate weight loss goal down into smaller goals. For example, say you want to lose 100pounds. Put that goal aside and divide that number up into several smaller, short-term, attainable goals. One of those goals may be to lose 10 pounds this month. That's a realistic goal that you have a good chance of reaching. Once you reach your first 10 pound goal, you will see that you can do it over and over again. Track your progress, and reward yourself along the way for improving your eating and exercise habits. On weeks when you get to the gym five times, treat yourself to flowers, a movie, or a ball game; whatever feels like a reward to you. (Make sure your rewards are not food related). As you go, your motivation remains high and your increased willpower continues to push you forward. All of these factors serve to keep your attitude positive and remind you of the benefits of a healthier lifestyle. Staying consistent is crucial. Inconsistency will sabotage all your efforts and will most definitely lead you back to where you started.

Don't compare yourself to anyone else. Even if you begin your weight loss journey with a workout buddy, a friend, or relative who wants to lose weight as well, don't fall into the comparison trap. Keep in mind that your journey is uniquely your own. Realize that everybody is different. Teaming up with a weight loss buddy is a great way to keep motivated, but your goals should be created from considering your own weight loss needs, not the needs of a weight loss partner. If your friend wants to lose 25 pounds, and your goal is to lose 50 pounds, be aware that your friend may reach her goal first, and that increasing the amount of weight you want to lose each month to match your friend's goal is not a healthy idea.

Develop new behaviors. The first few weeks of your weight loss journey should be devoted to learning new behaviors: healthier meals that consist of protein, vegetables, and whole grains; portion control; and exercising more. Permanently improving your eating habits requires a thoughtful approach. We will call this plan of action the "three R" method: Reflect, Replace, and Reinforce.

REFLECT on all of your specific eating habits, both bad and good, and on your common triggers for unhealthy eating.

REPLACE your unhealthy eating habits with healthier ones. This may take a while. Old habits are hard to break, but you can break them. Even with the busiest life or the most sedentary job, there are always healthy choices you can make. Making better choices puts you on the right path and, more importantly, makes you feel more in control of your weight, your health, and your future. Replace one unhealthy habit for at least one healthy choice each week. Be as consistent as possible. Some ideas are:

- Use part of your lunch hour for a brisk walk

- Look for one task, appointment, or to-do item that you could delete in favor of a workout session

- Find at least ten minutes each day for a quick workout

- Get up ten minutes early for a walk around the block or your local park

REINFORCE your new and healthier regime. I know it sounds repetitive; however, this information is so important to your journey that it bears repeating. Place emphasis on not only your diet, but exercise as well. These components are the formula for permanent weight loss. With regard to your diet, eliminate the temptation to gorge on your favorite bag of chips or cupcakes. Leave them on the shelf at the grocery store. Opt for a healthier snack like air-popped popcorn or strawberries and Greek yogurt instead of the donuts in your office break room or the chips in the vending machine. This may involve cleaning out your kitchen pantry or your desk draw at work that holds your "stress chocolate." Preparation is key. Prepare healthy snacks at night or in the morning to bring to work with you. Bag your favorite fruit and healthy nuts for your midday snack. Bring your lunch to work instead of buying something quick which may equal unhealthy.

Make a commitment to become more physically active and challenge yourself to move your body more. There are so many awesome benefits to doing so. Exercise increases energy levels and improves poor sleeping habits. Besides weight loss, physical activity helps ensure you maintain your results permanently as well as improving your mood and decreasing the risk of depression. Furthermore, exercise helps decrease the risk of serious health conditions, including high blood pressure, diabetes, stroke, and heart disease.

You don't have to start off full throttle, if you have not been used to physical activity and working out. Start small and build your endurance. For instance, start with parking the furthest away from the grocery store or mall as opposed to searching for the closest spot to park. Whenever possible, walk instead of driving. Exercising does not have to be a boring activity. Like dancing? Find out where Zumba classes are offered. Dancing incorporates fun into your exercise regimen. It's a good way to burn off calories, increase the heart rate, and work up a sweat. Aim for thirty minutes a few times a week. Check out your local park district or YMCA for salsa and line dancing classes— these are often offered at a very low cost and some are even free.

The Accountability Factor

Write your goals down, both long-term and short-term ones. Just put it in writing. It doesn't have to be anything fancy. Send yourself an e-mail, make notations in your calendar or journal, or simply write them on a piece of notebook paper. By doing this, you get the feeling you are making a contract with yourself, which makes you less likely to forget or ignore them.

Own up

Another aspect of reinforcing a healthier regime and overall mindset is to "own up" to your current condition. Taking ownership is perhaps one of the most difficult parts of the weight loss journey. Most of us know what we need to do in order to accomplish our goals. We know that we need to change our diet and exercise in order to lose weight, but we don't hold ourselves accountable. We often blame our inability to work out and eat properly on overloaded schedules, low energy and fear of failure. Playing the blame game not only gives us more excuses to skip workouts, it also distances us from the fact that how we live our lives is a choice.

Taking responsibility for your own choices may be the most important step you take to lose weight. When we own up, it forces us to really confront truths that may not be so attractive. We deny the issues instead of accepting them for what they are. Why the subtle denial of what we know is truth about our unhealthy lifestyles? Our brain generates cognitive blind spots that can make it difficult for us to honestly assess our actions and determine our responsibility for those actions and their consequences. In essence, our brain is inclined to flatter and shield our egos from blame. Despite how difficult it is to counter the mechanisms of our ego's defense system, the task is not impossible. Becoming intentional about losing weight and actively pursuing your goals in terms of improving your overall health may involve facing some harsh realities about your current lifestyle; however, the upside is that it then causes you to begin to take the steps necessary toward reversing those habits and slowly weeding out and eliminating what is needed to develop new, healthier patterns.

Needless to say, there are other factors involved with obesity in some people, such as genetics or certain medical conditions that make weight loss difficult. But for most of us, we're overweight because of our own choices. If you're tired of making excuses for your health, now is the time to take control; to take control of your health and fitness is to take full responsibility for what you're doing or not doing. It isn't easy to change how you live. In fact, it takes great courage, strength and will to look at your life, see where you're going wrong and switch directions. However, the more you do it, the more you realize you *can* do it, and that's what you really need to lose weight.

Keep Pushing Forward

Block out all the noise. Ignore the naysayers and skeptics. People close to you will question your decision but stand firm and don't give up on your goals. You know the reasons behind your decision to become healthier and lose weight. Don't be deterred. Not even by yourself. During this journey, the scale will play tricks with your mind; your weight may not move for weeks, but always remember that you are changing from the inside out. It's a process; if you are diligent and consistent, you will feel and see the change in your body. Remember, this is not just another twelve-week plan. You are changing the way you think in terms of food and how it will affect you. You are changing your life.

Affirm Yourself Daily

Wake up every day with the realization that this is it, that there's only one shot at this life, and we can both enjoy the ride and live it to its fullest or we can remain the same. It's always our choice. We can choose to relish in the negative or positive. The words that we use, especially concerning ourselves, have a great impact on our lives whether we realize it or not. Most people repeat in their minds negative words and statements concerning the situations and events in their lives and consequently, they create undesirable situations and defeat. Remember, what we declare serves to either build up or tear down.

When we want to remember something, we often commit to memory whatever it is by repetition. We put reminders on our phones and alarms to remind us of a certain task we need to do. Reminding yourself often about where you are headed keeps your goals at the center of your mind. When you begin to positively affirm yourself several times a day concerning your weight loss goals, your subconscious mind accepts it as the truth.

One of the methods I use to keep myself on task with the things I want accomplished is by writing them down and displaying them in different areas in my house. A simple pad of sticky notes can serve as a reminder to yourself to get moving in the direction you want to go. Stick your Motivational Love Notes to yourself on your mirror in the bathroom, your bedroom mirror, your refrigerator, at work – wherever you spend time at is a great place to place your love notes to yourself. In the Bible, God also reminds us to "Write down the vision, and make it plain/clear" (Habakkuk 2:2). Simply put, when you put pen to paper and lay out your dreams in written form then actively seek to achieve them, your dreams will begin to manifest themselves.

Try this. Write these short words of affirmation on a piece of paper. Attach them to the areas you frequent. Read them aloud to yourself each time you pass them. Mediate on them:

- I have tons of energy today!

- I am ready for positive changes in my life!

- Every day I get closer to my ideal weight.

- It feels good to move my body while working out, I feel stronger every day.

- I won't allow anything or anyone to hold me back from my dreams, not this time.

- I am a walking, talking success story. I see where I am headed and I am excited!

Allow these affirmations to soak in, especially during times of frustration and setbacks. (Newsflash: disappointments go hand in hand with your weight loss journey. No worries; you can overcome them, but just be prepared for them.) Tailor your own words of affirmation to yourself. Make them personal to you and allow those words to launch you to where and who you want to be. Believe it or not, your words and thoughts program your mind in the same way that commands and scripts a program on a computer. Repeated positive statements help you focus your mind. They also create corresponding mental images in the conscious mind, which affect the subconscious mind accordingly. In this way, you program your subconscious in accordance with your will.

Truth be told, you can lose weight on virtually any diet. But in order to maintain your body for the long haul and keep those excess pounds at bay for good, you must find solid, healthy strategies that can stay with you forever. They need to be specific, measurable, attainable, realistic and tangible. Making the decision to lose weight without a clear-cut plan that includes goal setting is like, getting in your car to make a trip to a new destination without ever looking at a map. You can't get to your goal unless you know what you need to do to get there.

Goal setting can improve other facets of your life. It will help you understand what is important to you, such as lowering your blood pressure or simply being able to walk your dog an extra block or two within a few weeks. Goals will also keep you motivated, so you will then be more likely to make and meet new, more difficult goals, not to mention finding your newfound confidence in what you can accomplish. You may even discover that other challenges in your life will begin to seem less intimidating when you see what you can really do!

Taking Back Your Temple

As chronicled earlier in this book, my eating disorder controlled my day-to-day life for over thirty years. For me and millions of other people around the world, whether obese or bulimic, food was the object that defined who I was and shaped my choices. As in my case, obesity and more specifically, binge eating, is associated with a wide range of adverse psychological, physical, and social consequences. A person who emotionally binge eats may start out just eating smaller amounts of food, but at some point, their urge to eat less or more spirals out of control.

People with binge-eating disorder lose control over their eating. Unlike bulimia, in which there is a series of binging then purging to rid the stomach of the excessive amount of food, periods of binge eating are not followed by compensatory behaviors like purging or excessive exercise. As a result, those of us who have experience with a lifestyle of binge-eating often are overweight or obese and are at higher risk for developing heart disease and high blood pressure. They also experience guilt, shame and distress about their binge eating, which can lead to more binge eating. Sufferers encounter a vicious cycle of self-reproach that can chip away at self-esteem. That is, until we come to the point when we are able to admit, confront, combat and deal with our underlying issues, in particular the condition of our hearts with regard to developing a true reverence for one's self which is the basis for a healthy life physically, as well as emotionally.

I can remember moments when I would look in the mirror and despise my reflection. I was emotionally depleted. I tried and failed so many times to lose weight that I began to just settle for the fact that I could never achieve want I wanted. I counted myself out of the fight before I even stepped in the ring. In reality, I settled for an existence that God never intended for me. Wearing a thinly veiled façade of the "happy fat girl" and internalizing the shame of failure, my esteem was at its all-time lowest. I simply could not forgive myself and that put the brakes on any attempt at even trying again at getting my body healthy. Then there were the pity parties. No one threw a pity party like I could, complete with binging on my favorite comfort foods like ice cream, cookies, and fries from McDonald's—any high-caloric food that would temporarily make me feel better.

Forgive Yourself

One of the most difficult parts of my weight loss journey was learning how to forgive myself completely for past failures associated not only with my weight, but for the poor choices I made in my past, that caused me so much unnecessary heartache. I could not move ahead with my life because I was too focused on the past. Forgiving yourself can be much harder than forgiving someone else. When you're carrying around a sense of blame for something that has happened in the past, a bundle of negativity burrowed deep within, can cause a never-ending, pervasive sense of defeat and sorrow. Forgiving yourself is an important act of moving forward and releasing yourself from the past. It's also a way of protecting your health and general well-being.

Making a decision to fight for yourself is not easy, especially when you have felt defeated most of your life. Loving yourself completely is a process. Give yourself time and don't feel down if you feel like what you're trying to do, is not going the way you thought it would go. Think of the areas in your life that are in need of serious inventory—whether it is ridding your life of a dysfunctional relationship, or striving for either personal or professional goals. Don't focus on shortcomings or mistakes of the past, instead, reflect on those lapses in judgment with personal pardon and make the necessary changes, rather than browbeating yourself for imperfection.

I decided to fight for the life I wanted with all I had, even after my first attempt did not go as planned. It's a decision that you must make too. How do you fight for your life? Decide to forgive yourself first. Forgive yourself for the times that you missed the mark. Give yourself permission to be human and imperfect. Release yourself from the guilt of past mistakes and appreciate the fact that you have a second chance to get it right this time. Remember, forgiveness is not a feeling, but a decision. Once you have made that decision, you can begin the process of not only changing your life, but concentrating on what's ahead, because you are no longer looking behind you.

Does God Really Care About My Weight?

What does God have to do with my weight loss journey? The answer is…everything. He is the One who gives you the stamina and the wisdom to make better choices for your life and that also includes your health as well. When there is nobody behind you to give you the encouragement you seek, God is there supplying you with all the physical and emotional equipment you need, even though you probably never figured Him into your weight loss equation.

I did not have a cheering section when I began my weight loss journey, nor did I have a workout partner whom I could call for a dose of inspiration. My friend who initially joined the gym with me dropped her membership after a few months and I was left with a decision to make. Do I stay active, or drop out too? My decision to stay the course, even if it meant flying solo, was the best decision I ever made. It was there that I discovered what my body could do and what I could achieve with determination and effort. It was there I realized that I am capable of doing whatever I set my mind to do on my own.

Your journey to change your life is ultimately a solo mission. No one can decide to change you but you. We can't wait for people to give us an extra push to reach our golden dreams; we have to propel ourselves to our greatest good. The road that you travel toward becoming healthier, won't always include someone giving you a pep talk or a girlfriend you can work out with. People can be finicky and everyone's commitment level is different. Everyone who begins with you on your weight loss journey won't necessarily stay there. Not everyone will be serious about actually adhering to a workout regime. Your feet must be firmly planted in accountability to offset ups and downs that come along with adhering to a workout schedule and a healthier eating lifestyle.

On the days you would rather throw in the towel and give up, you will need a source of motivation that will be a constantly at your disposal. For me, it was God. For those of us who are Christians, we are taught to turn to God whenever we are going through personal issues like financial difficulty or loss. But when it comes to asking for guidance and strength, both physically and mentally, to rid our bodies of excess weight, we don't immediately consider prayer to be a key component of our journey. I mean, does God REALLY care if we are overweight? Is the state of my health of concern to Him? The answer is a resounding yes.

I think we don't realize how much God has invested in us and in our health. He created the entire universe specifically to fit our physical needs—food, water and oxygen. When something like extra weight or obesity weighs heavily on our hearts and bodies, you bet He is concerned. God's desire is that we thrive in every way and that our quality of life is at its best. We are incapable of living the abundant life He promised us if our bodies are unhealthy due to the things we put into it. Not only is God concerned, He tells us in His Word how important it is to take care of our temples:

• One scripture that reminds us that our body is God's temple is 1 Corinthians 19-20. God's Holy Spirit lives inside a believer. After we accept Jesus into our heart, God gives us His Spirit to help us live the kind of life He wants us to live. Since God actually lives in us, Paul tells us in this verse that our body is His temple. Since God "bought" us with a high price, Jesus' death, than we are obligated to care for our body, which is His temple.

- In addition, being healthy is being a good witness to our loved ones as well as those around us. Acts 1:8 reminds us that we are to be witnesses for other people. As you go forward on your weight loss journey, there will be those who look to you for inspiration as well. Taking care of our health is one way that we can be a good witness.

- When you are healthier and not bound by excess weight, you will have more energy to do what He has called you to do. Ephesians 2:10 helps us see that we are God's masterpiece, created to do the good things that He had planned a long time ago for us to do. We all know that the more fit and healthy we are, the more energy we will have. The more energy that we have, the more we can put into whatever task, we are doing. We'll also be better able to sustain ourselves for the long haul.

God wants us to feel the joy and freedom that comes from living a healthy lifestyle. You were not created to live a life that is less than the one He intended for you. Once we learn to start relying on Him for our strength and willpower, suddenly the weight loss issue is a lot less lonely and a lot more possible. We turn to God for the many challenges we face every day. Allow God to be the One you turn to, when you face inevitable challenges and temptations associated with your weight loss journey. Keep in mind that while

God will grant us the strength to do what we must do when we ask. It is ultimately up to us to take the steps in order to reach our goals. God will give you the gas to get there; but you have to press the pedal.

Faith and Fitness

Faith and fitness…not terms we immediately tie in together upon making the decision to lose weight and live a healthier lifestyle, but I would venture to say, that it is the most important part of your journey. As we all know, losing 10 pounds can be a challenge, let alone a significant amount of weight and reversing years of bad eating habits, that we have grown accustomed to.

You will need extra enforcement to not only see your way to your goals, but also to maintain your weight loss permanently. Seeking God through prayer has made all the difference in terms of shedding the weight as well as keeping my focus to maintain it. God tells us in His word that we can be transformed by the renewing of our minds. True transformation can only take place when we begin to think differently. Asking God to readjust and renew your mind in terms of how you think about exercise and a healthier diet, is a great step in the right direction.

Talking to God and repeating His promises over and over again was my saving Grace and still is to this day, when I need to push myself beyond my pre-conceived limits. If we knew the power that we had to accomplish our dreams, it would blow our minds. In order to tap in to that place of power, we need to connect to the course from which it flows.

Prayer and exercise are two activities that we don't usually think of that goes hand in hand, but when combined powerful transformation occurs. God wants to be intimately involved in every area of your life; that includes your body as it relates to your health. Living a more abundant life includes a healthy, thriving, physical body that will enable you to live longer and stronger. I discovered early on in my journey, that the only way I would be able to make the kind of changes in my life that I desperately needed, was if I involved the God who knew more about me, than I knew about myself and my own abilities. His strength is made perfect in us. When you change your focus, incredible things begin to take place in your life. When your focus is on God's abilities and not your own, your whole perspective changes. We can do nothing without Christ but with Him we can accomplish anything, even our workout at the gym. Every time you pray for the strength to push on with your workout, He will give you what you need and then some.

My favorite prayer when I began to get weary at the gym is a short one, because when you are huffing and puffing, all you can get out is a short one!

"The Joy of the Lord is my Strength" (Neh 8:10). God will give you all that you need when you are physically and mentally running on empty; all you need to do is make Him your partner on your journey.

Here are a few steps to get you started on connecting your faith to your weight loss:

• Begin a conversation with God and invite him in to help you.

• Forgive yourself for all the times you've tried to lose weight before and gained it back.

• Surrender to God that you cannot do this without His strength. Ask for HIS willpower each time you are tempted to reach for that sweet treat or salty chips.

• Believe that His love is so real and so strong that He will never desert you, even if you slip.

• Pray about what step is next for you in your weight loss journey.

Incorporate those who support you and keep you accountable. Accountability blended with support, led by God, are very powerful tools to help you get started living well. Whether you are walking, jogging, or at your local gym, know that you do have a workout partner providing you with all you need to reach your goals. He is rooting for you!

Author's Note

It is my sincere hope that through my story, you have been fortified with the inspiration and reassurance that you need to get you started on your pathway to permanent change in your life. Not simply in the area of physical fitness, but in every area that has been stagnant with self-doubt and hesitation. Despite what you may think, you have capacity to break free from whatever binds your wings to the ground. Give yourself permission to soar.

You are tougher than you realize, more powerful than you dare to dream, and capable of achieving the personal success you long for.

The voice within you that says you can't is a liar. Resist the urge to give into it. Tap into the greatness that you were born with. Haven't you waited long enough?

Now is the perfect time to Dig Deep for your Change!

Born, raised, and currently residing in Chicago, Illinois, Susan is a health and wellness instructor, motivational speaker, devoted wife, and mother of three daughters and an adorable Jack Russell terrier pooch named Pepper.

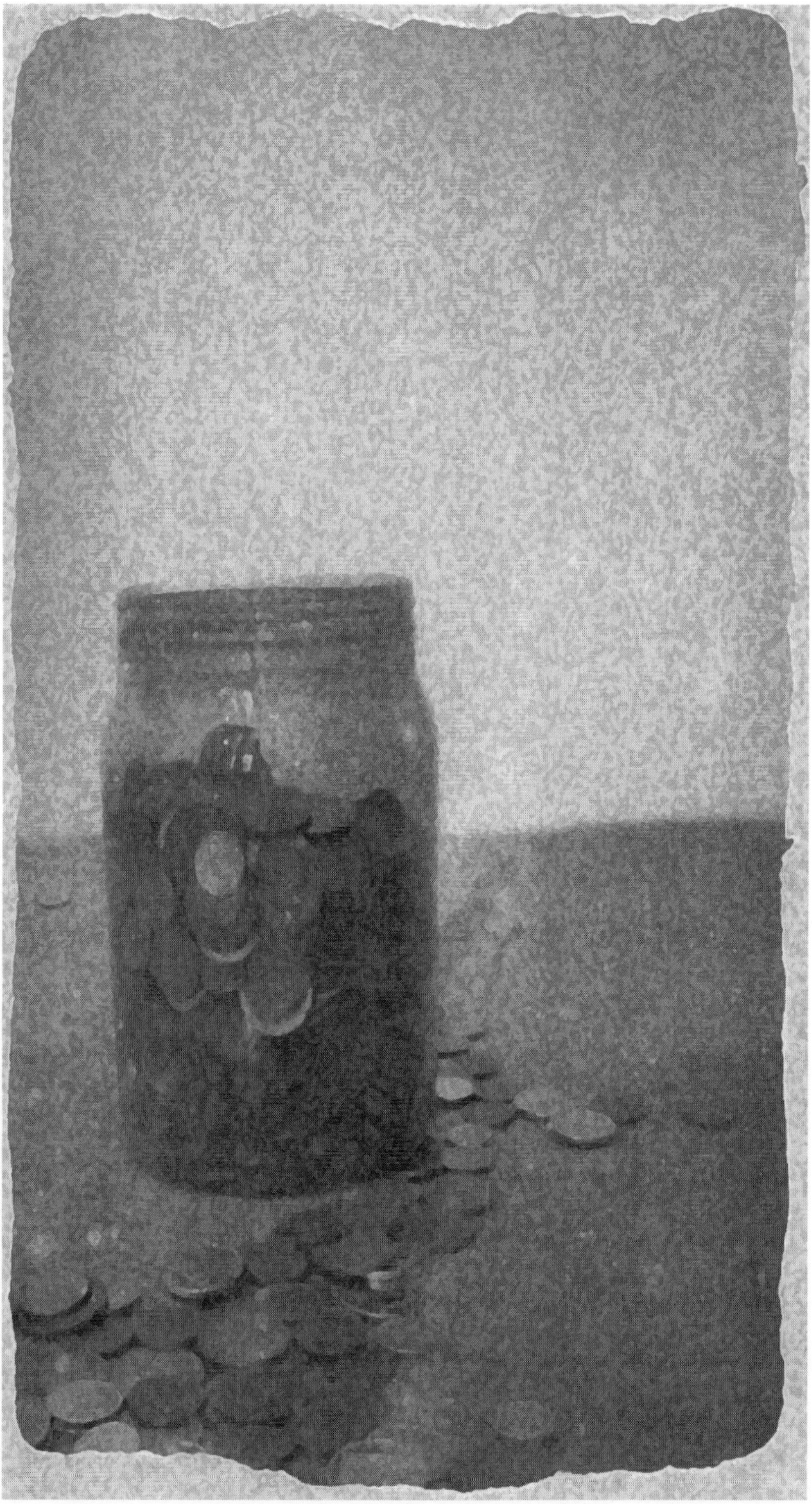